LETTERS FROM BRAZIL

LETTERS FROM BRAZIL

Reflections on Migration and Friendship
An Epistolary Memoir

RUTH ZELIG

SWP
SHE WRITES PRESS

Published in 2026 by
She Writes Press, an imprint of The Stable Book Group

1569 Solano Ave #546
Berkeley, CA 94707
https://shewritespress.com
Library of Congress Control Number: 2026904449
ISBN: 979-8-89636-352-1
eISBN: 979-8-89636-353-8

Interior Designer: Andrea Reider

All photos, unless otherwise noted, are courtesy of the author, Ruth Zelig.

Printed in the United States

Names and identifying characteristics have been changed to protect the privacy of certain individuals.

Author's Note

In this age dominated by social media, where many have a goal of surpassing 1,000 Facebook friends, when "BFF" (best friend forever) flies off our tongue without a thought, and when ties of friendship can be as temporary as a life event or as short as our attention span, it is easy to take a shallow view of the expression "my best friend."

But I have a lifetime best friend who was my lifeline when I was a migrant. The letters we exchanged for over twenty years after we no longer lived in the same country are as much of a treasure now as they were when I received each one. I kept these letters safe, and they form the basis of this epistolary memoir.

Dedication
Dedicação

This book would not exist if it weren't for a young teen who poured her heart out to me with earnest words in letters mailed across a hemisphere. Elana's writing is chatty but flawlessly articulate, and it comes from the heart. I am lucky she considers me a friend.

Obrigada, minha amiga de ontem, hoje e amanhã.

If you want to walk fast, walk alone.
If you want to walk far, walk with someone.
—African proverb

A bosom friend afar brings distant lands near.
—Chinese proverb

However rare true love is, true friendship is rarer.
—La Rochefoucauld

Table of Contents

Part One

In the Beginning

The past is a country that issues no visa.

—Janet Malcolm,
Still Pictures: On Photography and Memory

Prologue

Adrift in a Postwar World

We arrived, migrants, in January 1959 by ship. We left, migrants again, in June 1964 by plane.

Vera, Ernö, and their daughter, Elana, my best friend, accompanied us to São Paulo's Viracopos Airport to be with us until the very end and see us off. After all, who else goes along with emigrants to say goodbye at the parting gate. My parents and I were leaving Brazil on a night flight on the way to New York, and they were staying. We—fourteen-year-old girls—were on the verge of tears at this bitter parting. We hugged hard and long until we had to be peeled apart so that I could board the small Varig plane with my parents. As we waved goodbye, Elana and I and our mothers were forlorn: we were aware that the distance of a continent and a hemisphere was about to separate us. Our mothers never saw each other again. Our mothers had also been best friends.

On the way back from the airport to their apartment home in São Paulo, her father, driving, said, "Don't cry, you'll forget each other soon."

We did not forget each other. Instead, we wrote to each other every month or every few months for years to come. This was how our bond survived the distance across not just time but countries and cultures. The medium of this connection is now quaint. Now is the age of speed and immediacy, making us FOMOs (fearful of missing out) and indulgently impatient waiting for news and answers to be received without delay. We compulsively hit refresh buttons for up-to-the-minute updates. But in 1964 it was still the slow age of letter writing, akin to all analog processes that seem outlandish to us today. We now carry phones practically embedded in our flesh, but that was when phone calls were expensive, and international calls were unaffordable for most of us. Today emails swish across the globe instantaneously. Back then, even at the mercy of a notoriously unreliable, and as a result, comical Brazilian postal service, the letters were sent in faith (and sometimes registered), but replies were expected with certainty. We had patience then.

The narrative of our friendship was established in the diaspora of postwar migration, with Elana's family finding new roots, and my family looking for elusive roots for many more years to come. Having survived the Shoah in Europe, our young parents were set adrift. We were the offsprings borne along with their baggage, both physical and emotional. At the time, we were not consciously aware of this. Or maybe we were, but we accepted it without question as fundamental to our existence. We were migrants, children of refugees. But Elana and I were young, resilient, adaptable and were inclined to root anywhere we were taken. Our parents were the ones who had suffered upheaval of the most evil kind—racial persecution—that afflicts the personality. They dislocated us out of love, hope for a better life, and a desire to protect us. And so, our chronicle proceeded from Europe to Israel and then to Brazil, and in my family's case, continuing to Canada and the United States.

Why did Elana's and my friendship last? The friendship is now sixty-five years old as I write this. It has had its ups and downs with some cooler periods, but over its lifetime, a friendship formed by two girls, just children then, survived adolescence, young adulthood—the riskiest periods for friendships—and then solidified in midlife.

It would take years of letters, and a cumulative wisdom of later life, for me to understand why this friendship lasted so long. The resulting gift of understanding the essence of this friendship makes it worthwhile for me to impart this narrative by sharing a personal account, in the form of letters from my friend, and my reflections looking back at what I would be writing to her after we separated.

The most noteworthy fact about our correspondence, aside from its frequency and its duration, was the earnest nature of the writing, a fact I was to realize only after the letters were uncovered. These were not silly pen-pal letters. Even at the risk of my being partial to these letters I received from Elana, it says something that I kept them as a collection. Ordinarily, one rarely keeps papers for a lifetime, unless it's a reflection of their substantial significance. I did not keep them out of sheer sentimentality, weighing myself down with their emotional and personal value. I did not reread them until 2016. They were stored away, the way one stores long-term savings bonds. They had an intrinsic value, and I saved them and let them mature. I always knew where they were. Uncovering them was a question of when they came due. I also didn't want to have them uncovered after my death or hers. My intention for many years was to reunite us with the words of our former selves.

At last, after many decades, when Elana and I reread the letters together, the personal and historical nature of the letters and the basis of our relationship was revealed. And this discovery—not the old paper and faint ink—was the fortuitous surprise, the gift of friendship magnified. The letters were demonstrative and revelatory.

To understand us and to understand what made our friendship possible, a travel back to our origins is in order, as well as reckoning with the familial, social, and urban environment in which we lived. Our roots were seeded by history, our upbringing was determined by our parents' experience and worldview, and our distinctive environment shaped our experiences.

Childhood

Migration and Assimilation

Elana and I were born in Israel in 1950, and our parents were young European Jews who survived the Holocaust and migrated to Mandated Palestine prior to 1947. My parents, Edith and Victor, came from Romania; Elana's mother, Vera, also came from Romania, and her father, Ernö Weingarten, came from Czechoslovakia. The young survivors had married in Israel. All our elders spoke Hungarian. And so Elana and I also learned to speak Hungarian, our parents' mother tongue, not ours, an unusual detail for our generation. Our families were migrants and thus polyglots.

When I arrived in Brazil in January 1959, then just over eight years old, I spoke Hebrew only, with some understanding of Hungarian and German, because these were languages spoken by my family at home. My parents, however, abandoned their compulsory Romanian language, and so I never learned it. In Brazil, I was about to learn two more languages before the end of my first year in São Paulo. As I was learning to read and write the Roman alphabet and understand and speak Portuguese, I also started to become fluent in Hungarian.

My parents and I arrived in São Paulo with just a couple of suitcases and a paltry amount of money. Our first several months were spent in Curitiba, the capital of the state of Paraná, but for economic and employment reasons, my father moved us to the metropolis of São Paulo (population about 4.5 million), where he could find more opportunities. The Jewish community in São Paulo was rather small (less than 50,000 in the mid-1960s) but tight-knit enough for us to make connections via my parents' native tongue. And so Hungarian-speaking Jews living in São Paulo made up the network that welcomed us. My father soon found work as a mechanic, which was his profession ever since he was a teenager who landed in Mandated Palestine just before Israel's independence.

In São Paulo, word got around, and my mother found a former elementary school classmate from prewar Arad, Romania. Elsa was a Hungarian-speaking young woman living in São Paulo with her family that immigrated to Brazil after their short postwar sojourn in Israel. That family, the Garfinkles and Schiffs, consisted of Elsa, my mother's contemporary, Toby Schiff, her husband, and Miki Schiff, their only daughter, who was one year younger than I was. They lived in an apartment with the matriarch, Elsa's mother, old Berta *neni* (using a Hungarian honorific for an older woman) and Berta's taciturn husband, Rudolf Garfinkle. Old Mr. Garfinkle worked as a salesman, left home early, came home late carrying his bulging leather valise, and retired to his room every evening. A big, lumbering man, he walked studying the ground in front of him. The old lady scorned him, and his granddaughter ignored him. There was little chance that I was to ever get to know him. He sold leather material to someone named Ernö Weingarten, who ran a small leather glove workshop in his apartment in São Paulo on Avenida Duque de Caxias. It was through this connection that my parents met Vera and Ernö.

The first time I met Miki Schiff and Elana Weingarten, in the latter part of 1959, my mother took me along on her visit to Elsa, and I was ushered to a well-appointed bedroom where two girls were playing on the floor surrounded by many impressive toys. I did not speak Portuguese yet, but Miki and Elana spoke Hungarian, and Elana also spoke Hebrew, and so, in my Portuguese-muted condition I felt I was entering a comfortable and safe space.

Soon after, the only language we spoke consistently was Portuguese. The friendship was triggered by the fact that our parents were friends and that we had a choice of languages in which to communicate. And yet, as immigrants in Brazil, Portuguese was going to be the language of our discourse.

After Miki's parents' divorce, during the first year of our friendship and my tenuous hold on assimilation, the Garfinkle-Schiff household, minus the divorced father, moved to a fine two-bedroom apartment in another building. I say fine, because I could only compare it to my apartment and Elana's apartment. Elana and I were frequent visitors to the domain of Berta *neni*. She ruled in that household. She raised Miki autocratically, put her husband on a short and taunting leash, and catered to her only child, Elsa, the major breadwinner. The women, Berta and Elsa, shared a bedroom with Miki, and the second bedroom was the silent Mr. Garfinkle's. I only saw him walk to it directly from the front door when he'd return from work, and he never joined us during our visits. The apartment, in my youthful opinion, was finely furnished, with artwork on the walls, fine custom curtains and upholstered sofa and chairs, and a fine wood dining table with its matching dining chairs where the women frequently played a form of canasta.

Elsa worked as a saleswoman at a jewelry store in a highly ranked hotel in São Paulo in 1960. It was frequented by many American businessmen, with Elsa speaking about them as alien demigods. She managed to pick up many expressions in English, which she liked to show off. With such a plum job, she made a decent living to support her mother and daughter. Toby, of course, also contributed to his daughter's financial needs, being a loving father and an honest ex. Elsa wore an elegant wardrobe that kept me enthralled. For years thereafter, my view of women's fashion was determined by the clothing worn by Elsa in the early 1960s: suits, silk blouses, dresses with jackets, calfskin pumps, alligator purses. She'd habitually lay her day's costume on the bed her mother and daughter shared, to "air it out." It was a quirk that I took notice of and intentionally never copied. I always thought clothing should be hung to air out. She also had a boudoir table in the bedroom for makeup, hairstyling, and self-care. I have only seen those in movies. She was a darker Doris Day out of Hollywood, and in comparison, my pretty mother never had the means to indulge herself in such a way. In any event, Elsa not only dressed elegantly but also wore beautiful gold jewelry. I suspected some of it was borrowed for the purposes of modeling the goods for sale. (Since the days of Elsa at that jewelry store, I always retained a penchant for its jewelry, which epitomized Brazilian mid-century style in 18 karat gold. By the time I lived in New York and it opened a store on Fifth Avenue, that affinity had turned lackluster.)

As many times as I remember going to Miki's apartment to play, I spent far more time at Elana's apartment, and she at mine. Miki never came to my apartment, and I don't remember her at Elana's apartment either. Berta *neni* kept a close eye on Miki, and her playdates were closely monitored by the old woman, so the girlfriends had to appear in her domain and under her scrutiny. The short of it was that Miki was coddled and spoiled. And yet, Elana and I had a far richer life, if certainly not as rich as our friend's wardrobe. (My mother made my clothes.)

Under Vera's direction, our mothers exposed us to many cultural and educational experiences, and without fail, Berta *neni* made sure Miki was not left behind our pace. Art exhibits? Check. Piano lessons? Check. English lessons? Check. Ballet classes? Well, for a short time; Miki was chubby and not physically agile. Summer camp? Check. Except that one summer when we went to a Jewish *Habonim* (Labor youth group) camp by bus with the other campers and teen counselors. Having said goodbye to our mothers as we boarded the bus, Miki with her mother and grandmother were in a taxi following the bus so that they could check out the camp. They did. And they immediately turned around with Miki in tow. These summer camps had none of the comforts of home, not even hot water; they were not appropriate for Miki.

Elana roamed the streets alone, an independent and self-confident tween. Her mother worked full-time. I eventually was also allowed to go visit her alone, but never to "roam" alone. Not that São Paulo was a dangerous city. Traffic was a problem, and annoying men felt bold enough to catcall and harass young girls. But I never felt unsafe in the city. I did feel queasy in public, however. Poverty, begging, rampant physical deformity, and leprosy made many streets where public buildings were to be found quite wretched. In the early days, while I was very young, impressionable, and insecure, I found myself with my mother at the central post office. These civic buildings were very important in the predigital and pretelecommunication age, where letters could be posted, phone calls could be placed in phone cubicles with the help of switchboard operators, and papers could be notarized. This is no hyperbole: everything had to be stamped (with many glued paper stamps) and notarized. Places such as these were teeming with poor people. One day, I did not have a chance to avert my eyes when a person with a face missing many features passed by (facial transplants were unheard of in 1962). Frozen with consternation I buried my thoughts; I chalked it up to another alien experience.

And yet there were many small parks in the city full of year-long tropical lushness and birdsong. And without my being aware of it at the time, there were mid-century architectural marvels tucked away on different streets. This was also the period, the early 1960s, when the new capital, Brasília, was under construction in the hinterland state of Mato Grosso. As one of the three architects of Brasília in 1960, Oscar Niemeyer's modernism left an indelible mark on me, spawning an affinity for modern architecture. To this day, my head turns for any post-Bauhaus building, an example of Brazilian modernist architecture, whether in New York (the United Nations Secretariat), São Paulo, or Brasília. The most iconic structure, only a few blocks from our apartment building, and in front of which I passed frequently in my walks throughout the city, was Niemeyer's S-shaped *Edifício* Copan on Avenida Ipiranga. I knew it was a substantial design then in my preteens, as I know now it is an internationally known building.

In my flat leather sandals, I wore a track into the sidewalks between my apartment and Elana's: down two blocks from Rua Santa Isabel; crossing the street to skirt Largo do Auroche, a small park; veering slightly left for a block and turning right on Avenida Duque de Caxias; proceeding a few blocks northeast until number 428. If we were not in school, if we were not at the ACM (the Y) taking swimming classes and socializing, or if we were not at a Jewish youth group gathering, then we were visiting each other at our respective apartments, and that was most of the time. We had no telephone, so our visits were always spontaneous.

I lived with my parents for several years in a studio apartment on Rua Santa Isabel number 314, at the corner facing the entrance to the gated, pseudo-gothic, immense medical campus of the Santa Casa de Misericórdia on Rua Dr. Cesário Mota Júnior. In that small one-room apartment, my parents used furniture and some drapes to fashion a bedroom alcove for me. Elana and I played under the dining table with dolls. One day Elana was chastising one of my dolls, shaking her, and the doll's head split from her chest by the neck. I was devastated. But I swallowed my urge to cry. I knew then that a friend was worth more than a doll. If not with dolls, then we played games. Or we told each other stories. We talked about our recent past in Israel. Elana told me stories about her dear grandmother, and her beautiful young aunt, Yael, who was a first runner-up in the 1951 Miss Israel contest, and her aunt's subsequent life as a newly wealthy bride in South Africa. My maternal grandmother, Magda, who migrated with us, also lived in São Paulo, so Elana knew her and loved her as well.

It was always exciting to visit my grandmother, and sometimes Elana and Miki came along. I have an iconic photograph of us three girls in front of the house my grandmother rented in Jundiaí, a few hours northwest of São Paulo where she ran a pension for German expats working at Krupp SA (*Sociedade Anonima*, i.e., Incorporated). My grandmother had a German Jewish husband, Ziggi, so the language and the European-style room and board she offered appealed to the German Krupp managers.

Most of the time, I visited at Elana's apartment. Her building was on Avenida Duque de Caxias, almost at the corner of Rua Barão de Limeira. The apartment building was a narrow twelve-floor structure with only one apartment per floor. The elevator opened onto a staircase landing facing the front door. Their door was never locked during the day because upon entering you found yourself in the workshop—they called it their factory. It was originally the apartment's enormous living room in the rear of the building, facing southwest, and a large, airy, inner courtyard formed by the surrounding buildings. The large wall-to-wall windows gave an atelier or art studio feel to the space. The walls were lined with wooden shelves bowed by the weight of bolts of leather in every color, spools of thread, and various bric-a-brac, boxes, and detritus. Ernö saved every scrap of anything useful (or useless) and was not one to maintain orderliness. He worked hard: his workstation, where he could be found every day six days a week for long hours, was the cutting table. It was in the left alcove of the "living room." He cut the leather into glove patterns using various dies: size, length, men's hands, women's hands. A short stocky man, when he was ready to cut, he heaved his sturdy body and jumped, pushing down on the lever of the cutting press. While visitors came, he never stopped working, just continued talking cheerfully and kibitzing.

Along the long wall on the right of the room was a row of sewing machines. One of these stations was Vera's. She was the seamstress, running the glove fingers on the specialized sewing machine up around and down, up around and down, four fingers in succession, two gloves, eight fingers, and the thumbs pieced separately. I still have a cherished pair of blue leather Weingarten gloves. And while Vera sewed, she'd look up above her squarish black eyeglass frames at the person she was talking to, her glasses usually slipping down her nose. Or, with a view directly to the front door, she peered over her glasses at the entering visitor with the scrutiny of a receptionist.

Between Vera and the window sat their only employee that I remember, a young Black man with an oval, somewhat freckled caramel-colored face, and an ever-so-slight tinge of auburn in his close-cropped Afro. He was the presser. With a mallet without a handle, he'd pound the newly sewn gloves into a flat pancake, fingers slightly overlapping from pointer to pinky, thumb folded and tucked under, and facing each other as in prayer, the dainty pair slipped into a clear plastic pouch. Next to Vera was a chair where my mother sat for hours keeping Vera company while the two talked. Ernö sometimes participated in the conversation. Vera was my mother's older (by a few years) mentor. She knew the ins and outs of immigrant life in São Paulo, and she guided my mother on all topics: medical, marital, economic, educational, and emotional. My mother always had time to keep Vera company. Vera was her lifeline, and Edith was Vera's daily buoy.

While the adults were in the workshop, Elana and I would, after our dutiful check-in with them, slip along the long narrow corridor past the eat-in kitchen to the front of the apartment—the building side fronting the Avenida, where there were two bedrooms. The first, at the end of the hall, was turned into a living room and "formal" dining room that also acted as the parents' sleeping quarters on the pullout sofa. The bedroom on the right was shared by Elana and her older brother, Yoni. He was about two or three years older, an accomplished student, and his mother's pride and joy as an expected future doctor. At one point he tutored me in math. He truly was very intelligent and an earnest but bouncy young teen. He was tall like his mother and good-looking. He took the world seriously but with a grain of salt and a touch of cynicism. He liked to joke like his father. Most of the time Elana and I were alone; at others, she and Yoni bickered with reasonable sibling rivalry. Name-calling was just a game.

If Vera favored Yoni, Ernö favored Elana. Brother and sister were very different, each had a winning personality, a tenacity, a graciousness and sincerity, and a deep moral virtue and integrity. Ernö never hid the fact that he sympathized with socialism, although he chose to emigrate from "socialist" Israel in the early 1950s to a country mired in right-wing tendencies. Vera was not a pretty woman, but at the risk of sounding clichéd she had the moral soundness that Jews call *tzeddakah,* which is a beauty in its own right, deeper and more permanent. She did not allow her children to breach her codes of conduct, even as she gave her daughter plenty of freedom, a virtual elastic band, when Elana pulled harder. She worked her body into her sewing machine, never getting her hair done, never getting a manicure, never collecting fine clothing like Elsa. She always wore black pants and flat black shoes. She was a tall woman, with straight black hair cut in a blunt bob, and pinned on one side with a clip or occasionally with a tortoise shell band. She seemed older than she was. She found me a little spoiled, but was glad I was Elana's friend, as she preferred me to Miki. Vera liked that I was smart and a good influence on her daughter, who was somewhat disinclined to face the academic grindstone. Vera's guiding principle in parenting was education, preferably British education, which she admired most of all. We were supposed to become the intelligentsia and to make up for the fact that she and her contemporaries survived the Holocaust with barely an education. Grateful for survival, she worked tirelessly to raise the next professional generation. She instructed my mother, and my mother listened.

This is the interior environment where I spent the years from 1959 to June 1964.

Outside our apartment homes, the city provided the backdrop of a walkable living space. São Paulo was not a beautiful city. It is still not a beautiful city. In the late 1950s and early 1960s it had an old flavor of Latin America, what seemed to me Latin-et-French-Art-Nouveau, but with less grandeur than Buenos Aires, for example. By then past its prime, the way a socialite who is fifty years past her prime still thinks she's glamorous, still wearing her perfume-reeking and out-of-style clothing from her heyday, still wearing makeup that gets smeared from week to week until her liner is thick as grease, her lipstick oxidized, her powder puff caked like mud. Her hair is matted, teased by the attempt to fluff it a few days before, her voice deep and throaty with a coating of nicotine and tar. São Paulo's air was poisoned with automobile exhaust; the Rio Tietê poisoned with chemicals, garbage, and sewage; the streets festooned with garbage; and corners reeking of urine. It still amazes me how relentlessly modernity tried knocking on her door, and how modern structures attempted to pierce the decadent and passé colonial and Belle Époque elegance with an electrifying vitality, only to look dirty, decrepit, and misused within just a few years. Thus modern, colonial, Belle Époque, and Art Nouveau, erected side by side, were embellished by a mass of humanity looking for its next meal, *cafézinho* (a little double shot of espresso) or shot of *pinga* (alcoholic drink made of sugar cane). Aside from a small number of the super-rich, even in the 1950s and 1960s Brazil was a country of poor, uneducated people with a high rate of illiteracy.

I liked São Paulo as much as I would have liked living with this has-been socialite. When I arrived in Brazil, the culture shock was as intense as the tropical heat. It shook me to the core. I resisted my new environment. And in that battle, my body lost. An allergic autoimmune disease afflicted me during my life in Brazil, first as huge painful itchy welts that I associated with eating meat, particularly pork, which I had never eaten before. After about a year, this autoimmune reaction ceased, and I avoided pork, but a few years later, these same welts would reappear if I was exposed to the sun, a condition called solar urticaria that went untreated. That, too, eventually passed.

I endured the assimilation into Brazilian life—my first of several foreign migrations—because I had Elana as a friend. This is the blessing a friendship can bestow. Her friendship was indispensable to me, because I had no siblings. Israeli born, too, she had come with her family several years earlier, and by the time I met her, she was fully Brazilian. She had fond memories of Israel, but she naturalized into her environment more easily and seamlessly than I did. Until today, when I see her and talk to her, she is Brazilian, in speech, education, and naturalization. Even so, unlike Brazilians, she retained an internationalism, thanks to the upbringing by her parents and their Jewish faith. Her friendship was the psychological curative for my pseudo assimilation. Unlike Elana, I never quite assimilated into Brazilian life.

When I was ten years old, on recess in the courtyard of our local elementary school, Oswaldo Cruz, two blocks from my apartment, I usually ate my favorite sandwich my mother made me, two slices of bread with cream cheese and a slice of green pepper. After this lunch eaten outside, I loitered around the yard while other girls, including Elana, who was a sporty tomboy, played the game of *queimada*. One day a girl approached me and asked who my saint was. My own saint? I was stumped, and so I answered, "I don't have a saint." There was pity in her eyes. I was Jewish, and the girls around me were Roman Catholic. They each had their favorite saint. Nothing in my experience in Brazil, short of the priest wearing a floor-length cassock entering our classroom for the daily prayers, was as alien to me as having a favorite saint.

Foundations

My tentative integration into Brazilian life was helped by the fact that my family and Elana's were close. We celebrated holidays together, such as Seder and New Year's Eve, as an extended family. Our parents planned trips together, vacations, weekends, and frequent outings to the countryside. Ernö had a car, first an old Land Rover, then a small Renault, and in the former, we piled in together and went places outside the city. Then my father got a used Jeep (when he worked for Jeep SA), and caravan-style, we'd decamp to the countryside. Our destinations were an escape for the mothers and a lark for Elana, Yoni, and me. I cannot think of any of these trips without feeling a song rise in my chest. As an only child, I had acquired two siblings and another set of guiding adults.

We did not have televisions. My mother would frequently take me to the movies, her favorite pastime, because she loved American films. There was the ballet, opera, and concerts at the Belle Époque-styled Teatro Municipal. If you squinted and ignored the surrounding raucous city sounds and the smells of excrement, you could imagine yourself in front of its architectural source, the Paris Opéra. Otherwise, recreational life was about weekend outings in the country or to the "interior." São Paulo sits on a plateau in the eastern part of the state of São Paulo, but any trip out of the metropolis was a jaunt into the "interior." Brazil's vastness, the fifth largest in the world after the United States, was incomprehensible, because not much of it was accessible. There were roads, but not everywhere; there were states of impenetrable jungles, in which we as white Europeans were not intended to set foot. There was as yet no ecotourism, and not much travel except among the larger cities of southern Brazil and up the narrow band off the Atlantic coast.

In summers we frequently went to the beaches of the southern Atlantic north of Santos. During several summers we'd get away for a week to a barely finished beachfront hotel on Praia dos Sonhos in Itanhaém, our two mothers and the three children sharing a large room. The Miami Hotel was not quite completed and had no well-furnished lobby. It was owner-managed by a Korean family, making the place homey and casual, and it had plenty of ping-pong tables. The surrounding area was not developed yet. The beaches were pristine back then, and they were sequined with a trove of rare shells—or jellyfish—each morning.

We weren't unaware of the geographical richness that constituted Brazil. In 1961 and 1962 our geography class consisted of memorizing all the rivers of the Amazon basin and the names of all the known tribes. Little did we know that in our lifetime, the Amazon would start going up in flames. Our geography teacher, Professor Nunes, did not tell us that the Amazon was the oxygen and water engine of the planet, and that above the Rio Amazonas ran a river in the troposphere. Ecology was a very distant subject in that geography class. Just name the rivers and the native tribes with their unpronounceable names, as he asked, and we'd get a passing grade. Our real geography lesson was provided to us by our parents with their wanderlust.

There was plenty of nature to see outside São Paulo, past the hectares and hectares of coffee plantations. One year, our families decided to make a trek to Foz do Iguaçú in two cars, neither car large enough to hold seven people and luggage. At our young age, it was the adventure of a lifetime. It took several days over dirt roads, but we made it . . . and then turned around almost immediately. Iguaçú village was still undeveloped, with few decent hotels and lacking the trappings of touristy kitsch. There was only one historic, luxury hotel, which our parents could not afford. There were some guardrails on the edge of paths along the falls, but not many, and there were no crowds. Visiting the place at that time was like a meeting with earth's mighty force without encumbrances. For a young person, it was like an expedition into uncharted territory, one of the wonders of the world before the age of European exploration. The only other time I felt so close to this planet's majesty was on a raft for a week on the Colorado River in 1976, when there were no other rafts for several days at a time, an experience that now cannot be re-created. A few years later, on my first trip to Niagara Falls, for all its hyped greatness I found it disappointing: after you see a lion, a kitten is just a small cat.

It seems to me that my five years in Brazil were more gorged with experiences and memories than any other five-year period of my life. Perhaps my senses were on high alert with dislocation. Perhaps my sense of time had to slow down, because I found myself in an unfamiliar place. Perhaps it was because I was still a child, but changing, and had become aware of the world around me precisely because I was an alien in that world. Moving to Brazil awakened me from a protected infancy, and I became engaged as an observer. I was inhibited and fearful, unlike Elana, who was unrestrained and daring in her engagement with her surroundings. Being timid, I turned into a witness instead.

Our childhood life was experienced in a cocoon of Brazilian sights, sounds, and smells. The polluted air, the yearly Carnaval revelry and mayhem, the prostitutes propped at their doorsteps or windowsills. We also experienced the election and fiascos of Labor Party leaders such as the leftist Jânio Quadros and his vice president, João Goulart, becoming the next president, setting the stage for the Golpe de '64 (the military coup of 1964), just as my parents and I were leaving Brazil. During this period, however, news from the outside world also reached us: the talk of Castro taking over Cuba; the hush-hush talk about the salacious Profumo affair in London (the sex scandal between a government minister and a nineteen-year-old Christine Keeler, a fact our mothers unsuccessfully tried to hide from us); the capturing of Adolf Eichmann in Argentina and his trial in Jerusalem; the assassination of JFK; the transition of Pope John XXIII to Pope Paul VI.

We lived a charmed and protected life in a spartan bubble that was bound to burst eventually. We were not ready to swim in the raw currents of the second half of the twentieth century. We were still wearing ankle socks and flat shoes but were beginning to sense the thrill of wearing nylon hose we'd wrest from our mothers. And with it the need to shave our legs, which our mothers did not do. First, we needed to awaken to the antics of boys who were not yet astute enough to attract girls. And in the meantime, not yet fourteen, I had to experience a sexual assault by a stranger in my building's elevator. Luckily, I escaped as the elevator door opened, and I could run into my apartment. However, I was traumatized by the "close call," which made me afraid of men and elevators for at least another eight years, and during that time I never entered an elevator if there was only a man inside; if a man entered after me, I'd quickly get out. As we were slowly awakening to the opposite sex, good or bad, we were forced to part.

Language Barriers

When I arrived in Brazil, there was no language class for a foreign student, that is, no teaching Portuguese as a second language. I could not read the Latin alphabet, and there were no reading remediation lessons. I was assigned to a class and shown to a seat. And I put my nose to the language grindstone. Since everyone in my class was learning to write, I did the same. The Roman alphabet was revealed without any fuss or difficulty. Was the babel around me distressing? Of course, but I had no choice, and I was an amenable and dutiful student. So I stuck it out and persevered.

Nonetheless, my past was cut off. I had experienced a long and disturbing cross-Atlantic voyage, with a strange cultural phenomenon involving a Greek god, Neptune, which originally devolved into a sailors' hazing ritual at the crossing of the Equator and acted out by sailors parading in costumes in modern times. And after landing in a foreign country, I experienced the unnerving daily issues of settling in. Consequently, perhaps I felt classrooms were a safe place. In truth, my favorite class, unsurprisingly, was art. Surrounded by speakers of a foreign language, my muteness at first was compounded by the obstacle of a certain imposed deafness. It felt like being immersed underwater and hearing human voices above the surface. I think this lasted about two to three months. At someone's apartment where we first rented a room, the radio blasted traditional Brazilian songs oozing with dramatic cravings of love, and radio hosts made pronouncements in the intonation of football announcers. *Gooooooooal* is what comes to mind, even if I was not listening to a *futeból* game but to a declaimed advertisement for something or other beyond my comprehension. At that age, the prosody that I heard via the thickened space of this language barrier started to form the basis of mastering another language. I had already done that before: when I heard and listened to my parents and grandparents conversing in Hebrew, Hungarian, Romanian, or German. When it came to language, I did not feel passive, and I did not act oblivious: I was a listener. Cocooned in my inner world, I listened to and observed the outside, paying attention to and absorbing languages.

We spoke Hebrew at home while I was learning to speak, read, and write Portuguese in school. I flowed from a private inside (indoor) language, to a compulsory outside (outdoor) language, a phenomenon well known to children of immigrants. Inside being the family home, and outside being the newly adopted environment. Hebrew remained our language for communicating at home for several years, gurgling on but then rippling out, an evanescence of language into limbo when abandoned. My parents quickly learned to speak Portuguese because they already knew a Romance language, their second, Romanian. Therefore, I did not have to act as their interpreter as a preteen in our early years in Brazil, because they sustained their language independence.

This should not be seen as a revelation; after all, my parents had transitioned to a foreign language twice before: between their native Hungarian spoken at home and in their community, and the compulsory Romanian imposed by political boundaries that kept changing. And then in their late teens transitioning to their adopted Hebrew after they joined the clandestine migration from Europe to Palestine at the end of the Holocaust. This clandestine migration of survivors from Europe to Palestine, called *ha'apalah* in Hebrew, was a gathering of Holocaust survivors called *Aliyah B*, the second migration of the twentieth century, preceded by an earlier group of Zionist pioneers. Both my parents and Elana's, as survivors, were swept up in this historical migration.

It is not a rare phenomenon for European Jews who lived in the diaspora to experience diglossia—the necessity to speak one language at home, the mother tongue, and another language outside home, the official one. Once the expelled Jew must live in an altogether different country, however, where none of her languages are spoken, the migrant or refugee becomes alingual for a while, that is, not fluent in any language. My grandmother, Magda, was an example. Her Romanian was minimal, her native Hungarian, although fluent, became vernacular and lacked the high Hungarian grammar, her Hebrew was a patois, and in Brazil and then in the United States she also spoke a kind of Portuguese and then English patois. Her language acuity was superb, compared with so many of her Hungarian friends who could never utter a word of any other language, no matter the longevity of their residence.

In the meantime, our social circle consisted of other immigrants who passed through the same gates we did. They were also European Jews who escaped to Palestine but left after the formation of the State of Israel and landed in South America. Like my parents, other families, too, could not settle in for the longest time, being driven to pick up roots again. It occurred as if their original persecution and dispersion from war-ravaged Europe compelled them to keep on moving. Family units had been set into motion by an appalling force that overcame their inertia, the past assimilation that made many Jews blend into a European land, only to be excised by antisemitism, oppression, and ultimately, Nazi elimination. And some of them, especially my family, once in motion, they couldn't stop. There were at least a dozen families in São Paulo that I met and interacted with who arrived in that same, or an earlier, migrant wave. The parents spoke their native European language, some also spoke Hebrew, and finally their daily work and school life was conducted in Portuguese with a heavy accent.

I was swept up in this migration, and like someone who flips out of a canoe into the water, she does not think about the meaning of the event or why it happened, but only to bob up above the water to breathe and move, despite the current, toward something to hold on to. The current was the language, and learning it meant to be able to swim.

How to explain this except that Hungarian was embedded in me through spending so much time with my grandmothers during my early formative years and, in addition, listening to my parents speak among themselves and to their parents in Hungarian. Necessity is the mother of invention and the mother of speech. For me, learning three languages before age ten was necessary, and in my circumstances, I even heard another two languages spoken around me.

My closest friends in Brazil, Elana and Miki, were my migrant, multilingual doppelgängers. Within those first early months of arriving in Brazil and encountering my first lifelong friends, a strange thing happened. As I was learning Portuguese, I suddenly started to speak Hungarian. I transitioned from a single language to three. It was a spontaneous twofer.

Moving Away, Looking Back and Looking Forward

In June 1964 my parents and I left Brazil permanently and flew to the United States with temporary American tourist visas, and tucked away, to continue to our destination, Canadian immigrant visas. That was like throwing caution to the wind, including all the possessions accumulated in five years, plus friends to boot. We embarked into the wild blue yonder, during the early age of jet travel, with only what could fit into four suitcases, plus a curiosity that did not fit our lifestyle: a carry-on vanity case. All the luggage was in matching olive-colored leather. In Brazil, leather was cheaper than plastic. My parents had Israeli passports, which had gotten us to Brazil in January 1959, when I was eight. Although we lived in Brazil for five and a half years, we did not become Brazilian citizens, purposefully remaining unsettled and stateless, as if my father refused to set roots in a place where he had no intention of staying, using it as a placeholder without admitting it openly. Thus, we continued to use temporary Israeli passports, and I, having no passport, continued traveling on my mother's. The purpose of the layover in the United States was to visit family.

My father had formulated a plan. We were bound for Toronto, Canada, and he had acquired Canadian immigrant visas for us, though without any prospects, except his faith in his abilities to work. Canada, unlike America, would welcome us. The US State Department, led by white, patrician Ivy Leaguers, tended to be antisemitic and wanted few East European Jews to immigrate. Nineteen years after the end of the Holocaust, the State Department and American laws still considered that some types of Jews (and some others) were undesirable. The law that barred us was the 1924 Johnson-Reed Immigration Act, written by Rep. Albert Johnson (R-WA), a known eugenicist, and cosponsored with Sen. David Reed (R-PA). They were staunch isolationists and racists. In 1964 this law was amended, and President Lyndon Johnson signed the new law, which opened the opportunity for my family to immigrate to the United States in 1967. (There's an elucidating documentary by Ken Burns on PBS, *The US and the Holocaust,* in which the salient topic of the US State Department during the Holocaust reflects my family's experience.)

I remember trying to imagine what Canada would be like. With my prior two vantage points, one being the Mediterranean Levant, followed by the sojourn in the South American temperate zone elbowing on the wild tropics, Canada seemed like the North Pole. Of course, I had no say in the matter. I was always a quiet child, but my father's peregrinations made me withdrawn, because I became homeless. Each time I got used to a place and tentatively felt secure, another migration wrenched it away. I was so introverted that I felt the ridicule of adults who looked at me as an impenetrable object, a dismaying child.

I left Brazil in 1964 lacking self-confidence, perpetually insecure, and not knowing how I was to understand the confusing world outside the environment I had lived in temporarily. I took with me the knowledge of what friendship meant and the knowledge that my parents were still my protectors but not for much longer. Being already a teenager, I was expected to be more independent in a new place. I left Brazil with very few material possessions, and no understanding of how my experience until then was going to translate into another culture. I left behind a soulmate, and I went to North America as an only child again.

I was embarking on a migration to an education system of much higher rigor, with a distinct separation between church and state. I was embarking on my second migration, this time from a postcolonial Latin country with a racial checkerboard and a tenuous hold on democracy, to a thoroughly democratic English- and French-speaking bilingual country in the apex of a liberal era. My first dislocation from one home, at age nine, and arrival into another home, would have to serve as the basis of a repeat experience at age fourteen, but in a different environment. My frame of reference would not necessarily help me navigate the cultural changes, but the experience of having done so once before would be the thing for me to rely on in a reprise.

On our stopover in Rio in 1964, which was like a bonus mini vacation, we took the opportunity to sightsee: Christ the Redeemer on Corcovado, the cable car to Sugarloaf, the beach at Ipanema with its iconic wavy sidewalk designed by the landscape architect Roberto Burle Marx. We stayed at a hotel in the old city near the beach. We were well dressed, we had new leather suitcases, we were bound for North America, and my father was ecstatic. My mother was pregnant, in her first trimester, and already her midriff was bulging. I was disconnected from reality, experiencing a mental trip from so much stimulation on my first touristy experience. I wavered between the exotic attractions of Rio and the horror of soon being cut off from a sense of security, speaking the language, or understanding the customs.

Sightseeing in this Carioca World Heritage city could not mask the reality that we were just passing through on the way to the unknown. We were five years on from our penurious arrival, but better off. I had learned the language, and I had adjusted to the scholastic tempo of the country, both admirable achievements. I had had friends and many good memories. And now, an annulment of those experiences was to take place: a door closing, a curtain drawn, *finis*.

If free to choose, I would have remained in Brazil out of inertia. Dreaming of America was my father's dream. American films and the actors my mother loved were her passion, not mine. American movies did not quite give me a taste of what life was like in the United States, and none at all about Canada; I was too inexperienced. Not to mention that American films were holograms of American life. One of the last films I saw in Brazil was *The Parent Trap*, with Hayley Mills. It was set in a fictional American summer camp, and it seemed Martian to me, especially since my summer camp experiences in Brazil were so primitive and raw.

Why was America such a glittering idea to the rest of the world? Was it reflected by Hollywood? Did it really uphold the utopian vision of middle class (and white) life to everyone in the world? Was the Bernstein-Sondheim song "America" a musical gem that nailed this conundrum on its head? "Industry boom in America / Twelve in a room in America / Lots of new housing with more space / Lots of doors slamming in our face" sing the girls and the boys with different perspectives in *West Side Story*.

Although my parents made sure I got a head start in learning English, I also learned French at the same time. But we weren't going to France. Had my parents miraculously decided to return to Israel, I would have rejoiced, even with the loss of five years of my native Hebrew. Instead, my family had only one direction: going north. America was the goal. My father had been to New York when he worked as a mechanic on an Israeli mercantile ship in 1957, and he loved the experience. He brought back Corn Flakes breakfast cereal and a little bottle of Coca-Cola! Moving to Canada was a step closer to his goal.

Thinking back to five years earlier, in January 1959, we had alighted from the French ship SS *Bretagne*'s third class in the old, run-down port of Rio de Janeiro, and immediately looked for transportation to São Paulo, never leaving the antique, neglected, and economically dilapidated section around the port, never seeing the rest of Rio (that's why in 1964 it was a treat). The *Bretagne* was scrapped in 1963 after a serious fire while being retrofitted, removing second- and third-class berths. There were five of us new immigrants to Brazil: my parents; my grandmother, Magda; her latest husband, Ziggi; and a whole lot of suitcases. We piled into a taxi, where I was squeezed between my mother and the driver. The luggage was strapped in the trunk with the lid tied down and more luggage strapped on the roof. The trip from Rio to São Paulo, about 430 kilometers, took half a day before the days of interstate highways. January is summer in the Southern Hemisphere, and cars did not have air-conditioning, so we traveled with the windows open. During the trip a wasp flew in, and I was stung on my thumb. The commotion did not stop the travel, and somehow my mother provided a salve, either psychological or a first aid rummaged from the bottom of my grandmother's pocketbook. Ziggi, for his part, discouraged the dramatic attention to an eight-year-old girl's transient pain.

We were deposited in São Paulo late in the evening in front of the main train station, Estação da Luz, when its gates were already shuttered for the night. The adults went in search of a hotel for the night, and I remember tagging along and seeing an old, disagreeable hotel, a fleabag that the adults refused to stay in. And so, I was made to sleep on the luggage on the street in front of the train station. We were migrants and I was helpless. We were homeless. The experience of sleeping on the street engraved a breach in the plot of my life: unlike good memories or neutral memories, this one caused a crease, a rut, that like a scratch on a vinyl record would dislocate and persistently make the narrative of my life skip out of place.

In 1959, Brazil was a very poor and backward country. Compared with the Israel we had left behind, with its Zionist vibrancy, Jewish squabbling and optimism, construction, growth, energy, and a newly minted government, Brazil seemed a decrepit state. It gave an aura of a frontier territory awash in natural riches and a society on the verge of development stumped by the recurring setbacks to colonial mentality: the corrosive tendency of people in power to practice embezzlement and bribery instead of leadership. The construction of Brasília, the new capital in the interior of the state of Mato Grosso, was miraculous. There was no Hebrew TV broadcast service in Israel when we left, the first Israeli broadcast service with a single station was inaugurated in 1966, but in Brazil, with service available, there was only limited access to TV sets. Private phones and washing machines were also unaffordable for us in both countries.

It took us two days on the train to make our way to Curitiba, the state capital of Paraná, a distance a car can span in a few hours today. Bus service was just a tad better, with buses spewing poison. Even while I was seeing the countryside from the window of the moving train, once we got on board on our second day in Brazil, the view of lush unknown vegetation imprinted on my vision an incongruous green panorama. In Curitiba, where I was demoted to first grade, an art teacher taught us to draw Brazilian trees, and slowly I laid claim to the new country's landscape and iconography. Still, Brazil gave me the feeling that uprooted, I had arrived at the funeral of my old country. And so, I cried and cried. While living in Curitiba for about six months, I had succumbed to an untreated clinical depression. I stopped crying when Elana and I became friends soon after meeting at Miki's apartment.

Unlike my arrival in Brazil in January 1959, I arrived in America as a visitor in the summer of 1964 bedazzled by its wealth, orderliness, punctuality, cleanliness, delicious, homogenized milk, attractive and well-made clothing, slick highways, courteous drivers, obedient line formations; and stupefied by grievous racial segregation and the early involvement in Vietnam. I may not have shared in letters to Elana the degrading processes with arrogant immigration personnel at border crossings, because immigration to America was a humiliating experience that I kept to myself. If I did not share this experience in my first letter to Elana, then it's because our family reunion was an eclipsing, happy, and positive story, while the immigration process to get into the country was embarrassingly demeaning. My earlier entry to Rio de Janeiro getting off a ship in 1959 did not elicit memories of frightening men in authoritarian uniform. At least they did not wear flat-top hats, as officials in authoritarian regimes tend to wear. There was a comfort in that earlier swift and painless immigration procedure. American officials had softer hats, but not less power, and their mien was arrogant. They were guarding the entrance gates. As I look back, obviously Brazil wanted immigrants, but America did not, at least not us, and instead, we came as visitors on the way to Canada.

There was no direct flight to New York in 1964: São Paulo's airport could not handle the new large jets. In Rio, a transit between airports was required because of airport size: domestic flights arrived at Santos Dumont (SDU), and departing international flights took off from the larger Galeão (GIG), a military base built earlier that had longer runways. Not being long haulers, Varig jets could not yet connect directly to New York's

JFK. We traveled on a Varig flight that had to make a stop along the way in the Caribbean and then arrived at LaGuardia. A transfer at LaGuardia to an American Airlines plane bound for Detroit was also a transfer of mindsets for me. Detroit is where family, at last, would be waiting for our visit.

Unlike the self-confident and independent Elana, at fourteen I was still timid enough to accomplish no more than tagging along with my parents in a foreign land. My mother tagged along too. It was my father who was the brave, determined one leading us: through immigration, customs, airport gates, through a miasma of English I could understand a little and my parents not at all. My private English lessons in São Paulo had been with a congenial woman, born in India, who spoke with a British accent, Miss Margaret Fleury. Our limited conversations related to the readings she assigned to me. She taught me to read and write elementary English, and she allowed only English to be spoken during the lessons. But once on English-speaking soil, my ears perked up. My father would respond to the question regarding our destination that we were bound for *dah'-tro-eet* (Hungarian pronunciation). In response to which only the kindliest of Americans figured out we were bound for Detroit (*dih-tro'yt*). At no time in their lives had my parents heard how "Detroit" is pronounced. Is it their fault? They knew no Americans. And as a French-named city, it would have been *deh-troah'*, so in my opinion, Americans mispronounced it too. But it seemed humiliating at the time. I internalized that feeling. One more step down the ladder of confidence. However, once on board, aloft, above the clouds, observing those clouds I saw them as cities in the sky. Such a wondrous country!

My aunt Gitta, uncle Egon, and cousin Jack waited for us on arrival at the Detroit airport on a sunny, beautiful day in June 1964. We piled into their gorgeous American car. And they drove us on beautifully smooth concrete highways and roads.

Everything was so clean! My first impression of the US was that it was antiseptic. Plastic wrapping was the national tactile experience. As for us, our clothing and our bags, Gitta declared that we stank. We brought with us the smell of Brazil, which was foreign to her and to other Americans. People smell according to nationality. I thought Americans smelled of . . . soap and deodorant? Armpit odor was missing. That was a fact of life in the rest of the world. Soap, detergent, disinfectant, paint, plastic, medicine, and refrigeration were the American anti-odor salve. Milk tasted like . . . milk! And I started drinking it. There were no delicious tropical fruits, but there were sweet oranges (not a tropical fruit), juicy crisp apples, crimson cherries, and much more flavorful grapes. I could get used to this, I thought. And there were no more lepers on the street. I could put away my nausea brought on by so much human suffering. This time, migration did not induce in me an autoimmune illness as it did when I arrived in Brazil, just the buzz of dislocation.

We stayed with our relatives in the suburbs of Detroit for about a month, before heading to our destination in Toronto. Canada provided me with a different ambience from what I experienced in Michigan, where we were under the protective wing of my aunt, and where I had fun—first horseback ride, first bowling game, first drive-in movie, first drive-in hamburger joint and milkshake, first snow, first sled, first snowman. For years afterward, through the latter 1960s, visiting Michigan was always a vacation and always a treat for me. Having to cross the border from Canada was not a treat. We did not have valid passports, and entering for a visit required convoluted papers, translated, notarized, stamped, outdated, and seeming to provide no protection. Our papers and our bearing elicited obnoxious attitudes from the American immigration officials at the border. Each time we crossed from Ontario to Michigan to visit family, it was a demeaning experience.

Migration is humiliating. It belittles the migrant. It infantilizes the seeker who is unfamiliar with the new customs and is uncomfortable with the new language. It impresses on the seeker that the keepers of the gates feel superior and play for power. The incoming petitioner feels the implicit questions at the border, "Why are you here? What makes you sure we want you?" It is not a secret that only certain passports carry a cachet that allows their bearer to hold their head high. And an American passport was such a document in my father's eyes. It opened doors to safety and security. And it was something I desperately craved.

I must have shared all these other, positive impressions of America with Elana. I must have surely shared with her the excitement of meeting my cousin, aunt, and uncle after not seeing them for nine years, and my wonder at their lower-middle-class lifestyle, which seemed so much more elevated than the poverty I saw in Brazil or the standard of living my parents cobbled together. I'm not sure I knew what lower middle class was in Brazil, if it existed at all—maybe we lived the lower-middle-class or working-class life—but it did not compare to the comforts I encountered in America. I most likely did not share with her my feeling of loneliness and loss while implanting myself in the land of plenty. But did I share my family's devastation at the end of that first year? The letters will have to reveal if I shared any of this family tragedy.

Did I miss the disorganized, disorderly, tardy, nonstandard social customs of Brazil? No. The dissembling, the procrastinating, the insouciant and languid attitude toward schedules, appointments, goals, objectives, and ambitions? No. *Se Deus quizer* is the Brazilian motto and creed to live by: "If God wishes." Nothing in Brazil was in the hands of the individual; all was in God's hands. And not long after, I landed in a country where individual ambition, drive, aggressiveness, and objectives rule the overall American culture, even if "In God We Trust" is the national motto.

Part Two

The Correspondence

Sī valēs bene est, ego quoque valeō.
SVBEEQV: "If you're well, that's good,
I am also well."

—Latin salutation found in Roman letters
since the fourth century BC

The stack of letters

Letters 1964 to 1970

The Early Letters: Fourteen Going on Fifteen

Elana wrote to me in Portuguese. I answered her in Portuguese for a few years, then switched to English, first, because it became harder for me to write in Portuguese, and second, because Elana became a fluent reader in English. My letters have not survived. Elana kept them for decades, but with a large family and multiple moves, the boxes they were stored in were tossed inadvertently, which she deeply regretted. The existing collection of letters is like a one-way dialogue, where the letter-writer voice is heard across many decades and the replies are not; instead, they are filled in. After each letter, except when the letters arrive in a blitz later on, I recount what transpired in my life while we were corresponding. I speak back to her across the years from my current perspective a half century later, remembering and reflecting.

Since my letters no longer exist, they're not being novelized here. Instead, each of Elana's letters elicits an examination of the character of the sender and what she wrote. I reminiscence about our time together, relating how our bonds were formed before we parted. I attempt to explain some of her comments and memories, tying them to places, people, and events that were mentioned earlier. And finally, I recount my life when I received the letter, illuminating what I could be writing to her in return. My written responses to her letters are not divorced from my current state, however, because my responses are contemporary and represent how I feel retrospectively. They represent what I remember. While writing, I endeavored to bring up memories long neglected, which seem to have taken no space in my brain, as if erased. Except that I have proofs: my many albums of photographs from this period, with photos displayed in chronological order; and most of all, I have her contemporaneous words. Each of her letters can catch my lies if my memory deludes me; each of her letters can become a mirror to my recollection. And that kind of mirror does not lie.

If Elana's environment, family life, and internal struggles are the perplexing and bemused journals, then I am the docent guiding the reader through the archive. If her letters are the chronicles of a young woman growing up, as I was at the same time, then I'm the interpreter of our shared hopes and dreams, and I am also the oracle of what comes to be.

As a docent, I comment on my translations to clarify various cultural and language differences. When a word or phrase in the letter needs an immediate clarification, I place it in square brackets. An ellipsis represents the removal of a repetitive description or account, usually of her classes and grades. I elaborate on references to our shared experience while I lived in Brazil. I need not endeavor to paint a picture of Elana, because her letters are remarkable in demonstrating her personality and her essence. The letters are revealing and evidential. My goal in this memoir format, a dialogue across time, is to understand how and why we became friends, why the friendship lasted over the years, and mostly, to uncover how important these letters were to me in the situation I was forced to endure.

The first collection of letters spans the years from August 1964 until July 1970, when I traveled to Brazil to visit her for the first time since our separation. The letters were written in a stream of words, as in a diary, in the informal language of a literate young woman. The writing was always neat, there were rarely any erasures, cross-outs, or blotting. There were no paragraph breaks (I added them while translating), but the sentences were fully grammatical and very often expressive and evocative. All caps and interjections appear frequently. I kept these, and I kept all numbers as numerals. The writing was colloquial with a bit of occasional slang. As the years passed, the topics became more serious and dramatic. The language matured, and the writing became more poignant. We were growing up. We had lived through social experiences, and these experiences created memories. We didn't have TVs; films were few and far between. We were not controlled by or influenced by cultural trends. We had no luxuries at all, few clothes, and little paraphernalia; our lives were not replete with possessions: in comparison to today, we lived blissfully boring lives that seemed carefree. However, as our teen years ended, we were facing a new era, and describing it made our letters more thoughtful.

While translating Elana's letters into English, I did not rewrite or paraphrase them or adhere to English writing conventions. How do you translate this kind of epistolary language and straddle the fine line between an authentic Brazilian voice and an editorial-ready English-language pattern? As the translator, I chose to keep her natural Brazilian-Portuguese voice, turns of phrase, tempo, and emotional tones, and not use an Anglophone pattern that a Canadian or American young woman would use. The reader may sometimes find her letters stilted: I did that on purpose; I want the reader to hear a Brazilian young woman, not an English-speaking protagonist. If read aloud, her voice should be speaking English with a thick Portuguese accent.

Let me turn to her letters: after each one written with the voice of a young friend left behind so many years before, I answer in retrospect. I call her back across the years.

Adolescence: In an Alien Land Again

São Paulo, August 9, 1964
Dear Ruth,

How are you all? I hope this finds you healthy and happy. I don't know how to tell you how much I miss you. It even seems that I was suddenly left alone.

Flávia and everyone asks me how you are doing, and I answer everything that you wrote me. All of them send regards, hugs, kisses, etc.

Forgive me for this tardy letter, but you must already know that my grandmother died. I can't accept it. I was at camp when this happened. They didn't even call me out; my mother will probably travel in September to see my grandfather. But first, she will pass by London to meet my aunt who will come with Léon (second son), since she has a third girl who was born two days before my dear grandmother died, and in her memory my aunt named her Yudit.

I applied to be counselor at camp, and I made out well. I got Cabin One with only girls aged six and seven. I started school well. I am so happy that you did well in your English exam. I hope you will pass the next school entry exam even better.

It's a pity that you cut your marvelous hair. Did you at least save it? If yes, send me a little of it (if you can) as a memento.

Estelinha misses you a lot. Our English teacher [Miss Margaret Fleury] *sends kisses and regards.*

Ruth, I have a million things to tell you, which would not fit on these little pages. It's Sunday, and I can't find the pad. I think this will do this time, right?

Don't do like me. Send a letter soon, because I'm going crazy wanting news from you.

More than anyone, your friend who always cherished you, who cherishes you, and will always cherish you, guaranteed,

Elana

PS Don't worry about Miki, I will not give her your address, OK? Estelinha sends a letter together with this one.

Toronto, August 1964

I received Elana's first letter soon after settling into a new apartment and preparing to enter a new school in Toronto, Canada. The experiences of the migration that summer were still vividly raw. My life had not yet settled into a comfortable and secure routine. I did not resist this, but I also did not buy into it: I was living it in the third person, in some form of dissociation. I was on autopilot, and I was going to wait and see what would come to pass. This was a defensive attitude on my part; I did not wish to relive the trauma I suffered at age nine when my family moved to Brazil.

In this first letter, Elana sadly reveals that her grandmother died. This is the grandmother she used to talk about so much. And Elana's mother, Vera, who had not set foot outside Brazil since the mid-1950s, flew to London to meet her sister, Yael. This is the first of many such notices that I received from Elana over the years. Yael's newborn at the time, Yudit, would become Elana's favorite cousin.

Elana mentions Estelinha, my classmate. She was my friend during my last two years of living in Brazil. She was a petite, gentle, and quiet girl with straight, inky black hair, beautiful dark eyes, and long black lashes. An orphan, she lived with her aunt in São Paulo. I corresponded with her for a year or two and then stopped. Aside from our timidity, we had less in common than what tied me with Elana. Someone can be a good friend, but the longevity of a friendship is not guaranteed by the depth of the friendship, and with Estelinha, the distance was an obstacle. She would have been a good friend for much longer had I stayed in Brazil, and yet, whatever magic potion existed in my friendship with Elana, it did not appear with this charming, quiet, and beautiful girl. Between Elana and me there was more fire, and we were going to keep that magic ember alive.

When I arrived in Michigan at my aunt Gitta's in the summer of 1964, being a hairdresser, she gave me a haircut. It befitted a new older-than-you-really-are American teen, a pseudo-adult. I desperately wanted to feel grown-up and secure, but in fact, I felt I was an impostor, and a haircut masked what I had been so far, an immature girl. Elana mentioned she wanted a locket of my hair. I don't remember if I sent it to her, but my cut-off brunette ponytail is still in one of my drawers. After all, as odd as this sounds, this was hair I had grown in Brazil.

At age fourteen, having become a summer camp counselor, Elana stepped away from the experiences we had together attending several seasons of austere Jewish camps. Her summer job was more consequential in the development of adolescence than my mere mature haircut. I could only imagine that Elana must have been a terrific counselor. She was energetic, enthusiastic; she loved games and physical competition, *horah* dancing, and singing. She was a model to her young charges, since she herself had always been a dedicated group participant. Elana was a comrade-in-arms that in semi-Hebrew is called a *chevrehman,* a portmanteau word.

It was many more years before I would land my first summer job. As much as I would have liked to be a camp counselor, I could not even garner babysitting requests. Almost no one knew or trusted me as a new immigrant. I had not gone to summer camps in Canada, so I had no contacts and connections to such places and the people who run them. I did not have friends in Toronto who either went to summer camp or worked as teen counselors.

At the end of summer, with trepidation and unease about the unknown, I was about to enroll at Vaughn Road Collegiate Institute (VRCI), a high school in Toronto, Ontario. We had moved into a small apartment across the street from the school on Vaughn Road at the corner of Winona Avenue. The instructions I received from the school in August to prepare for the start of ninth grade included a list of stationery to buy at a small store a few blocks away, the likes of which I never used in Brazil, where we only needed some notebooks and pens. What was a three-ring binder? Included was a combination lock to be used on a locker to store books, coats, and sundries between classes. I had not had a locker in my Brazilian schools. I can still open this lock with one hand (I used to hold my books in the other), so ingrained in my brain did the number combination become.

Why did something as insignificant as this become seared in my mind? Maybe because I was in a new environment that was foreign to me. I barely spoke the language, and every action, every activity had to be done with complete conscious attention. It was emotionally exhausting. I was anxious and apprehensive about the strangeness of it all. If humans think in fast or slow modes, according to the renowned behavioral economist Daniel Kahneman in *Thinking Fast and Slow*, then as an immigrant, every minute outside home I spent in slow thought mode. Home was a haven, outside home was a challenge course. In other words, everything had to be done purposefully and analytically; nothing was done automatically. Every minute of my day in the new school required intense concentration. Therefore, the smells, the sights, the teachers, and the educational customs of a 1964 Canadian high school were seared into my brain, including a lock combination. I was on hyperdrive.

In my Canadian high school, there were no priests in floor-length cassocks like in Brazil, but each morning the intercom piped into the classroom the voice of the principal praying "Our Father, who art in heaven, hallowed be Thy name . . ." Didn't take me long to memorize it, but at least I didn't have to stand out as the only one not crossing myself. Torontonian Presbyterianism seemed a little more benign than Brazilian Roman Catholicism, before I learned more about religions. I tried to stand respectfully and not show that my feelings about public school prayer were in turmoil.

In Toronto, my father continued his habit of not joining a Jewish congregation or club. In São Paulo, I had access to such clubs because Elana joined them and their summer camps, and I did as she did, under my mother's guidance as suggested by Vera. In Toronto, we were outside the Jewish community. I did not know enough to feel this disadvantage. It was lost among the many other disadvantages of a newcomer. My life in Toronto seemed as thin as the frigid winter air. And summer or winter, I felt I was living out in the cold.

In my new environment, I started grade nine without support or any tutoring for English as a second language. I was expected to dive in, like I had done in first grade in Brazil. I had to jump in and swim. No one was going to help me float. English class started off with reading *Twelfth Night*. I was horrified; I understood nothing of Shakespearian English. It was followed by *Julius Caesar*. I was numb. I floundered with writing essays. While my teacher, Miss McGrath, noticed me, she did not extend me any favors, extra attention, or extra time. She treated me like any English-fluent Canadian in her class and critiqued my minuscule essays with "You need to elaborate." As if I could. *If only I could raise up my voice, Miss McGrath!*

I did well in French. I started German, why not another language, my sixth could be just as easy. Science with Mr. Ferguson was bearable because we had hands-on labs, and so I felt comfortable and proficient. Algebra and geometry should have been easy but weren't, because Brazilian schools did not prepare me well in math. In history (English, not Canadian, for some obscure colonialist reason) I was on a par in lack of knowledge with other ninth graders. In geography, I could indulge in my sense of world travel of which my fellow students were ignorant.

My father found a job as a tool and die maker at a small machine shop, then switched to working in an auto dealership service shop. He was a talented mechanic, and being a tool and die maker is the apogee of that craft. He was still a heavy smoker in 1964. He made his own lighter out of machined stainless steel. I've kept it as a remembrance of him, because it's a marvel in workmanship. My mother managed the domestic work and spent time visiting her elderly great-uncle and great-aunt on Winona Road. Mr. Lajos Sipos was my grandmother's uncle, and he was the one part of that large maternal family that had moved from Transylvania to Budapest before World War II, changed the family name to Sipos from Schächter, and passed for Christian. They were the only modern *conversos* (Jewish converts to Christianity, a naming from the time of the Spanish Inquisition) of my family. The Sipos clan had escaped the Nazi atrocities by migrating to Venezuela and then to Canada. In Toronto, they were family, and Lajos, an artist, was a tenderhearted man. They had only one son, mustachioed, pipe-smoking George, "Gyuri,", who had two much younger daughters than me. This tenuous tether to Canada was thin, temporary, but indispensable. However, it did not match the powerful bond with the Weingartens that we had left behind in Brazil.

São Paulo, October 12, 1964

Dear Ruth,

I think you have not yet forgotten us, but you'd have a reason to. It's been a month that I've been telling Estelinha and your grandmother: "Tomorrow I will write to Ruth." But as you know, mine [mother] *has gone, and I'm left lacking. My father seasons and cooks, I help (set the table, wash, boil). I must straighten out, stay at the factory, etc. I don't even have time to move a little finger. To write this letter, also to Miriam G. and to my mother, I had to skip class and go to Flávia's house. It was "nonsense" (Theory) class.*

Your grandmother has been so good to us. Thank her for me. Sometimes I eat at Flávia's. This happens when my father makes beans. How I don't like beans.

. . .

Ruth, very happy birthday (I am late) since the date was September 16, repeat it more than a trillion years. Prosper in culture and in love, and in everything. I feel so alone. I just have Flávia. I feel like this because I'm acutely and seriously in love. His name is Arie (mon amour). I go to Ichud Habonim [Jewish youth club] *and met him there. It's just that he has a girlfriend.*

I will write to you when I can. Don't wait for a letter from me. Write! It's not for the lack of wanting that I don't write. You know how it is. Before anything, I want to congratulate you for entering the first level of high school. I guarantee I was left jealous. Our teacher, Margaret [Fleury], *was super content.*

Ruth: many hugs and again, congratulations, and don't imitate my tardiness.

Kisses, hugs, and everything better than the best you write.

Elana

São Paulo, October 1964

Dear Ruth,

Since I am on my way by the post office, I won't miss the opportunity to send you a letter. How are things there? I hope everything is going well. And your grandmother? Ask her to write.

My mother left September 16. She did not write, except once [received] *on the 27th. We were very worried not having news from her. On Saturday, September 17, on her birthday, I was asking for money from my father to go get bread—there, where he cuts the gloves. From there the front door can't be seen. My brother was sewing on one of the machines that has a view of the door. Suddenly he looks at the door, his mouth agape and says, "Hine Ima!"* [Here's mother!] *I told him not to talk nonsense, but it was true. My mother arrived. We hugged and all was so good. In the afternoon, as she laid down because she was so tired from the trip, I went out to buy cake and flowers and went skipping with happiness on the street. She brought me so many beautiful things, that I was flabbergasted.*

. . .

In conclusion, my closet is renovated.

Is it nice to have a TV? Do you have friends now? Send me some pictures of you. How are your parents? and your cousin? Are you happy there, or do you miss Brasil [Portuguese spelling]*?*

I hope one day we will be able to see each other, right? Estelinha is a darling. Poor girl. I promised to give her your address and always forgot. But I already gave it to her. She must have written to you by now.

I am doing well in studies, with good grades in everything except History, which I must pass with an 8 or 9 to advance without an exam. The rest I don't need. I'm doing well in French and English, and piano, too. I am thinking of returning to ballet. I miss it.

On the 30th of October I am going to Rio de Janeiro with SNIF [a Jewish youth group]. *I rejoined. That's at night because the team there is throwing a party. On the 31st* [my] *group will join the Rio group to go to Itatiaia* [pretty destination town between São Paulo and Rio]. *November 7 and 8 there's weekend camping for the ACM* [YMCA]. *This month is full of trips. I will write you shortly. Missing you, hugs and kisses, your friend who wants you very much.*

Elana

Toronto, October 1964

Elana liked to recount a story in minute detail. It shows in her letters, which she wrote like a journal. I am somewhat like that too: too many details, not enough brevity. (If Miss McGrath could see my writing now!) When we were together, I used to let Elana recount her minutiae as we talked, and she clearly was delighted to continue to do so in letters. Her emotion, her happiness and energy, permeated these pages, and it cheered me up. She was grounded and on land, and I was afloat on choppy waters.

These letters from 1964 are suffused with Elana's exuberance, accounting for all her social engagements, particularly when it involved social clubs and sports. Elana was powerfully built, physically active and sporty. She was not sedentary like I was. She loved being part of a group and was an enthusiastic participant in social clubs. Her passion had always been belonging to Jewish youth clubs. From 1960 to 1963, I went with her to summer camps. Vera had persuaded my mother to let me go too. Elana loved to be active and out of the house. My mother used to scoff at her *csavargolás,* a comic Hungarian expression for roaming, little realizing that it showed Elana's bravery and her mother's workload.

All my extracurricular activities ceased when we settled into our small apartment in Toronto. Aside from going to school, I did homework, read, listened to the radio, and watched TV. We finally had a TV, and I loved watching American shows. In São Paulo, Elana and I did not have TV sets before I emigrated from Brazil to Canada. We would watch TV in other people's houses. They were mostly dubbed American shows like *Lassie, Rin Tin Tin,* and other westerns.

Outside of my school in Toronto, I knew only the elderly relatives in the neighborhood. My life felt insubstantial. Elana's letters sustained me. Did I miss Brazil, she asked. Well, I missed her, my social life, and a deeper family life. Alone with my parents in Toronto, just the three of us, I intensely felt the isolation of being an only child. By age fourteen I should have been accustomed to being an "only." But in our circumstances, it was hard for me to bear the singularity of being my parents' only child. I acutely felt the weight of their attention, not only during my adolescence, but throughout their lives. I yearned to give away at least 50 percent of that attention to a sibling, to rebalance their gaze, their expectations, their purpose for living as survivors.

Elana's writing in detail about grades and schoolwork are mostly her paying lip service to a topic important to her mother. She faltered in school, because she was not consistently studious. She was intellectually capable but preferred to go out with her groups. She loved belonging to these social groups that partied, had athletic competitions, and involved traveling to other states such as Rio de Janeiro. Elana was socially gifted. She loved making friends from other cities. She desperately wanted to achieve an academic level to keep abreast of her brother and me, but not if it meant missing a social gathering. All of this she showed in what she wrote to me.

By the time I received the October letters from Elana, I was going through the motions of becoming acclimated to a strange environment. I was experiencing the difficult effort to understand what I heard and read. And I had to cope with the feeling of being disconnected socially from peers. I was isolated and alone when I was not in school. Even when with my parents, as a teenager, I felt alone. I wasn't in need of their company; I needed the company of peers. It took months for my language muteness to clear and for me to enter the next stage, reticence. Ninth grade English class was hard to understand; Shakespeare was confounding. My former private English lessons in São Paulo with Miss Margaret Fleury consisted of reading *Reader's Digest*. Elizabethan English in comparison was a foreign language.

Curiously, I continued to read *Reader's Digest* in Toronto. It is easy today to snub my nose at this publication, but I subscribed to it then. The articles were easy for me to understand and improved my fluency. The word games were vocabulary builders and instructive. And I liked to copy the drawings.

My mother often visited her elderly relatives nearby. Lacking my own friends, I often accompanied her. It is thoughtful that Elana asked me if I had friends yet. I was going to have friends, I was sure of it, certainly by tenth grade, the following year. I think I stayed positive when I wrote to her. I don't think I poured my broken heart into my letters. I was not a complainer, and in view of her cheerful letters full of daily facts, I must have reciprocated. Nowhere in Elana's letters does she address my insecurity, apprehension, fearfulness of a new environment. It's proof I did not write about it. My goal was to match her journal with my journal of facts and acts of Canadian novelty, which to Elana were a view of North America.

In the meantime, I lived for the anticipation of visiting my aunt and cousin in Michigan. My grandmother followed us out of Brazil later in 1964. By then her husband, Ziggi, had chased after another woman, and my no-nonsense, self-confident grandmother sent him packing. My aunt, uncle, cousin, and grandmother came to visit us in Toronto. I was so happy when they did! They were US citizens, they had a car, and it was easier for them to travel. My grandmother could travel, too, because she had a Green Card, which she acquired by having a citizen daughter—immediate family—living in the US who sponsored her permanent residency petition. (Some call this "chain migration"; however, one could not sponsor a sister.) My father did not own a car in Toronto. We would travel to Michigan for visits by bus. There was a world of difference in living in Brazil, with loved ones we longed for in the United States, and living in Canada across the border from them. As difficult as it was to go through the border from Windsor, Ontario, into Detroit, Michigan, with inadequate papers, it did not stop us from visiting.

Before the next letter arrived in February 1965, my mother lost the baby she was carrying. Life with my parents was as somber as the aura in a funeral home. When we arrived in Toronto, my thirty-three-year-old pregnant mother, with an Rh-negative blood type, should have sought an obstetrician who specialized in Rh-negative patients. Instead, she relied on her relatives to recommend a general practitioner (who probably spoke Hungarian). He misguidedly accepted my pregnant and high-risk mother as a patient. She had previously lost her second child in 1953. The baby lived a day and could not be saved, notwithstanding transfusions, which was the prevailing protocol through the 1950s for an Rh-positive baby born to an Rh-negative mother. And so, eleven years later, in 1964, my mother's labor was induced in a Toronto hospital after we spent Christmas in Michigan. The baby girl was stillborn.

My mother slipped into a long and profound depression. My parents lacked a community that would help them grieve, and my mother was adrift in her boundless pain. They lacked the religious rituals that usher the bereaved through the fog of sorrow. The loss of a second full-term birth was a disaster, and like a virus, it embedded in her, festered, and with a vengeance broke out less than ten years later into a mental breakdown. Did I relate this to Elana?

(RhoGam, the inoculation that could have saved my mother's mental health and the life of her third child, became available three and a half years later, in May 1968.)

São Paulo, February 27, 1965

Dear Ruth,

How happy I was to receive your letter! Thank you so much for remembering my birthday. I didn't do anything nor received anything. [Except] *Miki gave me a book: "The Romance of Leonardo da Vinci." It's beautiful.*

My brother is finishing his Vestibular [university entrance exams]. *He will finish tomorrow. They will select 800 out of the 2,500 candidates, and he also must take two practicals* [exams] *which finish tomorrow and only 400 will be selected. I don't know if he'll pass. He said he did poorly yesterday, and well today. We will see tomorrow.*

I hope you have done well in your exams, although I do not have doubts. You all look so lovely in the photograph. Was it you who made the snowman? Is it fun to horseback ride? I would like to try.

During vacation I went to 3 camps. Two in Jundiaí and one in Mauá (near Rio). Total of 54 days. Super, right? I took a selection exam but did not pass. I continue at Oswaldo Cruz—science and medicine [high school].

I took pictures during camp, and when they're ready I'll send them to you. I miss you so much. I don't forget the good times that we spent together. Flávia moved. She sends you greetings, just like everyone else.

I'll excuse myself here, leaving you a big hug, from your friend who wants you so much.

Elana

Toronto, February 1965

According to this letter, did I tell Elana my mother lost the baby? It seems I didn't. Was I a heartless and frozen creature? This time I was not depressive; I was simply numb.

My mother also corresponded with Vera sometimes; perhaps she told her eventually.

The long break in correspondence between October and February points to the despondency that permeated the atmosphere at home. I had lost my mother when she lost my sister. Trying to adapt to life in an English-speaking country sapped all my ability to see a broader or deeper view of life. I was in survival mode myself, bent on taking care of my own needs. I heard and saw my mother's loss across a distorting element, like water. Her loss just flowed over me like a water skimmer passing over a submerged fry. Maybe I did not tell Elana because I was trying not to speak of my own loss. Or perhaps, and this is hard to admit, I did not see this baby, this would-be sister, as a real person, and I just could not imagine the possibility of interacting with a sibling fourteen years my junior. If I pretended, selfishly, she did not exist, I could save myself some heartache. That is simply and utterly being in denial, and so, I didn't tell Elana.

At the time, my mother managed to function, but in the long term she lost. I kept going. Although my mother is ninety-three years old as I write this, she has been suffering from schizophrenia since she was forty-two, and now also suffers from dementia. I have been her caretaker for fifty years. Justifiably, I have been doing penance for my lack of attentiveness to my mother's loss. Imagine, I could have a younger sister who most likely could help me and alleviate the lonely burden of care for a senescent mother.

In my first Canadian arctic winter I soldiered on. And my letters must have been an improvisation to complement the concreteness of Elana's letters. She could describe no drama that could match the gloom that descended on my family in Toronto, and I was not the type to lament.

Depression and lamentation are not foreign to me. Although not diagnosed by a psychiatrist, since no such care existed in our migrant and isolated environment, I experienced clinical depression before I turned nine during my first six months in Brazil. I was debilitated by a depressive state, crying if anyone even dared look at me. I clutched and curled up with my one or two toys and was terrified by an incomprehensible world for at least six months. However, I did not learn to lament until I became an adult. I don't think children know how to be deeply sorrowful until the language of sadness grows and matures. It's an emotional language that is learned later in life. I was utterly sad in a new South American country, and all I could do was cry. I could not express my sorrow in words. I was utterly sad in Canada as a teenager, but I still did not know how to express sorrow. What I did find is the ability to dissemble. I learned to feign maturity and confidence. To do so, I hardened my heart and cast myself in bristly skin that eventually became permanent. Over the years, I've been told I am cold to my face, and in many instances I do indeed feel cold-hearted. It's in fact a misunderstood intense reserve. It's also possible I inherited some of this ramification of upheaval from my father, since he was encased in steel, becoming a hard man because of his experience during the Holocaust.

Undoubtedly Elana experienced sadness. She was very sad when her grandmother died. But Elana was not a downcast or despondent person. She was by nature cheerful, positive, and buoyant. Her letters were the life ring she threw into the water for me. Because of that, if they're full of minute and mundane details of her daily life, there was nothing boring about them to me. I clung to it all.

São Paulo, April 24, 1965

Dear Rutinha [diminutive form in Portuguese],

Ah, how your letter was late. But it arrived!!! Your mother wrote that you were studying hard and didn't have time to write. You are forgetting Portuguese, eh?

Selection exams mean what you wanted to do for Caetano de Campos [a public school], *just that it can be done in other series. Exam is to enter the state high school. Got it? If you have a hard time in Portuguese, I'll take your letters in English.*

I am doing well with Miki, we are friendly. Imagine she has joined SNIF, Ichud Habonim, and goes more often than I do. She's A-OK. On the 15th it's "Holiday on Ice—it's very beautiful!!!" [written in English].

How did you spend your vacation at your cousin's? Was it nice? and Judy [my new friend in Toronto], *is she well? I am not going to the YMCA like I used to. More often, I go to Ichud Habonim. If only you'd know how nice it is there! I have so much to tell you, but so much, that if only I could meet you, or it would fill a whole pad of letters. The subject, I think you know what it is.*

...

Ay, what a pity that I can't talk to you about everything in a letter. There are so many things that you can't even imagine!!! Is it possible that we will yet meet one day? How I miss those days we were always together!

You know, my grandfather came here on the 11th of June. My father already bought him a house [apartment] *near us. About 2 blocks from here. My brother is going to live with him, because he told us he can't study here for all the noise we make (same story as before).*

...

If I move, don't worry, I will write you my new address. "IF I MOVE" there's little chance. But we pray that we will. The super would give me the letters, you can write all you want. And look that you don't delay, OK? Together with your letter, I am also sending two to Rio, one to Recife and one to Porto Alegre. (Imagine!!!!) Aside from these I correspond with seven other 'chaverim' (amigos/as) in various states. It's so good to be corresponding!

Ruth: I hope you write me quick. I must stop here, because I have to study Chemistry for the sabatina [exam]. *They say this teacher is the devil himself. He has no heart or pity. There are 7 who had failed his material, aside from others, Physics and Mathematics. Well. Now I really must stop. I already stuffed* [the page] *enough. Write about everything and everybody, OK? 1000000000 kisses and hugs. (I think you can calculate this, "né?")*

From your friend who wants you much and is dying of longing.

Elana

PS Remember me to your parents.

Toronto, April 1965

In the early years after separating, I wrote to Elana in Portuguese, which was not my native language. The day came when she noticed my mistakes. Fortunately, she was learning English, so eventually I switched to writing in English, but not yet. I would not have been able to continue maintaining the correspondence in Portuguese for several reasons. I had no one to speak it with in Canada or the US; I was not reading Portuguese books or newspapers or seeing Brazilian films and shows. During my first year in North America (Canada included) I had to immerse myself in my new language. My goal was to fight to maintain my academic standing: I started high school in Toronto in grade nine, on track with my age group, but with a huge deficit. I needed to surmount it at any cost, which meant letting fluency in Portuguese slip. I understand Portuguese to this day; I can still converse in it casually. I can read it fluently, and I can watch Brazilian films and understand them. But I can no longer write letters. Today, Elana is fluent in English.

It is with wonder and relief that in my memories of this difficult first year in Canada, I don't recall experiencing rudeness or bullying, and none of the girls in my class (or the other ninth grade class) would be considered mean. I was isolated but not an outcast. I can't explain this surprisingly passive benevolence that I encountered in my Canadian high school among fourteen- and fifteen-year-olds. Also, my parents and I did not encounter intimidation around the city, whether shopping or carrying on day-to-day activities. Benign? Civilized? Toronto was in fact a haven.

São Paulo, May 15, 1965

Dear Udi,

Ah, how good it is to remember the old days we called each other Udi and Nanica! But it's also good to use that in letters. What "saudades" [longing]*! When I look back to those days of our childhood, it seems they were yesterday. In the meantime, the longing is immense. How I wish we could spend a month together! Who knows, one day this opportunity will come. Until then, our friendship should be preserved the same as always. I think it's not because of distance that we will forget everything quickly. In letters it seems that you are there on General Jardim* [my street in São Paulo].

Yes. The 9th was Mother's Day. Seems like yesterday. How time passes!!! It's been a year since we have seen each other. Miki is in love as always. I hope you will have a good time at your grandmother's. How is she? Send her a thousand hugs and kisses and tell her that my mother will write her soon, and I will write her even before that, OK?

Oh, before I forget. Wait. I found it. Estelinha asked for you to write to her. Write her, because she sent you mounds of letters to which you didn't respond, or at least none that arrived. Something went wrong. I gave you her correct address, and I gave her your correct address. Write her right away, she's anxious. Estelinha Vargas . . . [address]

Ah!!! Now that you are going to your grandmother's, tell Gabi to write me, OK? Thanks.

...

To resume. I will have a stupendous weekend. I already planned my vacation. Encampment will be the 2nd half of July. Before that I will go to Rio and stay with a "chaverah" [friend] *from there. You know, they also have a SNIF and I know many people there. The encampment will be interstate again, I will join with them and then will return to São Paulo. Neat, right? I will get to know Rio. But all this will only happen if there are no surprises. But really, I would exchange all this if I could spend at least ONE day with you. Believe me, I miss you so much, and our little fights.*

Ah! I have so much to tell you, you know, they're prattles but would require an entire paper pad to write about. But if one day someone would go there [Canada], *I will send you a whole pad written up, OK?* [Postage was expensive.] *I don't have any photos ready, but I will take some during encampment, OK? Remember those photos taken at the Y picnic? Well, I'll see if my brother "inclined himself" to have them developed, since he has not done it so far. I think I'm overstuffing this whole pad.*

The Science curriculum is horrible. And see, that this year I am not playing around with studies. I AM studying a lot. (Can be seen by "AM.")

Tomorrow I'll go to the post office with this letter and 5 others to Porto Alegre, Recife and Rio. I got none from Curitiba. Well. Until next time. I really need to finish this. I stop here, all the kisses that can be given and sincere hugs (ibid) from a friend who will never forget you and hopes never to be forgotten.

Elana

Regards to your parents. Your mother's letter arrived, my mother will respond, but you know it takes a century.

Toronto, May 1965

Like other close friends, we had given each other nicknames at the age of about ten or eleven, and when we corresponded, we started to use them again. She called me Udi Udi, and I called her Nanica. These were not standard abbreviations or diminutives for our names; we made them up. In reading *My Brilliant Friend,* by Elena Ferrante, the girlfriend protagonists call each other Lina (for Elena) and Lila (for Raffaella), which are conventional diminutives for those names. Elana and I were more playful and unique.

Elana corresponded with many friends as she recounts in her letters to me. I finally only wrote to Elana. I stopped corresponding with Estelinha after two years. Miss Fleury also wrote me letters and I answered for a short time, then stopped. As I mentioned before, Miki and I did not correspond until years later, and even then, sparingly. I didn't have time. Writing to Elana was important to me, because the correspondence and the friendship was important, more so than any other friend or acquaintance from Brazil.

I, like Elana, took piano lessons. She mentioned playing and practicing in almost all her letters, sometimes with a detailed repertoire. To this day she still has the old piano that stood in the living room in R. Duque de Caxias. My parents bought me my first piano in Toronto from a Hungarian piano dealer, a beautiful, but touchy, upright August Förster. It was the cheaper one made in Bohemia, not the expensive German-made piano. In Toronto, I no longer took ballet. My parents couldn't afford the extra tuition (the Municipal Ballet School in São Paulo was inexpensive), and I was struggling to keep up with school and the Royal Conservatory.

In this letter, the details of Elana's busy events are spelled out with such enthusiasm, it was obvious she lived for sports and participation in clubs. It's the focus of her letter.

I belonged to no such clubs and participated in no such social events. My life in Toronto the first and second years was staid and even somber. It lacked the cultural enrichment I had experienced in Brazil, such as attending ballet performances, concerts, and social activities. I did not rebel against this fate; on the contrary, it reinforced my passivity. My second migration to a foreign environment stifled any hope that I could overcome my natural shyness. I am convinced that had I lived in one and only one country, among compatriots and cultural norms where I was born, I would have developed more confidence and become more outgoing.

In Toronto, I succumbed to the long, cold, and dreary winters. Even attempting to learn to skate did not alleviate my gloom in drab surroundings and bland social connections. I did not learn to skate. Spring and summer were only improvements in weather, but my personality, my family, and my circumstances were not going to match the blaze of Elana's "coming out." There was no coming out for me; at fifteen I was in suspended animation.

I longed for but was not jealous of her social engagements, and my letters surely did not express any of it. Instead, I probably soldiered on and recounted my current interests and tame activities, illuminating them as much as I could in the light of a sedate Canadian atmosphere. To Elana, Canada and the United States were wonderments. My reality was not a wonder. One of the reasons I never regretted leaving Toronto and moving to New York, becoming an American immigrant, was because living in Toronto was a sluggish and sad experience for me. I did not feel that my family was part of a community.

It was obvious that an alternate life in Brazil would have been so much more engaging. Even so, I met a few friends in high school, and my relationship with them started to develop in 1965. Among them was Judy Riesz. (Elana asks about her.) And a year later, a long-term friendship was established with Phyllis Cohen, even though I spent more time with Judy. Judy's parents were

Hungarian Jews who also survived the Holocaust, then escaped the Communist takeover in 1956, and they befriended my parents in Toronto. Phyllis seemed to me the Jewish intellectual counterpoint to my family. Phyllis's father was the drama critic of a major Canadian daily paper. Her mother was a confident, educated, engaging woman who created an art-loving environment for her daughters, and that was a living environment I aspired to.

São Paulo, June 21, 1965

Dear Ruth:

Ooph! Your letter finally arrived. You make my heart explode when I wait for your letters.

My grandfather arrived here on the 11th. How wonderful! But I'd really wish my grandmother would have come too! He is 73 and in good health. [In June 1965, my grandmother was fifty-two years old.]

How much longing, is it possible that we will see each other one day? I would love it to be.

Even if I have many girlfriends, I can't find one like you. It's been a year and 3 days since we said goodbye, and one year since you left Rio, right? Well, hope is the last to die. Because of that and because I long to see you, I hope that we continue to correspond, continuing our old and dear friendship.

Classes end in 9 days. My grades until May were bad, but in comparison to the course difficulty and others' grades, they are good and I'm among the best.

. . .

These are castles constructed in air, theoretical. In practice, it will be harder than pissing [an idiom that does not translate well into

English]. *But I will try. Maybe I won't go anywhere at all, having an operation of the meniscus.*

Ay, Ruth, don't cut your hair! So beautiful, but now that you have cut it, if you kept it, send me some strands, OK? Thanks. And send photos, OK? I still haven't developed the one my brother took. But I am nagging him to have them developed. I think next time or after that I will have some to send, OK?

Well, I must stop here because tomorrow I have a make-up, and I don't want to get a low grade.

Regards to your parents.
Thousands of hugs and kisses from your sincere friend,

Elana

PS It's a bummer waiting so long for you to write with news. Write soon, OK? Thanks.

Toronto, June 1965

Back in the days before digital photography, the notion of Elana sending me photos was like a running joke. They were promised in every letter, but hardly ever delivered. Occasionally I'd get a few pictures, and it made me happy to see her. In Canada, and later in the US, it was easy for me to take the 35 mm roll and have it developed in local photo shops or drugstores. So I sent Elana many photos. It's no wonder that Instagram is so popular; we possess an instinctive need to behold the visage of another person, and Instagram fills that need.

For a few more years, Elana continued to give me a rundown of her grades. After a while, the difference in our high school education made it harder for me to understand her categories of tests, exams, and the sequence of academic advancement. Something got lost in translation. I left Brazil when I attended what in America is called middle school.

In the 1960s middle school was called *ginásio* in Portuguese, and high school was called *colegial* (grades nine to eleven). But a course of study or college was *faculdade.* The terminology does not translate well. Illiteracy was prevalent in almost half the country when I left. The most competitive schools and supposedly the best schools in Brazil requiring entry exams were the "public" (free) ones, but the private schools were more accessible and available. In Brazil, entry into a university and a *faculdade* was based only on the very rigorous and competitive exam, the *Vestibular.* If applying to more than one *faculdade,* that is, college or academic division, then more than one *Vestibular* was necessary, since this rigorous exam was not generalized. As a result, most students who wanted to advance and had the means wagered everything on one *Vestibular* at a time. Just like SAT prep courses in the US, there were private courses in Brazil to practice taking these exams. But the American process is more streamlined: SATs are national, general, and widely accepted, and aside from the Verbal and Math sections of the SATs, they were not specific tests of knowledge in a particular subject like the *Vestibular.* In contrast, American advanced degrees in law, medicine, and business require more subject-specific proficiency exams.

Brazil's education system varied over the years after I left, but while I was living there, "high school" spanned three years starting at age fifteen, ending at eighteen. Schooling was eleven years in length but could end at nineteen years of age for repeaters. Failing to advance was common and repeating classes happened often, so graduation could be at age eighteen, nineteen, or never. It took a special dedication to academic studies to complete secondary and university studies. Elana's brother, Yoni, was an example of such dedication.

São Paulo, August 6, 1965

Dear Udi-Udi

First, I want to apologize for this letter's delay, since yours arrived on the 16th. On the 18th I went to an encampment, there, in Jundiaí. I returned on the 26th, and a friend from Porto Alegre stayed at my house until the 28th. Then, since all the "chaverim" [gang/friends] *were still here, we went on outings every single day.*

Classes started on the 2nd. I had horrible grades in June. I should be ashamed. But I am going to recover this month. Until today I've had no excuses for not writing. A little lack of time and a lot of laziness. But I will not forget you, oh no!

How do you want me to go there? It's not that easy. And now, have you bought the piano yet? Yes, it's so nice to have my grandfather here. We have a new home where he and my brother live. It's still not completely decorated.

. . .

You know, your old class always asks about you and sends you congratulations for entering first year of high school. Now you must have passed into second year, right?

. . .

I am on good terms with Miki. She has changed a lot. She's no longer the former spoiled girl. She spent 2.5 weeks in Santos (near Itanhaém) with a classmate of hers. She returned changed. She will come here today, soon, and we will go to the post office, then we'll go to her house, there she'll have a math lesson, we'll have dinner and then we'll go to Ichud Habonim [Jewish club] *for Kabbalat Shabbat. Isn't that neat? We've moved from the SNIF, Ichud is big and beautiful. It's near Miki's house, only about 3 blocks away.*

I was so happy that you have a good friend. Send her my regards. Who knows, maybe one day I'll arrive there on a magic carpet, and then you'll introduce me to her. OK?

I had English class yesterday. I already showed her [Miss Fleury] *the photos, and she loved them. How about you send me more? The other ones are already in an album (I won). One year has passed already, you must have changed a lot. I promised you pictures, but my brother has not sent the film to be developed, and he won't let me have them developed. But I will ask him every minute.*

Ruth, how about you write me in English? Only if you wish. I can already understand English pretty well. And I will not show the letter to our teacher. I have a dictionary in case I don't understand something. It's that your writing in Portuguese is funny, and I almost wet my pants from laughing. Don't be offended, because I know you don't have anyone to speak Portuguese with, and this way we forget very quickly. But I understand your letters very well. If you want to, continue in Portuguese.

Ruth, I must finish this here, because Miki is coming soon, and I still haven't practiced piano. A huge, strong hug from your friend who misses her Udi-Udi so much.

Elana

PS SHMAK!! (kisses)

Toronto, August 1965

The Brazilian school year started at the end of February and ran through December, with a one-month winter break in July. June exams were mid-year exams, and as she recounts in this letter, Elana realized that she was falling behind. Even so, in this temperate climate, it was possible for Elana to go on encampments during the July break. Further north of São Paulo the climate was warmer. Christmas fell in the summer, and by January school break we'd go to the beaches or summer camps.

On the date of this August letter, 1965, I was still on a languid and lonely summer vacation. I was slated to return to Vaughn Road and grade ten in September. I was conquering English. Understanding it came naturally, and speaking was getting easier.

I was not an exceptional student, however. I started to take a heavy load of foreign languages besides English: French, Latin, and German. Aside from English, the three language classes elevated my grade point, because I found them easy. Math, biology, physics, geography, gym, and swimming were on my curriculum. And of course, English history, as in the history of Great Britain. So why English but not Canadian history? I don't know the answer except to surmise that in 1965, English-speaking Ontario, Canada, considered itself a colony. After all, we all had to sing "God save our gracious Queen, long live our noble Queen . . ." And Queen Elizabeth was on every Canadian dollar note and coin. In 1967 the coins were reminted with the maple leaf symbol. Subsequently, ancient history was also added to my curriculum. American history was still a mysterious empty book to me.

We were required to change into a gym uniform consisting of baby blue bloomers, making the girls such a comical sight! The school had a pool, so gym included a swimming class. I remember the girls were weighed, something that's frowned upon today. In 1965 it was still the pre-hippie era, and the coming cultural and generational divide was not apparent to me in Toronto or São Paulo. The Beat Generation may have already come to light in some circles, but we lived in the shadow of a postwar and early rock 'n' roll era; it was hard to shake the 1950s. Officially we were part of the Baby Boom generation. In that year's class photo, most girls still wore bobby socks or knee-high socks. Only one girl in my grade wore fishnet stockings, astonishing the rest of us. My first friend was Judy, who was a frequent topic in my letters, and Elana, with generous warmth, sent her regards and expressed wishes to meet her, knowing that the possibility was as far-fetched as a magic carpet ride.

I was not particularly tuned into popular culture. Canadian news was transparent and bland; life in Canada was securely tepid. It felt like living in a cocoon, swaddled and protected from nationalism or chauvinism. It was an environment where we could safely shed our Brazilian aura and language, and easily acclimate to an English-speaking country. The news from the United States revolved around the fight for civil rights and the French exit from Vietnam, creating the vacuum filled by the United States. These were momentous political developments, but we were just observers. All the lively elements of popular culture and historical developments were televised and broadcasted from Buffalo, New York. Now that we owned a TV set, we had a window across the border. And every Sunday my parents and I would watch *The Ed Sullivan Show*, getting our education in popular culture.

Elana did not pay much attention to popular culture. She was immersed in the social network provided by the clubs in São Paulo, which connected her to others throughout the country. She paid scant attention to international news or, for that matter, to Brazilian politics or historical events. Just before we left Brazil, a coup d'état had taken place, the Golpe de '64, and a US-instigated military dictatorship took over that lasted twenty-one years. Its first appointed president was General Castelo Branco. Four more generals would take turns running a right-wing government with the blessing of the United States, to protect Brazil from communism, left-leaning labor politicians, and socialists. The Golpe was a bloodless coup, but not all Brazilian citizens were in support. As seen in later letters, Elana awoke to the tortures and excesses of the military, as secret resistance and demonstrations on campuses intensified. The current president of Brazil, Luiz Inácio Lula da Silva, and one of his successors after his first term as president, President Dilma Vana Rousseff, were revolutionaries opposing the dictatorship, and were imprisoned and tortured in the 1960s.

By this time Elana and Miki became closer again, but only for the time being. In the long run, they remained friends for the rest of Miki's life. Elana was never spoiled, so the rapprochement described in this letter signified Miki's spasmodic maturation. Eventually, Miki resented her grandmother's strangulating hold, and she must have rebelled, with the blessing of her mother. Elsa had a way with her elderly mother and used her as child-care provider, cook, homemaker, and admirer (Elsa being the admired). I have an intense memory of deeply aromatic chocolate babkas, the best ever made that Berta *neni* used to bake. My impression, however, had always been that Elsa had the upper hand and did as she wished. I have no doubt that eventually she wanted her daughter, Miki, to be independent and escape Berta *neni*. Whether Elana and I were going to rebel against our elders was yet to be seen.

Even so, Miki's mother and grandmother created a phalanx that drove the teenage Miki in a supercilious direction. As a child, she was spoiled, coddled, managed, and curated. She loved her mother and did not rebel. In some of the following letters, she acted under the theatrical direction of her matrons, and the results were not always pretty or to Elana's taste. Their friendship was like a rollercoaster ride for a few years, and eventually matured into a steady lifelong bond.

One more letter, and one more entreaty by Elana to switch to writing in English, I think, made me start to heed her suggestion, but I was still resistant, trying to hold on to my former Brazilian speech a little longer.

São Paulo, September 9, 1965

Dearest Ruth,

Yes, it's been one year and one month since we've seen each other. Another birthday when I cannot give you a wee hug and a wee kiss. Yes, we have changed a lot, we've grown more, and we enlarged our "noggins" (intelligence). Time passes, and I don't have much hope of seeing you soon. But one day we MUST meet, don't you think?

Ruth, or better: Udinha, a million kisses and hugs, much happiness for your whole life, which should last for eternity, and I'd like to see for one instant to tell you in person what I need to write to you. But your photo is here in front of me. How I miss our little squabbles of little value. How much better than being apart like this? What can we do?—accept it. How are your parents? Send them my regards. And you? What have you done for fun? How is Judy?

You know that here it's September 7 and a holiday [Brazilian Independence Day]. *Since the científico* [science and math] *and the clássico* [humanities] *high school has let out, I went to Peruíbe* [beach].

...

We went to the Sonhos beach, where our old Miami hotel is. We were collecting shells when a young guy came from the direction of the rocks saying: "There's a woman drowning! Funny that she went down there!" Ruth, I became so enraged, just the way the guy was talking I could have killed him. Someone from our group ran there, and we followed. You remember how dangerous it was there? The husband was taking pictures, when a "little" wave took her. The husband didn't even see it. When the lifeguards arrived, imagine it was just to get her out of the water with her head still underwater, she ended up passing out after still fighting. By the time I got there, she still had her last movements, and the lifeguards right there. They swam around the rocks and came out to the beach. If they had taken her head out of the water, given her CPR for 2 hours they could have saved her. But no, they took her out of the water and called the mortuary. Is this what you call lifeguards? Ruth, you have never seen me with so much anger. Imagine there were more than 50 people there, and no one lifted a finger to try to save her. She was 29. I could not even manage to open my mouth. If I did, something ugly would have come out. I was affected by seeing the dead woman, as I was by the reaction of the crowd. Ay, Ruth! How people are egotistical! I'm not saying I'm not an egotist. But now I learned a lot from this!

Well. You see, the rest of the day we were silent, or better yet, we could not utter a word. We couldn't put it out of our mind. I arrived home at 11:30 p.m. We were on the train for 9 hours, and the train was delayed. The train was called "Cata osso" [bone rattler]. *Get it?*

Well, Udinha, I know I've written a lot of nonsense, forgive me. Sometimes I can't help myself.

I wish you a happy birthday on the glorious day of September 16, the day you appeared in this strange world. I apologize again for this poorly written letter. Answer me quickly. What is new there? Write everything. I must excuse myself right now.

A big hug from your little friend who is dying with longing for you.

Elana

P.S. Regards to your parents.

Toronto, September 1965

A very peculiar coincidence happened to me in Toronto that summer; therefore, I understood Elana's stirring experience. On Toronto's Lake Ontario waterfront, there was a park called Center Island with many inlets, coves, and protected water, which made it feel like a smaller lake. My cousin Jack was visiting us in Toronto, and we were on an outing to Center Island. We rented a rowboat and were out on the water. We saw a commotion very close to us, and a person was struggling in the water. Some people were screaming, some people were trying to grab the man and get him back on the boat. The attempts were unsuccessful, and Jack and I saw the man slip under the water and not return. We were in shock. We were about fifteen years old, and it did not occur to either of us to jump into the water and try to find him and grab him. Neither did anyone else. There were no heroes that day. Elana's story, her anger, and her agitated feelings echoed my experience. However, I don't remember being as angry as she was at this senseless loss of life. Once again, I discovered a difference between us: my hardness compared to her compassionate sympathies. My attachment to her friendship and her letters were a moderating influence for me, in view of this lifelong contrast.

Where was this hardness coming from? It surfaces even today, more than fifty-five years later. At what point and with which experience did I deep-freeze my feelings? Clearly, this buttressed me against becoming debilitated by the trauma of my previous two migrations. The first one is always hard; my second one was not any easier. When my father left Israel, for all his good intentions, which I understand now and don't hold against him any longer,

I underwent an amputation, or a deracination. Whatever I have said until now about moving to Brazil and then migrating again, how I learned the language fluently, how I adjusted, how I had to assimilate, how I made friends and learned to be world-wise, the fundamental trauma never went away—because it wasn't what was done to me, but what was taken away. In other words, it was not a trauma of commission but of omission. Said more plainly, it was loss. And in Canada, for all its comfy blandness, it was another uprooting, all over again.

São Paulo, October 19, 1965

Dearest Rutinha,

News! My mother said that if we win the lottery, I will come to visit you! People must collect receipts of up to CR$50.000 and I already have CR$500.000. [In Brazil, the thousands marker is a period, and the decimal follows a comma.] *I will collect more so that at least one of them will have to win. Imagine? Me going there? How fab, Ruth! I can hardly wait!*

What are you studying? Ruth, I thought I already wrote you! The Maestro passed away if I think I'm correct on February 3rd. Suddenly! He was in the hospital for 3 days, poor man, he was such a good man! We only see this when it's too late.

My brother has not resolved to have the photos developed.

...

You know, I think I will have an operation on my meniscus. It's getting worse and worse. When I sit, and the knee is bent, it starts to hurt. Then I stretch. Then soon after it starts to hurt. I bend, and it happens again. ENOUGH!

I think my aunt in Africa [Johannesburg] *will be coming here this year! How wonderful! My cousin Philip has written us in English.*

Yesterday evening Florita [Flávia's sister] *celebrated her birthday and I went. Hm!!! I did not like the little group that was there. I think I was born to be a "schlepper"!* [Not sure what she meant, but not the "schlepper" that has been incorporated into English jargon from Yiddish.]

Congratulations on entering the 6th piano level at the Conservatory. I think I will be passing into the 7th. I switched teachers. I am no longer with Dona Fausta, I'm with a Maestro Pelavsky, and he's no softie!

...

Did you see Miki in the photo? What did you think? Don't forget to send your photo, even if it's a 2×3. Which I'd prefer because it would fit in my little wallet. Thank you.

Without much more ado, I shall excuse myself now, with infinite kisses and hugs, from your friend,

Elana

PS And a big hug for your parents.

Toronto, October 1965

Elana tells me in this letter that Maestro Andrelino Vieira from our Conservatório Oswaldo Cruz passed away. His daughter had taken over directing the music school even before I left. Her father, although elderly, was still active, and his mind was sharp. Elana says in this letter we don't see how someone is a good person until too late. And yet, we all esteemed and respected the man. His gentleness and his caring as an educator and musician were hard to equal. We had been in the hands of a gem of a man and teacher. He started our little group of four recorder players: Elana and I and two boys our age. We practiced outside of our regular piano and music lessons, and we gave concerts. One time, his daughter arranged for us to perform on a popular children's TV show, a talent competition. We did not win first or runners-up level, but we did win consolation prizes.

Maestro Vieira wrote a musical piece he dedicated to me in 1961 or 1962. He titled it *Valsinha da Mamãe*, "Mother's Little Waltz." It was one of the pieces our group played on the recorder in all our concerts. He had the song published, including the dedication. I cherish the musical piece he wrote by hand, and the published version. I'm not sure why he liked me enough to write a song for me. I was quiet and meek, and the simple waltz must have been befitting. I was not a star musical student. But I did play the recorder, which I learned in first grade in Israel, and Maestro and his daughter loved the idea that the instrument would be an ideal vehicle for children to learn to play music. It was decades before I listened rapturously to a professional musician, Michala Petri, playing Vivaldi, Corelli, Telemann, and Handel on her recorder. And so, Elana and I, Israeli-born, introduced to the recorder at an early age, contributed to this step in early music education in São Paulo, under the auspices of a wise musical educator.

In winter 1965, I was in level 6 of piano at the Royal Conservatory in Toronto. Elana played well, much better than I did, and she and I continued to study piano until our early twenties. She eventually taught piano lessons, fulfilling her dream of teaching music.

It was Elana's mother, Vera, who instructed my mother in rounding out my education with piano, ballet, swimming, English private lessons, and social clubs. My mother had no mentor in Canada, and so my mother's influence on my education vanished as she struggled with living her sad, quietly grieving life in Toronto.

São Paulo, December 3, 1965

Dearest Udinha,

Ah! How good to receive your letter! Seriously! When I saw your photo, I don't know if my heart stopped or raced. You're beautiful. I can't see your mother well. You're wearing your hair well this way, you know?

Ooph, I had a piano exam yesterday. It was hard! I was afraid I didn't pass, but I did. I don't know the grade, because I had to leave in a hurry. Will tell you why later. I'm no longer studying with Dona Fausta, I'm with Maestro Israel Pelavsky. I don't think he's Jewish (I'm just kidding). I passed to the 7th year. You caught up with me on everything, little lady! Aren't you ashamed? Leaving your friend behind like this? Boohooo! One day I'll catch you there. [Misunderstanding, I did not catch up with her in piano.]

We still haven't won [the lottery]! *I think this will pass till next year.*

...

Lucky you! you're already on vacation. Mine only starts on the 17th. I'll know about the exams on Monday, the 6th. These last months' grades were bad. I would have to take all the exams, depending on this last grade.

...

You know, every time you send me a photo it's as if I'm meeting you again. Send me all the time when you can, that way I will always meet you! Thank you! I will arrange to get you the lyrics for "Girl from Ipanema" and mail it to you, I don't know it.

...

Miki must have gone today to Jacareí until Monday. The lucky bum is already on vacation, because she passed everything and has no exams to take. Well, my dear. I have nothing more to add.

How is your love life? Do you have a boyfriend? You don't tell me anything. Do you remember Nescafé? Ah! the good old days! (I'm talking like an old lady.) But ah, the good old days. Ruth, I'll write soon, so that your letter will arrive before my encampments. Thank you. I will leave space here for the lyrics of the song:

...

I was writing this in the morning. My father must go to the post office this afternoon or this evening, so he'll take this letter. If I find the lyrics I'll send in another letter, but don't wait, write to me right away. Answer me soon, OK? That one will be an Extra.

Without delay, I part here with big kiss and a huge hug for my unforgettable Rutinha.

PS Regards to your parents and your grandmother, how are they?
Elana

Toronto, December 1965

This last letter of 1965 was Elana's longest, chattiest, and one of the happiest so far. Of course I did not have a boyfriend, and of course I had nothing to tell her about my "love life." It didn't exist.

Elana reminds me of Nescafé in this letter. That was a nickname Miki gave a boy, Michel, who sat next to me in fourth grade. Miki liked to discuss boys, and she'd extract from Elana and me any mention of a boy who then became the "boyfriend" and to whom she would assign a nickname. Despite all her naiveté, and she was far less naive than we were, she claimed to know all about love. She'd explain to us what it means to "fall in love." She considered herself (forevermore) an expert on love, infatuation, attraction, and relationships, an expertise I considered as sham and tenuous as reading coffee grinds in a fortune teller's cup. But we listened and played along. We did not know any better, so we didn't laugh at her, although her expertise was comical. (Her mother, Elsa, was far more sophisticated in this topic than our mothers, Vera and Edith.) We were like the blind being led by the blind. Miki was always enamored with someone, and she always considered it serious, until the next one came around in rapid succession. Elana and I were laggards in that realm.

This boy and I were not even friends; we never spoke to each other. I sat at the last desk of the last row on the left of the class, and he sat at the last desk of the row to my right. I found out he was born in Israel, a Sabra like me, and that he must have understood some Hebrew. I never asked him. Perhaps we were placed in those seats because we were not favored by an antisemitic teacher, which is not a farfetched assumption. Antisemitism ran as an undercurrent in Brazilian Catholic culture, where the presumption was that we killed Jesus. Perhaps he and I were placed in those seats because we didn't make any academic impression or verbal distinction. Or perhaps I was in the last chair of the class because my last name started with "Z." Did I like this boy? I probably did. Why? Because he was an immigrant like I was, from the same country, and I missed Israel with the acute pain of a captured, wounded bird. Israel was my home; this classroom in São Paulo was my birdcage. And a boy-bird I pined for was in the cage next to me. If only I had the voice to sing and connect via airwaves. Instead, I was mute.

This letter came from Elana during my second winter in Toronto. Dark, cold, and wet, a city that lost whatever sheen it possessed when the sun would move up in latitude to bless it. Toronto sits higher than Chicago or Portland, but not as high as Minneapolis. It does not sit higher than London, but neither is it awash in the Atlantic gulf stream that brings London mild winters. Toronto does not have an airstream furnace to warm it. The Great Lakes create their own winter weather. And with no major mountain range between Toronto and the North, it can welcome the arctic air mass every winter with the open arms of its flatness. In the 1960s it was not a world metropolis. It was a staid city without its future sky-high needle or night clubs.

Elana mentions that I'm beautiful in the photos. I never thought I was beautiful. I had intense feelings of inferiority. I knew I did not attract boys, and I was resigned to being a Plain Jane. On the other hand, I thought Elana was gorgeous. Not her body, which was powerful and solid, not her walk, which had the gait of a warrior, not her stance, which was angled despite years of ballet classes, but instead she had the facial features of a gorgeous doll. She's blonde with hazel eyes. Her hair is wavy, but she abused it by always pulling it tightly on the scalp, willing her hair to be straight. She inherited the wavy blonde hair from her father. She never let her hair flow. And how it could have flown! Compared with my mousy, thin, straight, and unruly hair, she had a lion's mane she perennially attempted to tame.

As acclimated as my family became to Brazil, we were not truly assimilated. Being Jews, we lived parallel lives in tandem with Catholic Brazilians. We mixed in classes, at university, in ballet class, or at the Conservatory. And yet, Jewish immigrants were not embraced as national kin; after all, none of us had formalized our citizenship. We were happy to remain outsiders, in a social structure where parents befriended each other, partnered in businesses together, and sent their children to social clubs. That is not to say we did not have Catholic friends. I had Estelinha, as sweet a friend as one would wish for. And Elana also had Catholic friends. She was friendly with everyone and did not feel insecure or constrained. In her free time, she ran from one club and event to another, which brought her such joy that she spilled it into her letters time after time. And I? I had none of it in Canada. My parents were deeply occupied with making ends meet, and for some reason neglected their cultural and religious foundation and social needs. They had very few friends. They could not provide me with a deeper social environment, so I relied on my school and my own ventures. I did not reach out to Toronto, and in turn, Toronto barely acknowledged me. I stayed satisfied with the few friends I made, none of whom had extended lives beyond school and family either, and so I lived vicariously through Elana's accounts.

Turma is the Portuguese word for a social, friendly gang, or *chavurah* in Hebrew. Elana loved her gangs. I missed experiencing such a social life at the age when it's most important, the teen years. As sexually reserved as Elana and I were, in comparison with Miki, who fancied herself as seductive as her mother was—the crux of femininity—Elana had a social outlet to help her transition to the next phase of her life, and I did not. I remained zygotic.

São Paulo, December 28, 1965

Rutinha,

I promised and here it is. I'm not sure it's correct, but if I find an error, I will send it again. The girl who gave this to me is not sure either. Here it goes:

Garôta de Ipanema

"Olha que coisa mais linda . . . etc."

[This is my translation, not the official English version: "Look what a beautiful thing, so full of grace . . . etc."]

Toronto, December 1965

In 1965, a recording of "The Girl from Ipanema" won a Grammy Award for record of the year, and it was played often on the radio.

I wanted the lyrics, and interestingly, Elana didn't know them. She had to ask a friend for the lyrics, and even her friend was not sure she got it right.

I used to listen to the radio in my apartment in Toronto, trying to get to know the current musical trends. I remember a lot of dull crooning by Frank Sinatra. I was listening to the wrong radio stations. The new wave of songs popular with teenagers came from the Beatles, the Rolling Stones, Petula Clark, the Righteous Brothers, the Byrds, the Beach Boys, and others. If I did not hear the Beatles' hits in 1964 in Brazil, I certainly knew these soundtracks the following year or two. Subsequently, I became more interested in the folk songs of Pete Seeger, Peter, Paul and Mary, Simon and Garfunkel, Leonard Cohen, and others before entering college.

While I lived in Brazil, Elana and I were in our callow years, and we were far behind Miki's hip sophistication in popular music. She had her ear attuned to American pop music, and she mimicked her mother with less-than-convincing fandom excitement. While her starry-eyed mother would talk up Neil Sedaka or Bobby Darin, she missed the coming of the Beatles. I corresponded for a short time in early 1964 with an American pen pal from rural Illinois, and she is the one who enlightened me about Beatlemania. She asked me if I heard of them, and unfortunately, embarrassingly, I had to say no. It was my English tutor, Miss Margaret Fleury, who found this American pen pal for me. It didn't last. We had never met, and we had nothing in common. Eventually, there was nothing to write about, not to mention that my English was elementary. Elana, in contrast, was not a pen pal. Our correspondence was not a hobby, it was a lifeline to a friendship.

It was not until I was friends with Judy, who, just like Miki, was also supremely knowledgeable about popular trends, that I was taken by the hand and introduced to who's who: Judy was mad about the Beach Boys.

Consequently, I had to ask Elana to help me get the lyrics for a hit song that was associated with our background, the bossa nova that came from Brazil, even though Elana was rather uninterested at the time. When I visited her in 1970, I asked her to take me to record stores, where I could buy Brazilian records to bring home to New York. She helped, because she was fond of me, not because she was fond of popular music.

São Paulo, January 11, 1966

Dear Ruth!

Everything well there? There's little news here. Yes, I remember when I slept at your house [reminiscing about something I wrote]. *I am studying English with her* [Miss Fleury], *of course! The Michigan Exam* [yearly standardized test] *is on the 17th. I passed into second year at the Aliança.* [Alliance Française. I also attended the Alliance for several years in Brazil. It gave me a very strong foundation in French, which lasted over a decade.] *I am ashamed to say, I flunked. And you, yes, I know you, an 80 is not enough, must be higher, of course.* [She's making fun of me.]

We also have a lot of nonsense on the radio. Did the letter with the "Girl from Ipanema" lyrics arrive?

You are so lucky! You have snow! I would love to see it. Be patient, one day I will come knocking on your door and we'll go skating together! I am so happy about this, that our friendship continues. I thought we'd forget after a few years, but praise [the Lord], *we're not forgetting.*

I am taking a shorthand course that will end on the 22nd. I already know how to write it, all I need now is to speed up, that is to be more agile. I don't think I will go anywhere on vacation this time. And! I need to study, right?

Well, Rutinha, write SOON and don't forget photos (I am now direct: with plural).

Without ado, a big hug from your always,

Elana

PS How are your parents and your cousin? Regards to all of them.

Toronto, January 1966

Elana's letter is brief, with curt sentences. Her usual exhilaration is not present. Perhaps she was bummed out from failing to advance in school. I, on the other hand, was back at school for the second half of tenth grade, struggling through my second arctic winter. A visit to Michigan was a reprieve; somehow Michigan snow was more bearable thanks to family.

Also more bearable was the fact that my maternal grandmother, Magda, had finally immigrated to the United States from Brazil. She waited for a visa in 1964 so that she could join her younger daughter, my aunt Gitta, in Michigan, who sponsored her immigration. But she moved to New York City and found work right away. She was always independent, and she came without Ziggi, her third wayward husband. Her first employment in the summer of 1965 was working at Kutcher's in the Catskills, a summer resort and diversion for established Jewish New Yorkers. She worked in housekeeping—she never shied away from menial work. It is what had sustained her during the Holocaust in Romania while raising two young girls alone. She was no bourgeoise, she was hoi polloi, and proud. If my mother suffered from extreme lack of confidence, which she passed on to me, my grandmother counterbalanced it with her admirable strength and unshakable self-confidence.

São Paulo, January 28, 1966

Dear Rutinha,

I didn't have time to send the letter, and on the 20th, I went to encampment. Yesterday the group from the encampment went on a one-day excursion. The encampment was great, and I made more friends, from Rio, Curitiba, Porto Alegre and Recife. One guy from Recife, called Isaías, nicknamed Izinho, wrote me this verse [it was an acrostic in Portuguese]:

> *Today is a happy day,*
> *Tomorrow—who knows?*
> *Equal days don't exist*
> *Equal beings don't exist, so*
> *Humans keep walking to*
> *Unknowns! Until when? . . .*

Do you like it? I liked it. We went on several hikes, and one was to Ermida, do you remember it? There, near the lake.

. . .

My aunt arrives here with my cousin on the first of February. I would also like if she brought my older cousin and the little one (Yudit). But only Arieh is coming. It's possible I'll go with my aunt to Rio.

I have Math and Chem exams on the 7th and 9th. I'm ashamed to say it. OK. Before I have to say I flunked them, I'm going to study. So, I leave you with a big kiss and a big hug to my big, big friend.

Elana

PS Write right away, eh?

Toronto, January 1966

Elana restated countless times her dream to go to Rio. She loved traveling, going places; she was like a vagabond, not because she had no home, but because she couldn't stay still. The wider world beckoned to her. It is curious how she recounts her social activities with such gusto while also recounting how she barely passed her classes.

She was crazy about her aunt. Our affection for a maternal aunt was another parallel between Elana and me. Elana's aunt Yael counterbalanced Vera's plainness. To Elana she was resplendent. My aunt Gitta counterbalanced my mother's timidity. To me she was vivacious and spritely. Neither Elana nor I resented our mothers for their shortcomings. They were virtuous and dedicated. They taught us humility. I never met Yael, but for all her wealth, I believe she was humble, or Elana would not have been crazy about her.

My aunt Gitta was my lifeline when, later, my mother succumbed to mental illness. Gitta was my other mother. The two of them, at ages eighteen and seventeen, gave birth to babies a month apart. My mother used to cheerfully tell me that they sometimes exchanged babies to nurse us. They were truly little girls. And their mother, Magda, my third mother, so to speak, was the hen who clucked after them through continents, relationships, grandchildren (two: Jack and me). She was the psychological powerhouse for the young girls, especially for my mother. My grandmother meant so much to me, that Elana, knowing this, was always asking about her, sending her regards. Surely, I wrote about her in many letters. Surely, my mother loved me in a possessive sort of way (as her only surviving child), but my grandmother bathed me in her effusive love and unconditional veneration. My mother always claimed that children should not be praised in public; my grandmother ditched that poppycock the way she crushed her spent cigarettes. Elana's interest in my grandmother, aside from having known her in Brazil and fallen under her spell, mirrors her feelings of closeness to her own grandmother she left behind in Israel, and who died in 1964. For Elana and me, aunts and grandmothers, our inner circle, held a very special place in our hearts and our being. Unlike ours, Miki's relationship with her grandmother, Berta *neni*, was complicated and unsettled. All three grandmothers, however, Elana's, Miki's, and mine, were formative in our young development.

São Paulo, February 27, 1966

Dear Udi-Udi!

Thank you for your birthday wishes. It was as if you whispered them into my ear! It reminded me of all the time we spent our birthdays together! Ah! They were good times, weren't they? I'd love to see you soon! The years are advancing, but I am not, obviously, because I flunked. And yes . . . your friendship repeats itself. My brother is already in 2nd year of pre-med. My aunt left yesterday. I adored my little cousin. He's a love. It looks like he'll be well. I hope so.

At the Michigan exam [English as second language] *the lowest passing grade is 13.*

. . .

But you are laggards in Mathematics there, eh?

I liked the "meditacau!" Ha ha! Maybe he wanted to say "medita cão" [a play on words in misspelling and homophones].

The guy who wrote the verses for me who's named Isaías, that is, Izinho, he lives in Recife, and I met him at an encampment. He's very nice, and we are writing to each other. His first letter that he sent took half an hour to open, I was so afraid of ripping it. But it turned out easy! It was about holding it just so, and it opened automatically. I will fold your letter the same way, OK? (If I succeed!)

Carnaval was the 19th to the 23rd and 24th was Ash Wednesday. I went to Jacareí with Miki. They have a house there [condominium at the beach].

Yesterday, not the 23rd and not the 25th, was my birthday. I didn't have a party (haha), but I was invited to 2 birthday parties, and in each there were two of us celebrating. Isn't that great? I had a good time.

...

How are your parents? and your cousin?

Well, Rutinha, I must stop so I can study piano. That's why I'll excuse myself with a sincere hug and kiss, from your friend who's dying from missing you, your always,

Elana

PS do you have a recent photo? Thank you.

Toronto, February 1966

Well, I guess I was still writing in Portuguese and making mistakes! Elana was teasing me very gently. In a prior letter she said it made her laugh so hard. And finally, her English was also improving from the looks of it: the Michigan exams were standardized English exams in Brazil, and she did well. The more she struggled with her other subjects, the more it seemed that Yoni, her brother, was speeding along in his.

By this time, I was fluent in English, although I spoke with an accent. No one tells me now that I have an accent, but I do hear it: there is a vestige of ghostly language sounds in the way I speak.

And it also looks like I made a mistake with her birthday. It is on February 26th, and again, she reminds me gently. It is also around the usual date for Carnaval (this is the Portuguese spelling), which would throw the city into a frenzy. Carnaval fever would begin early, and Brazilians would put up with a lot of shenanigans on the streets. Pedestrians just passing by minding their business would be pelted with colored water, streamers, or loud horns. We usually did not go watch the parades on the evening of Carnaval. But it was hard to avoid the fever pitch of the festivities. Of course, Fat Tuesday is celebrated anywhere in the world where there is a Catholic population. In Canada, the date was silent. It was not until I moved to the United States that Carnaval entered my awareness again, as New Orleans's Mardi Gras.

São Paulo, May 9, 1966

Dearest Rutinha!

It's been so long! Your letter arrived in my hand this minute!

I didn't know if I should cry, laugh, or yell, I was so surprised. Even yesterday I nagged my mother asking if she took the letter directly to the post office. I thought you didn't get it. I didn't know what else to think, because I didn't want to think that our friendship would stop like this, no more, no less. But . . . now that your letter arrived, let's forget everything and be in the present.

Yes, me too, for all the kilograms of friends that I have, no one is like you. Have you heard this: "Things can be imitated but not duplicated." In this case "things" is our friendship.

. . .

As for my studies, after the last letter, something happened:

[Here Elana describes failing a class and requesting to move from the science section of high school to the liberal arts section, and she selected evening classes so that she could study piano during the day.]

Soon I gave up the ideas of doing the cientifico, because I loved the classico! I'm studying in the evening. There are two of us girls (she's called Ana Maria) and 57 guys. The class is wonderful, they're all so kind and friendly. You know, when you enter a classroom and you feel insecure and ashamed, even if it's not co-ed, but when I entered this classroom, I felt so good, so willing! The teachers also seem friendlier, finally—everything is better [the schedule explained] *with 40-minute classes.*

A new friend always gives me a ride home. When he can't, there's always someone else who volunteers to give us (including Ana) a ride home. She's very sweet, and we get along. We always go out at the same time, and the guys, too. I've improved in everything: piano, which I haven't played in audition for two years, I will play 3 pieces (Bach, Beethoven, João B. Julião) on the 27th. I already told you I switched teachers, it's now a maestro who is now the director, since Maria de Carmo stepped down. That's very good.

I'm doing well in French and English. Also, in the Conservatory subjects.

. . .

[In other subjects] *not great marks, but in comparison to last year, they're excellent. Latin was hard, I studied a lot for it.*

. . .

Yesterday was Mother's Day. I gave her my grade book (including the Conservatory's 8,0 in piano). The other subjects have not yet been graded. I made lunch and a cake. She was pleased with my improvements. And I am ever more pleased, because I see it's fun to study and see these results. Well, enough of studies.

I loved your photo. You're gorgeous. It's obvious! Give my regards to your cousin. You are well?

As for Miki, she has deceived me a lot lately. She's starting to be insufferable. It makes no difference to want to see another side of her. You know, right? She's already 15.

Ruth, you said your mother is studying hairdressing. Look at the dictionary and see the different between "cabeleira" and "cabelereira." [I made a mistake in spelling and in meaning.] *But do you have a dictionary? I'm asking because in front of me sits a memento you left: the dictionary which I use now all the time. And whenever I look in it, I see you sitting at your desk, doing your lessons and studying. I remember well your little room, where we spent so many wonderful hours together. Yes. This dictionary and other things bring beautiful memories.*

But what is this? We will see each other, right? Of course, sooner or later one of us will visit the other, right?

. . .

How is piano going? How is Judy? What have you done for fun? And your parents? My mother always says "Ay, I must write to Edith!" But she never writes. I'll see if I can make her write this time.

I see it's time to finish this, but . . . it's so good to talk to you! It's so rare that you feel like writing pages upon pages. Ruth: write a lot, even nonsense, OK?

Without ado, with difficulty, I excuse myself awaiting a LONG letter and SOON!!! She who cannot forget you,

Elana

PS Did you answer already? And did you mail it already? NO? What are you waiting for?

Regards to your parents and a little sweet kiss on the point of your little nose.

Toronto, May 1966

Elana described in these letters the complicated nature of the education system in Brazil. It was simplified years later, but back then there were three tracks of studies beyond elementary school (from fifth on). Elana entered middle school and high school in the *científico*-track but had a hard time hanging on. She explains in a convoluted way that she switched to the evening *classico*-track and finally found her footing. And how ecstatic she sounded! Better teachers, friendlier classmates, and so on. What she meant by global average must be something like a grade point average. She may have had a hard time in *científico* (math and science) not just because of the rigor of the subjects but also the arrogance of teachers and the snobbery of the strong students. Or it could have been her insecurity alone preventing her keeping pace.

My high school had no tracks. It was not a question of having a homogeneous class of students, but somehow, every year carried the slow ones and the fast ones in a resolute course from ninth to tenth and eleventh grade. I don't remember anyone repeating grades, but there were students who excelled far above the others. One of my friends in tenth grade was Susan S., who was at the top of our class (there were only a couple of sections of tenth grade). She was exceptionally intelligent and studious. I did not stay to graduate, because we migrated again, but she no doubt was the class valedictorian at the end of high school. Canadians entered university at nineteen, not eighteen, making it upward of two years beyond Brazilian high school.

I'm not sure what I wrote Elana about school. She and I were on different tracks, although she mentions that we were lagging in math, based on what I wrote to her about studying algebra, geometry, and/or trigonometry.

It seemed as if many letters showed a waffling in the friendship with Miki. This went on for a few years until Miki left Brazil. I don't think it was Elana who changed; it was due to Miki's teenage volatility. She had vain tendencies and inconsistencies that Elana was not comfortable tolerating. When Miki came down to earth, Elana was happy seeing her, because she never held a grudge.

Does this mean that I showed opposite characteristics to Miki's? I'd like to say yes. I was consistent and constant. If my love for Elana was not as ebullient and visible as hers was for me, at least I was devoted and unwavering. That is not a trait I exhibited with everyone. Elana urged me to write to Miss Fleury, who considered me her favorite and intently followed my progress. Eventually, I stopped writing to her. I also stopped writing to Estelinha, who was such a delightful and gentle person. I don't stand by all my friends all the time. As I look back, there were many who fell by the wayside, most likely through my neglect. But not Elana. My commitment to our friendship was firmly cast. It was archived into several decades of correspondence; it was generated in the past going back to our parents' shared early life; it was also a historical Jewish and Israeli expatriated bond. It was a bond that came close to the familial.

Was it the correspondence that formed the glue? And what drove the relentless urge to keep writing to each other? It seems like a tautological process. The longer we wrote to each other, the stronger the glue. The more the stack of letters grew, the more precious the friendship grew in value.

Was it the letters, was it the correspondence, was it our character, was it our background? Maybe all of it made this a unique relationship. Another driving force behind the correspondence and the connection across the hemispheres was that we needed each other. I'd say I needed her more than she needed me, because I needed a consolation for my loss of home, and I also needed to assuage my loneliness. She was not lonely, so her motivation was different. She needed a sister, and she also needed to fill a very deep well of love she could feel for another person.

São Paulo, July 27, 1966

Rutinha,

It's incredible! Is it you?? You look like your mother! Did you gain weight? Or is it the hair that gives that impression? How are you all over there? Here we keep living.

I returned today from Guarujá (do you remember, past Santos, crossing on the ferry). I went the 17th, a friend's invitation. It was nice, but sometimes she planned distasteful activities that I didn't like. I was to stay till the 30th, but I returned today.

Some guys from my class who are working on a play written by one of them, who helped me with my audition in May, asked me to play several numbers. I accepted, but I still must practice. It will take place August 6. I'm studying Chopin's Valse Brilliante, Monti's Czardas, Lake Como and a Samba by Zinbo Trio. Maybe I'll also play Bach's Gavotte from the English Suite III. I think you know them all, they're not hard.

Continue to write in English. I only used the dictionary for one word, "schedule," and I read the rest correctly, it's clear—"understanding it." [Written in English.]

Did you know I will be an aunt in two months? No! My brother did not get married! Haha. I bet that's what you thought. It's my cousin Ruth in Israel.

You know something even better? Yesterday by the sea, or better yet, by the beach, I learned to ride a bike! But it took its revenge on me. I got completely smeared in grease.

Congratulations on passing your grade. And now? do you have any plans for your vacation? What have you read? Have you continued with piano? Of course! What are you playing? I loved your photo, it's here in front of me. But I insist on a small one for my wallet. I think tomorrow I'll get some photos my brother had developed (at last). I will send one. Yes, I continue literature with Miss Margaret. She always asks about you. But I won't intervene, it's just my opinion, you should write to her.

Who do you go out with? What do you usually do? Ruth, write about yourself! Write a lot! And your parents? How are they? Do they still remember me? How's your cousin? Regards to all.

The other day I passed in front of your house with a classmate. We were on our way to USP [Universidade de São Paulo] *Philosophy. You can't imagine how much went through my head, my memory, looking at your window. Ah! the old days, I seem like an old lady talking, eh?*

Have you heard of Roberto Carlos? I think you have. He's an idol of Brazilian youth (haha). He lives in front of my house.

Ruth, could you do a simple little favor and answer a little more speedily? This year, this is a shame, it's the 3rd letter. Tell me something of your life. How and what do you like? I know you like air and food, what else?

Well, I carried on long enough. 'Plis' [sic] *answer quickly!!!!'*

I end, pardon my nonsense. I big tight hug, and a well-placed kiss (haha) from your forever friend,

Elana

PS Continue writing "em English, all right?" [This was written in a mixed Portuguese/English sentence.]

August 17, 1966 [Letter mailed as a continuation of the previous.]
Udi-Udi!

I'm sorry for the delay. Yo! forgive me, eh! How's everyone? Today I received the postcard you sent from Niagara Falls. Beautiful, marvelous, I envy you. But which is more beautiful? [She's comparing it to Foz do Iguaçú.] *I think each has its different qualities.*

...

Rutinha: "plis," 1,000 "plis," answer quickly! You leave me crazy! Take care, one day I'll show up there. Beware. On Saturday, Miki is having a very fancy ball [15th birthday]. *Hm. A chic ball!!!* [sic]

OK, I'm done here, imploring you to respond soon. And I'm sorry I'm not sending a photo this time either. Still don't have one.

Ruth, a big and sincere hug, from your forever big friend,

Elana

P.S. You ask if I remember Iguaçú! Yes. I don't think I'll ever forget it, especially the travel there. Yes, we did it together. I'd love to go back to those days, who knows, maybe one day we will return. "Bai." Answer soon in English. All right?

Toronto, July 1966

I finally abandoned Portuguese and wrote to her in English. I remained fluent in Portuguese for two years after leaving Brazil. Portuguese, my third language, was not ingrained in me as a native language, and I spoke it for only five years. It is easy to forget a language when you are young and stop speaking it. However, I did not forget it; I got "rusty." I can still read and understand spoken Portuguese, but ironically, I speak it with an English accent.

My visit to Niagara Falls that summer was a pleasant vacation, but the memory of the trip to Foz do Iguaçú in 1963 was strong and prompted a comparison. Of course, one day we did travel there together again. My impression, like Elana's, was that above and beyond the natural wonder of both falls, it was the experience that Elana and I had with our parents at the Foz that made us recall the vivid memory of it in 1966. Iguaçu is vaster than Niagara, it's in the interior of Brazil and less accessible except by air, whereas Niagara is easily reached by car. The former is also wilder, spread out in innumerable cataracts, and is affected by seasonal levels of water flow that can reach gargantuan proportions. The largest is called the devil's throat, Garganta do Diablo. I was awed by Iguaçu's expansive majesty, wowed by Niagara's taut and concentrated rumble.

São Paulo, September 14, 1966

Dear Udi-Udi,

First, I congratulate you, and wish you many sincere birthday-wishes, good surprises and happiness this year. Sixteen years! Boy, where are we headed? I wanted this letter to be in your hands on the 16th, but unfortunately it didn't work out.

...

How are you? How are your parents? You hardly wrote anything about them! Does your father still have a playful spirit?

Here we are managing. My parents work like always, my grandfather watching, Yoni studying at the medical college. He leaves at 7:30 a.m. and returns at 6 or 6:30 p.m. He's not studying the whole time, he also has swimming, library, discography, everything they have there. He's tall and strong, as the girls say, a "pão" [literally bread, or as we say, a hunk]. *I don't know if you knew that expression from before. I sometimes study, and I'm sometimes lazy. But I think this month I will complete all my subjects with at least 40 points. Till August my worst was Math at 31 points and the best was 39.*

So, you are already playing Beethoven's "Moonlight Sonata?" I will do it alone without the teacher, because I already have a Beethoven piece ready, and he doesn't want to cover another. I find it beautiful. One day I'll show up there to hear you play it. I'm not kidding. Do me a favor? stop laughing. What a thing. It's almost as if I just told a joke.

Roberto Carlos is the actual "Youth Idol." He sings ye ye ye. You're not missing anything by not hearing anything about him.

Hm. Miki? I concluded that I'd prefer not to have a friend like her. I think that to have a friendship, both must GIVE, and not always look to GET. As for the ball, it was nice, but it was not for me. Snobbish? No. Not just at the ball. She is now permanently like that. Phooey. But let's leave that. She now likes two guys, but they don't reciprocate.

Me, I was going with someone, but it ended. All my anger at Miki, and of dating, all of it is relative. Especially the END. But it's too long to tell you about it. As I said, one day I'll show up there, and I'll tell you about it. How marvelous! all this while looking out the window and seeing snow fall! Enough of dreaming. I want to think about snow, like the sun burning my eyes.

Ruth, how is your grandmother? Send her my regards, OK? Do you have a car? How did you go to Niagara?

Here's an epigram: "However rare true love is, true friendship is rarer." La Rochefoucauld. Do you have other epigrams? In English.

Well. I'll stop here, wishing you again a happy birthday and Shanah Tovah. A big strong hug, your friend, always,

Elana

Toronto, September 1966

In September 1966, I was sitting on the front rightmost chair in the class photo of eleventh grade. I was smiling. I spoke English, had friends, and found my equilibrium. One more school year in Canada until the next migration. I did not know that at the time. My family was still persona non grata vis-à-vis American immigration quotas. In other words, the wait was so long that one tended to forget that America would ever open its doors.

These quotas set by law and followed by the State Department were a consequence of years of antisemitic sentiment. Germans could be welcomed. My parents were of Romanian birth; therefore their native country was currently "behind the Iron Curtain." Never mind that they escaped from there at the end of the war! They could not be welcomed to the USA. The imposition of tight quotas on East Europeans was a backhanded and convoluted way to restrict Jews. East Europeans were unwelcome, not just Romanians. Did this population amount to a front categorized as communist sympathizers? Just another generalization and catch-all classification? My father was such a staunch capitalist that this immigration selection was akin to a joke. This is a man who didn't want to stay in Israel because it was too "socialist," and he could not abide the collective atmosphere there (although today it is a far cry from its early socialist inception). It's the irony of life that was turned on its head and made my father's quest a tragic one. Once again, he did not intend to stay in Canada. Once again, we were not on track to naturalize as Canadian citizens. Once again, we were in a holding pattern. Landing was going to be difficult.

At last, in 1965 the United States Congress passed the Immigration and Nationality Act to end the prior exclusionary law, the Johnson-Reed Asian Exclusion and National Origins Acts of 1924 signed by President Calvin Coolidge, which had selected for North European (and white) requests "to preserve the ideal of U.S. homogeneity." President Lyndon Johnson signed the new law, stating that it would end the "cruel and enduring wrong in the conduct of the American Nation." Whereupon my father contacted a lawyer to assist in the process of getting a Green Card (a wallet-sized document in a green hue that designates the holder as a bona fide permanent American resident). It took over a year to get our immigrant visas. On the other hand, my father had not needed a lawyer to help apply for the easier Canadian immigration in 1964.

Elana's letters were repetitious, of course, and mine were too! We didn't make copies, and we had no modern digital folder of

SENT MAIL. And we were still immature correspondents. We relied on our memory after a month or two, and we sifted through our daily lives to share what touched us. And so, the sagas were repeated like "previously on" at the beginning of the next episode of a TV series.

We had so many things in common, even if we had different personalities. But nothing was as deep and continuous as our ongoing expressions of friendship. La Rochefoucauld was correct: "However rare true love is, true friendship is rarer."

While Elana wavered in her friendship with Miki, there was no such equivocation between Elana and me. The letters show their on-again-off-again friendship. However much Miki was connected to our past and to our bond, by character she was capricious. Despite her protestations about Miki's behavior, and her shifting affection for Miki, Elana continued a sincere friendship with Miki for the rest of her life. My friendship with Miki had been tenuous. For me, Miki came part and parcel with Elana, like an inverted isosceles triangle—Elana and I on top, Miki connected to each of us below. We were a peculiar threesome; Miki was an important part of our relationship, and our triumvirate had not been insignificant. We had a collective past. But for me, Elana stood alone and needed no buttressing. My austere patience with Miki was thin, but Elana's was admirably solicitous and long-lasting.

As for the question in the letter, we did not have a car in Canada; my father could not afford one. We went to Niagara Falls by bus. We met my aunt and family there, and we did our sightseeing together.

São Paulo, October 26, 1966

My dear Udinha,

You know, every time I receive a letter from you, I can't resist waiting for another. It is so good to get news from you. "Saudades" are many. There's a saying: "When we're separated by an ocean, I feel your hand on mine. When your hand is on mine, I feel an ocean separates us." What do you think?

You want to say that you are studying hard now? So, study even more, because the payoff will be soon. That's what I wish for you. I have already passed. In November I could get zero in everything. Yes, I am still at the Alliance Française, but I like English better. I am so happy that I can read your letters without a dictionary, and I read them correctly. Miss Margaret is a marvelous teacher. Yesterday she taught me to crochet. It's super. Do you play rugby? [This misunderstanding must be Fleury's influence.] *Is it neat?*

I think I will go to Argentina this vacation for a seminar of volunteerism via Ichud Habonim. But my mother doesn't want to let me because of the situation in Argentina [a coup d'état formed a military dictatorship].

Yes, Rio is beautiful, but I didn't see enough of it, I want to go back and see more. Try to.

...

This is how it went. She invited me to join them [the older women] *in Jacareí for Carnaval, when we met Tomi, and she started dating him. OK. He was part of a group. We were introduced at her place, but I thought I would be in her way, so I did not go out with his group. Tomi has a friend who I know for a long time, since we were little. He and Jean Louis, my favorite, were with this group. I tried to avoid going out with them. I went maybe a total of 2 or 3 times. Well. On the first day of vacation (July) I went to Miki's house. And he also went. Since he lives on Barão de Limeira at the corner of Duque de Caxias, a few steps from my house, he brought me home. He asked me why I don't go out with the group, and maybe the following day he'd come get me. I said I couldn't. In the meantime, Tomi and Miki fell out. I called him on Sunday, to tell him I wanted to return his jacket that he lent me. He said there was a birthday party at his cousin's place for some of the girls in the group, and we should go along. I accepted, and said I'd be there at 4 p.m. It was then 1:30 p.m. At about 2 p.m. I was by the window when I heard an insistent ringing. I looked and saw Jean Luis. He was wearing a tie, etc. He came up and said he came to get me, because Miki said I was coming to the party. I changed and we went to the party, but first we went by Miki's to pick her up. At the party I thought I ought to stand aside, because he'd certainly be with Miki. But it was on the contrary. I liked him, but had not yet told Miki, because they were friends, and she would have told him. So, he was talking with me, and on July 3rd we started dating. OK, in the beginning everything went well. He studies in a classroom next to mine. My mother doesn't like him, but I do. Since "Mikikeh"* [Hungarian diminutive] *did not have a boyfriend* [right then], *her mother went above us, calling him at the office asking urgently to come by their home in the evening to tell him something. In conclusion: Elana, me, went home alone, that is, with another classmate, being afraid to go alone at night.*

Ruth, I have so many important details for you to understand, that in the end I could not bear their falsehood and mockery that could fill pages upon pages. In the end, it couldn't be, I was more unhappy with him than without. And so, it's over. August 23 at the same time, we had been at break, and I was certain we'd go home together. But DONA Elsa found a way to trick him to go there. And I, raging, venting, and . . . "finita la comedia." It was horrible, Ruth. I had a few terrible days, I lost 3 kilos (and this is good). After they got what they wanted, they took pleasure in private. I was still calling her [Miki] *but rarely. Then one day she started asking questions left and right, thank God I answered with dignity. A few days later, she said this to me: "You know who I was on the phone extension with? Jean Louis!"*

When we parted, she said: call me! I only responded: Miki after what you all did, I don't know why I should. Since then, "Bye." However, I don't feel a grudge against her, because all of this was because of her women [mother and grandmother]. *Now for sure, when I find a friend, first I will look both sides before extending my friendship.*

Well, let's talk about something more interesting. Yes, my father still has the Dauphine [small French car], *(dirty, so as not to be different). Yes, I also remember all our trips together as if it was yesterday! What "saudades!" Is it possible we'll take trips together? Yoni is in his 2nd year and there are 4 more. He loves it. He studies and does sports: swimming and water polo. He's on the university varsity. He's big, robust, gorgeous. We still speak in 3 languages at home! Yikes! what confusion.*

Do you like these epigrams? If you have some more in English, send them. Thanks. I hope I made you pleased with this letter. We changed a lot. Before I did not know how to write to you. But, as much as we have changed, I think our friendship stayed just the same, and even got better.

And you, do you have anything to tell me? How is everyone? Send them regards. How is piano? I played in audition on the 21st. It went well, the best so far. Well, I hope you answer soon, because I'm anxious to receive letters from you.

A huge hug, enclosing a sincere and huge "saudade" from yours, always,

Elana

Toronto, October 1966

Finally, Elana writes about some boys, in addition to her piano repertoire and school schedule. And she admits we have entered a new stage in our correspondence, albeit we were still adolescents.

Miki took no time to start dating, of course. She changed boyfriends like a seasonal wardrobe. And so, at last, Elana started dating, too, but was thwarted by Miki's "director," the mother. That would set her back a while, because Elana was not a coquette or a flirt. Miki could model after her mother, be self-confident, and believe in her ability to attract boys, but Elana could not. Neither could I. In 1966, without social media, without visual entertainment such as TV, without reading romance books, and without an older sister or cousin nearby to emulate, a teen girl had nothing to go by but her mother's feminine comportment. Most girls we knew were not different from us. However, Elana and I had unsexy, inhibited, and overprotective mothers.

If I think back to the girls in my high school class, most were incredibly innocent. Our generation, in our environment, São Paulo or Toronto, may have entered puberty at around age twelve (today it's much earlier), but several years later, we were still innocent. It may seem shocking today. Puberty comes earlier, sexualized clothing, makeup, body movement, and sexual fixation result in very early sexual experience. Is that for the better? Maybe not. With the craving and addiction to social media starting in the 2010s, I suspect this early awakening can usher in depression, eating disorders, possible coercion by boys, perhaps in the extreme, even suicidal thoughts. There's also the possibility of sexual abuse by older men to contend with: whether girls are innocent and as unworldly as we were in such matters, or whether girls have more sophisticated sexualized aspirations leaving them vulnerable, they're at risk either way. And as for the girls who are aggressive in their pursuit of sexual excitement and experience, the competition among them to be sophisticated probably benefits boys more than themselves. There's no sense in being prissy about it—we were to remain virgins a while longer, but that fact was not out of the ordinary then. There's nothing titillating to recount here, no promiscuity, abuse, or descent into mental breakdown. There's no drama here, only innocence that has become out of fashion. We weren't Victorian, but we did not live in a psychologically toxic female environment. Our mothers were our role models for better or worse, and neither Hollywood actresses nor TikTok influencers affected us. I'm by no means making a case for how wonderful those days in the 1960s were for girls, they weren't; I can only describe our life, even if outdated and cringe-inducing to a teenage girl in 2010, 2020, or 2026. And even Miki, who was far more sophisticated navigating the dating scene than we were, she, too, was never a loose girl. Compared with a teen today, she was innocent like us.

I was still feeling the fear that overcame me, body and soul, when I was assaulted in the elevator of my São Paulo apartment building. I was coming home from school and pressed the elevator button to my fourth floor. As the door was closing, a tall young man stopped the door and entered the elevator. As soon as the door shut, he turned toward me, placed one hand on the wall, bent down a bit, and with the other hand lifted my skirt, feeling for my panties. Frozen, terrified, I could not find my paralyzed voice to scream or yell vile words at him. My brain was also paralyzed; I could not summon the strength to fight back, of knocking him against the wall, of kneeing him in the groin, or poking his eyes and scratching his face. I didn't save myself, luck saved me. He had no ability to lock the elevator door, so the door opened, and since he did not pin me down, I ducked under his arm and ran down the hall. He looked out the elevator perplexed to see me go and to which apartment, but I didn't care (how dare he assume I was interested), and I barged into the apartment through a providentially unlocked door. And there my mother stood shocked at seeing me in a state of terror. I gathered my poise, said a stranger was in the elevator, but nothing happened, and went to my room. Later, after my father came home from work, he made a pointless and short attempt at looking for a stranger without having any details, and then the matter was dropped, since I was intact, as they say. I insisted nothing happened, because I controlled my anger and fear, locking it up forever, but with repercussions.

The result of this experience is that for years, I avoided an elevator if a man I did not know was standing inside. When I was followed into the elevator, I would quickly go out and wait for another ride. But I also avoided all men whom I was not acquainted with. I would not speak to or respond to a male stranger for the next ten years. It left me even more timid and mistrustful of half the world's population. I suppose this is called trauma, but it resolved itself in time.

I never told anyone about this experience until the #METOO movement came about. I only told Elana when our children had already grown. It is assumed that good friends share everything, but I don't agree. There are things that I was not capable of sharing, without loving her less or trusting her less.

São Paulo, February 24, 1967

Dear Udi-Udi!

It was such a good surprise to get your letter. I thought you'd never write again. But one letter got lost. Which is the last letter you received from me? Your last letter was dated October 20, 1966, and I answered. Either you did not get the response, or I did not receive yours. Anyway, let's go on from here.

Many thanks for your birthday wish. I thought this year a letter would not come from you, but happily, it did. Truly, it would have been missed. I would also wish that you were here. But . . . there's this thing called DISTANCE. I have a lot to tell you.

. . .

But I've made a lot of progress. Until today I have not needed to use the dictionary for your letters, just one word in your first English letter. What I'm missing is conversation. In French, which I never liked, I got a "passable."

In general, this year has been the most successful, and I think my parents would be pleased. On vacation, I started with 10-day at Solelim [Jewish] *encampment 12/24/66 to 1/3/67, then there was a selection of 12 volunteers (2 from SP) for a seminar in Argentina. There was a mix-up with the documents. I had to get a permit to travel alone with an Israeli passport. I managed the Argentine visa in the last minute. I went Jan 11 and returned Feb 6. It was lovely, I loved Argentina and Uruguay, including the EU do Sul do Brazil* [the southernmost state of Brazil].

The movement there is a MOVEMENT and will function even where there's already "Aliyah" and "Hagsharah." [Jewish groups preparing for life in Israel.] *There is so much antisemitism! The place is full of swastikas.*

. . .

But now down to business, this year will be very tough. It's my 3rd year in Classico, all the subjects plus piano AND studying for my Vestibular. I won't take a [prep] *course, I will try to apply for Psychology and Pedagogy* [Education]. *The weather is wonderful, very warm and some passing showers. But how did you study Malagueña? It's hard! This year, I'm in 8th level* [music]. *I am practicing Revolutionary Study by Chopin, Sonata Op.31 #1 by Beethoven, Souhaite d'une Jeune Fille by Chopin, Liszt!!! And 2 more I haven't been assigned yet.*

The rest consists of exercises, and Bach Preludes and Fugues ("Well-Tempered Clavier").

But you have so many exams!

I think this coming year I won't do English or French. I left the YMCA. I had enough. We are all at the Maccabi [Jewish sports club]. *Did you get to know our new club? It's spectacular. A huge swimming pool, and a very beautiful place.*

"My family is very well, thank you. And you?" [Elana writing in English.] *My brother passed to his 3rd year of Medicine, and if I'm not wrong, he will start Interning. My parents work, and my grandfather is testing our patience. Hmm. And yours? Everything OK? Does your father still joke? And how's your mom? Your cousin, you get along? I remember you'd talk a lot about him. And your grandmother? Give her my greetings. Yes, I liked your epigrams. Here are some more:*

...

For now, it's enough, I'm going to have dinner, then to the post office and then for Kabbalat Shabbat.

I thank you again for your good wishes, I excuse myself for now, expecting a letter soon and not 3 months from now!

Your friend who really wants you, and who misses you so much.
Elana
PS I bought a camera in Porto Alegre but did not have the film developed. Next time. Send me some too!

Toronto, February 1967

I am not sure why I didn't write to her between October and February. Maybe it was due to the dreariness of winter, and there was nothing to say about it. Or as she said, I had a lot of exams. Maybe we had gone back to Michigan for Christmas, two years after the misfortune that befell my mother and my father, but the visit was not newsworthy to me this time around.

Being in different hemispheres, we lived through opposite seasons. Besides driving the school calendar, seasons also affect our moods. It is a wonder that we plugged away, still sending our letters akin to ostensible diaries to each other.

In historical terms, Vietnam droned on in the background, with the war's casualty numbers conspicuously reported and displayed on TV. And President Johnson's term trudged on monotonously toward a fated appointment date. There was also an unacknowledged, barely noticed, political force that passed liberal laws in the United States such as the Voting Rights Act, Medicare, and so on. Even racist Southern Democrats participated in the negotiation of the passage of such socially progressive trends (although they did so in lieu of support for the Vietnam War), but this trend was numbingly normal until a conservative movement took ascendancy later with Nixon and Reagan. If I describe this era as the apex of the liberal era, I may be wrong, but that was my impression.

Brazil was a military dictatorship, and there, civil darkness was not due to weather. To live an ordinary life under a dictatorship, one must force one's political orientation into a state of denial. It is not easy to describe how personal lives are transformed in authoritarian states or dictatorships. Individuals and families who don't choose to rebel, agitate, or revolt must turn inward and put blinders on for the purpose of making life tolerable. They must also relearn how to navigate civil society's altered norms. Elana's family, and many other families we had known, coasted through this era, heads down, successfully. I had additional, secondhand knowledge about life under a communist regime (another form of dictatorship). My father's brothers did not leave Romania like he did in 1947, when the incoming communist regime left an exit door open for them through 1948. In short order, the Iron Curtain was shut solid, and they were trapped. They could no longer tolerate their situation, yet they could not leave. I remember my father reading letters aloud when he received them from his brothers, and they were coded: he had to read between the lines for meanings, because all letters were opened and read by the communist authorities, requiring the writer to obfuscate. It was not as grim in Brazil, and so it was easier to ride through the dictatorship to its end. In Canada, with daily news from the United States, my interest in world news became intellectually active, awakened from my youthful state of denial. I was living in a free country.

São Paulo, May 15, 1967

Udi-Udinha!

Geez! Do you know what you deserve? A spanking! How do you make me wait 3 months for a response? I thought either the postal service is lazy, or that you forgot about me. I was wrong: you are lazy! Don't do this again, or I'll go there, and we'll settle accounts! Stop laughing! do you think I'm joking? You know I'm so happy, my parents said that if I pass the Vestibular we will go visit you in July 1968! What do you think? It would be terrific! I won't believe it until I set foot there. It even seems impossible. I'd want to go by car to see everything. Thank you so much for the photo. When I opened the envelope, you came out jumping, smiling. Everyone here thought it was your mother, you look like twins! You're beautiful, your mom did your hair well. Enough of admiration! Why did it take you so long to respond? I wait anxiously for your letters. Seriously, could you write more frequently? Do you go to a lot of parties? When does vacation start? What have you read?

Do you have good films there? How is everyone? How's your grandmother? Give them a thousand regards.

I am cutting back on going to the SNIF, because I have so much studying to do. It's very hard. Outside of high school, I'm preparing for 2 Vestibular exams: Psychology and Education. Then there's piano, music and English. I stopped taking French. If I get into college next year, I'll take French again, and German, too. Do you know of the confusion at the universities here? It's awful. There are 21 candidates for every seat. And next year will be worse. I am so scared. Students are striking. They're angry and with reason. Some are even on hunger strikes. Do you have problems getting into university?

My parents are well, working as always. My grandfather is doing nothing all day. My brother is doing sports and studying in 3rd year Medicine. And me—around. No, the factory did not change, it's still the same. It was Yoni who sent the last letter, and he said that he paid Cr$380,00. Let's see how much this is going to be. Yes, the prices went up.

Ah, Ruth, Brazil is going to the dogs, it's worse than before. What confusion. There came this character Fou-Fou (Sr. Fontenele) to make changes in public transit, there were blowups and accidents, and people were walking on foot for kilometers, there was hardly any public transit.

It's a little better now. There has been a change in the currency: Cr$1.000,00 [one thousand] *is now NC$1,00 one Cruzeiro Novo. They are making more and more plans for changes, and people wait, right?*

And you? Are you satisfied there? And your cousin, how is he? I am reading "Native Son" by Richard Wright, it's about racism in America. It's a good book. Have you read it? I've been reading a lot. With piano

I'm going slowly. I stay 3 hours at least, sometimes 5. I love to play more and more; I can't stop it. What are you playing now? The rest of the day I study and prepare so that one day I can go visit. This month my average was 9,2 and the lowest was 8,0.

I bought a beautiful pair of shoes today. Oh, I haven't told you yet, Colégio Oswaldo Cruz moved. It's a little further from Miki's, on Marechal Deodoro [street]. *I must take public transport and sometimes, since I must go twice, do you know what it costs me? It's a big building, I think 8 floors high. It's humongous.*

OK, I must stop and ask "plis" [sic] *respond soon. Seriously, you make me crazy waiting so long.*

I'm sending you a picture from the encampment in Jundiaí after I returned from Argentina, and I gained 4 kilos (but I've lost 5 already). It's the most recent I have, but at first opportunity I'll send more, OK?

Here goes a sincere hug, from your friend for always,

Elana

PS Regards to all

"The heart of the insincere is in his mouth; the mouth of the sage is in his heart."

São Paulo, May 27, 1967

Udi-Udinha!

What a surprise, I found your letter on the table when I came home from the Conservatory. I thought it would only come in 3 or 4 days.

But I was so content. I would love for you to repeat this, it felt so good. I don't know how my letter arrived to you so quickly. Strange. Did you finish your finals? Did they go well? Don't even respond, because I know you did! What will you do during vacation?

Ay! a flea! Do you have fleas there?

I was baffled about what you said regarding the photo, that you didn't recognize me. The only thing that changed was my hair which I haven't cut in a long time. Otherwise, I have lost a little weight, but my face is the same. The contents: identical!!! I will send you another one soon, OK? If you have, send to me too, including your parents, all right? Thanks. How are your parents? Why don't they write to mine? [Only my mother would write.] *Your cousin and aunt and uncle? And your grandmother? Is she still the same? Regards to all.*

...

Yes, I heard the 1967 Exposition must have been interesting. My teacher already talked about it. If it wasn't for this damned Vestibular we'd go this year and take advantage of the Expo. I have not read anything of James Michener, but I will look for it. I don't remember seeing "Hawaii" here. You know I'm always behind and out of touch with films. "The Bible" I'll go see because it's playing here.

Last Thursday the 25th I saw the Ballet Barioska. Beautiful, spectacular, marvelous. Did you know where I sat? on the steps of the 2nd floor, and I had a terrific view, and didn't pay anything.

Yes . . . the problem of vacancies at the university is not a piece of cake. There are marches, strikes, demonstrations even hunger strikes. But there are students who have good grades and can't go to classes. Soon only the geniuses will go.

...

The only problem is that the teachers are old and rusty. Do you know who always asks about you? Leni. She is also going at night, she's short, skinny, pretty. Ruth, what do you think of what is happening in Israel? Tomorrow evening all the groups will organize an event at the Hebraica [Jewish Community Center] *and we're hoping the entire Jewish community will attend.*

This evening I'm going to the inaugurations of "Casa Chopin de São Paulo." The pianist, Ninfa Glasser will play her own composition, she's my favorite. She lectures on History of Music and Pedagogy at the Conservatory. It's very nice. Ah! on the 22nd we danced at the Teatro Municipal, and we also sang. All the groups together. It was hard practicing for it. There was also an Israeli pianist (Frank Peller), choir and orchestra, an "Israeli Evening" to commemorate Yom HaAtzma'ut [Israel Independence Day]. *It's getting late, and I still must go to the post office.*

...

Rutinha, better Udinha, excuse this letter, it's hurried, and I wanted it prettier. PLIS, answer soon, don't wait months, or weeks. Even if it's just one page or a fraction, would be great.

Regards to all, and a special hug for you from your friends of always, for always.

Elana

P.S. Guess . . . no . . . no . . . no . . . maybe. Ciao.

Toronto, May 1967

My mother and I used to go to Simpson's or Eaton's to shop, or sometimes just to browse out of boredom. We wandered through these department stores for hours. We enjoyed a lunch of hotdogs and orange juice at a counter. I didn't mind spending so much time with my mother; we kept each other company, and that continued until my early twenties, way longer than other girls who break away from their mothers by their middle teen years. Either I didn't have that option, or I chose to be her companion out of expediency, or I was meek enough to tolerate her as a teen, or I had a bond with her as a traumatized fellow migrant. I think it was a combination of all these factors.

I've often heard of teen girls who'd speak of their mothers as ogres to be avoided and survive the parent-teen ordeal. I did not understand that. In my early twenties, I had dates who wondered why I liked my mother (these did not foster repeat dates).

One day we had to go to Simpson's to buy a party dress for me. I was introduced to the North American custom of the high school prom. I didn't have a date, but I was going to go. There was a recent immigrant in my class, a Hungarian boy with a disabled left hand. He was very quiet and self-effacing, he had a peculiar smell, and consequently I was not attracted to him. However, he asked me to the prom. But he also asked one of my friends, Maria (another girl of Hungarian descent), and so he had two dates. Looking back, I find that comical. The prom was not a big deal, I didn't enjoy it that much, and my dress became quite useless after that. But with hindsight, it is not a surprise that three non-natives upended this high school custom by breaking the rules of "dating" to go to an overrated, ceremonious prom. As astonishing as this sounds, the reality was that my girlfriends in my class were not dating.

By eleventh grade, my friend Judy had moved and was attending, in her opinion, a "better" school. She may have been right; her neighborhood of small private homes was on another social level, but it made no difference to me. I continued seeing her, and we'd meet at her house. At Vaughn Road, I had also had other friends. Except for Phyllis and Judy, all were going to fall away when I moved to New York City.

In passing, Elana mentioned the unstable events in Israel, and the Jewish community of São Paulo mobilizing in support.

São Paulo, June 16, 1967

Dear Udinha!

I received your letter yesterday, and I was so happy, since of 8 correspondents I have in Brazil and Argentina, no one writes. And two letters that arrived were open. I was scared that yours would not arrive. You passed your grade, as usual? Congratulations!

Yes, it's clear, here too, everyone talks about the main topic, the war in our Israel. You know I continue to go to Ichud. We had meetings upon meetings about how we should proceed. The older ones went to Israel. Our pack was left under the guidance of Raymond (remember him? [I did not]*), Fabio, and me. It's hard, we didn't expect it. First, because there are encampments to arrange, places, comrades, etc. Some comrades will work in São Paulo, in Porto Alegre (if my mother allows me to go), and in Recife, imagine. But for now, no one feels the difference that the older ones have left. But we feel their absence. Here in Brazil, Uruguay, and Argentina, there were many who collected money, clothing, blood. Really, in 90 minutes you can collect a lot* [funds]*. All over the world Jews came together. Too bad it only happens during such an occasion.*

Here at home imagine my father! When the war ended, he himself said "I was resurrected!" And we had news that my aunts and uncles are safe. Ah! did I tell you I have a nephew? Yes, I did, I remember now. As for me, when I read the newspaper, I wanted to cry. First because we were winning, we were not losing, and we reacted quickly, second, because there were people dying. Ruth, I don't think we have to talk about this, we're both Sabras, I think our sentiments are the same.

With me, all is right. My conservatory exams start on the 19th, and the break, too. You know, I've been thinking lately of continuing only with piano. I really feel like it. When I try to study a subject, and it just doesn't go. But I go to the piano and play for 5 hours, I love it. Now, for those in the 9th level, there will be a State Governor's Medal [competition] *each year. The best in every Conservatory will win. Until last year, I didn't feel it was hard, since there were only two other students at my level, but this year many new students arrived and they're good! But I won't achieve anything with laziness. It's my business to study since I don't lack inclination.*

...

What is "nightmare?" I'm nuts, the dictionary is next to me!

Ruth, I have a class at the conservatory in 15 minutes. So, expecting you to write soon, I part, with an enormous hug, which contains "saudades," your friend of always,

Elana

PLIS [sic] *WRITE, NOW!!!!*

PS Regards to your parents, write about them. Why does your mother not write?

Toronto, June 1967

This letter arrived after the end of the Six-Day War. The news affected both of us very powerfully; we considered ourselves expat Sabras, and the country of our birth was at war. Elana was able to turn to her fellow colleagues to bond, discuss, plan, and support each other emotionally through the nail-biting news that came to us from Israel. In Toronto, with bated breath, we continued to follow the proceedings at the UN on television news. Abba Eban, the Israeli ambassador to the UN, was the eloquent voice that stood for every Jew in the world who cared about Israel.

I hung on to every one of his words. I marveled at his fluency and preciseness, at the calmness of his logic and the legitimacy of his perspective. I wanted Eban to be the voice of Israel and to speak for all Jews, Zionists or not. But I had no connections with anyone who had a personal interest in this event, not even my relatives in Michigan, who lived a life of hidden Jews. It was another war; it was intensely suspenseful and had historic consequences that most non-Jews didn't dwell on, but it was physically removed from us, as expats who were not able to get on a plane to go back as volunteers. Certainly not our fathers, who hovered around forty years of age and had not served in the Israeli Reserves since emigrating many years before. And we were too young by one year to be drafted (at eighteen years) had we remained in Israel.

At times of crisis, like my mother's loss at the end of 1964, I needed more human connection and caring empathy than at any other time. It's a human trait that can't be dismissed. For me, the acute pain of not being there, of not helping or being a participant in any way, because I had been severed from the country, was like being shut out of a meaningful life. War shouldn't be a vehicle for a meaningful life, but we're tribal and we have an urge to belong to a group and play the defending acolytes of that group. And so, I was nothing but an observer. My parents did not have much to say that they could share with me, or with each other, so I really felt disconnected. They did not communicate their feelings and fears about the war. We watched TV to listen to the news and see all the reports for as many hours as they were broadcast. But I felt no emotional support between the three of us. My father and I were reticent, and my mother was still grieving.

At about the same time I had read James Michener's *The Source,* and I became so immersed in it emotionally that I proceeded to create my own Jewish bubble with no extensions to reality. The book influenced me much more for the history it presented than for its literary merits. Perhaps Michener's book stood in *loco fraternitas,* a verbal object that was a metaphor for my belonging to a group. I had not yet started reading extensively about Jewish history. I did not yet resent my father for being a loner who would not join any groups. His choices affected me for the rest of my life, because, consequently, I did not gravitate toward ethnic groups or national attachments. With every subsequent attack on Jewish lives and Jewish customs and existence, I'd observe my fellow Jews embattled and on guard in defense of their raison d'être. I could only stand by and sympathize—not an apostate, but an outsider. It was several years later when I started to immerse myself in basic, starter history books such as Paul Johnson's *History of the Jews* and Simon Schama's *The Story of the Jews.* While in high school, my Jewish education had lacked depth.

There was a major change in my life forty years hence when I took leadership roles in a synagogue for many years, rising to the level of the congregation's president. I learned to upend the path my father had modeled for me, and I became an active member of a Jewish community and found a deep satisfaction in its social connection. To his loss, he was not capable of achieving this, but as I rose through the lay ranks of my community, he beamed with pride.

Another Migration: Third Time

São Paulo, July 8, 1967

Dear Udinha!

Hi! I was so happy yesterday! The mail arrives around 11 a.m. And nothing came. In the evening, I was getting ready to go to Kabbalat Shabbat, when my mother asked, "Who wrote?" I said no one. My father who was passing said, "Yes something came, I forgot." It was on his table at the factory. It was yours. Imagine! It was almost pressed [by his machine]!

This morning, I woke up with a pain in my left thumb. Tried playing the piano, couldn't. If I move the finger, it hurts. No, I will not go on vacation. I must study. Ah! The Petropolis Tennis Club, I remember. Do you still have our 3rd place medal of distinction? I still have it. After that I never played again. Did you find a way to play again? Do you have the results of your final exams?

Yes, I love piano.

...

But aside from this, I sincerely like to sit at the piano for 5 hours.

Miki [friends again, of course] *was here yesterday. Many people from our gang will go to Israel on the 17th. I think some are doing the right thing, others, not. These people are doing the prep course for university and are halfway through.*

My grandfather left early on the 4th to Africa, by boat. My father took him to the port. It's now calm in the house! How are your parents?

...

You know, Miss Margaret is doing well. It's been a while, she broke an arm last year, and she had broken the other one, many years before. Now she has a hard time carrying heavy books in both arms. She always has problems with her feet, and she doesn't know what it is. She's been to doctors, but each one says something else, so she quit. Last week she fell. Who knows, all of that, I think, won't be good, but no one has been able to rally her. But she's still the same, so kind. We are now translating booklets on philosophy, and then literature from her encyclopedia. I think when we meet, we will be able to converse in English! OK, Ruth, I don't have anything else to say, only: answer soon, as you said, "a couple of words are better than nothing."

With nothing else, parting, your FRIEND who wants you a lot,

Elana

PS Do you have a new photo? Maybe with your parents?

BAAI!

New York, July 1967

The big event in my summer of 1967 was moving to New York City. Immigrating again! But this time to our destination at last. And with a Green Card, there was no more humiliation at the border.

Leaving Toronto was like "Get out and don't let the door hit you on your way out!"

Canada and Toronto don't deserve this disparagement. Canada may have been the most inoffensive country I ever lived in. I am sure there is plenty of Canadian patriotism, but it was not rubbed in the face of immigrants then. Democratic, free, amiable (aside from shameful past abuses on First Nations people), it should have been a welcoming haven.

But an introverted family of three cannot thrive alone anywhere, no matter how welcoming the place is. We had relatives in the United States. And my father had a dream—the United States. So, it beckoned, and we settled there.

I do not remember leaving Toronto. Or packing up of the apartment (we did not have many possessions). Or how a few pieces of furniture arrived in NYC. I just don't remember! And how did we travel? The memory is blocked. What mattered more to me was to be joining my grandmother soon. If I have memories of leaving Israel, of how everyone in my second grade class filled beautiful drawings, writings, and decals into a red leather diary, and if I have memories of leaving Brazil, of hugging Elana at the airport while our parents looked on, there were certainly no goodbyes in Toronto. I knew I could call my friend Judy from New York or send her and Phyllis postcards and letters, which we exchanged. Otherwise, the separation from the city and the country was easy.

How easy was the adjustment to NYC going to be? I do remember that we moved to an apartment building on East 167th Street in the Bronx where my grandmother lived, and where she had pulled strings to get us a larger apartment. It was more spacious than our tiny one-bedroom apartment in Toronto.

With a Green Card, we were free to travel for fun. In the summer, my father got a car, and we drove to Expo '67 in Montreal. This time around, we went to Canada as American landed immigrants. Now we could go back and forth across the border. It was such a relief, and it made for a pleasant trip to Quebec.

My grandmother lived in the same building a few floors below us. I finally had an extended family nearby. My grandmother was very social, and she had friends. Her friends always wanted to talk to me, inquiring about my interests, books, music, and school, which made me feel so much older than seventeen. She helped my mother get a job as a hairdresser across the street at the Daughters of Jacob Home for the Aged, where she worked as the head of housekeeping. My mother styled the old ladies' hair and interacted with their adult children, so she had a healthy outlet to engage with people—and that was a reprieve that maintained her mental health. The proximity to her own mother was certainly also a stabilizing force for my mother. That stability at home seemed pervasive through the first year in a new country and new city.

My father ran an auto mechanic shop, and being a terrific mechanic, he had friendly, grateful clients. One of them even had an elderly mother living at the Daughters of Jacob Home, so it seemed our social circle was real.

My grandmother, in turn, was mentored by an older Polish Jew named Moshe Halpern, a short and stocky man with an overlarge head, who also lived in the same building. He had some management position at the Daughters of Jacob facility. He was wildly attached to his two beautiful and spoiled Schnauzer dogs. He was married to a very calm and quiet wife with a speech impediment, or stroke-stricken, who cooked and baked superb dishes. She was large framed, wore cotton shifts, and exuded an aura of Eastern Europe she had left behind decades ago. He was a rather crude and loud man, and he drove a massive Cadillac, his other baby besides the dogs. He'd take us out in the Caddy to have Nathan hotdogs in Yonkers on weekends. He flirted with my grandmother so conspicuously, it was almost embarrassing. My grandmother, however, was expedient and not above playing games that would benefit her and her daughter's welfare. She could outdo any weasel of a man. After divorcing three times so far in her life, she was experienced.

My father came home one day with a lot of old books left in a garage he rented, many of them musty-smelling Russian classics, which I started to read. I played piano, the one my parents brought from Canada. I took private lessons with Ruth Fishman, a petite, elderly Jewish Bronx doyenne. Her black Baldwin baby grand, her custom cabinets full of sheet music, her antiques and Persian rugs filled her apartment with the touch of unfeigned culture that attracted me. She was exacting, demanding, and ultimately very aware that I did not possess a future in music. Nevertheless, I continued to study with her throughout the next four years, and I felt my affection for her was deeply reciprocated.

As such, Elana and I both lived the musical life that started when Vera convinced my mother that I must study music at the conservatory just as Elana had to. For the eight years after our departure from Brazil until I went to graduate school and stopped taking piano lessons, a shared musical thread kept us bound up together and was a recurring topic in our letters.

Elana's letters are a microcosm of piano pedagogy: every piece, composer, and arrangement was spelled out in epistolary progression. I was far below her talent and depth of engagement, however. In reviewing her letters and the detailed enumeration of her musical repertoire, one might believe that it was the start of a brilliant musical career.

São Paulo, August 9, 1967

Dear Udi-Udi!

One thing you can't complain about: travels. You already know some of this world, hey? I would really like to take your place. Miss Margaret got your postcard. She taught me to knit socks. Since my brother has a birthday on the 12th, I made (making) a pair to sleep in, because his feet are cold in winter. How is your grandmother? Parents? You don't write about them. Will you spend some time with your cousin, too? Regards to all. You're on a real vacation. And what a vacation!

I am studying a lot, it's real damn hard. The Vestibular is in 6 months. I'm behind, but I hope to catch up soon. Most of those taking the Vestibular take a prep course, which covers material not taken in high school, and practice taking the test. I am not taking the course, maybe I'll take the intensive 2-month course before the Vestibular. I try to study what I can until then, then review everything.

...

When are you going back to Canada? Send regards to Esti and Gabi, I wonder if they remember me!

No, it's not that we're glad my grandfather left, we miss him, he was the one who brought bread and milk and now we must go get it. You know, Ruth, when a person gets old, they have their habits and selfishness, and we must understand that. But all this is not unfortunate. Not just lately, but this has been a trait since his youth—what's most upsetting is that he was always an old man, but—we like him. You know my parents. They never fought. But when he was here, everyone was on edge . . . I don't know . . . Doesn't matter. If he returns, he's welcome. Maybe I feel this way because I was expecting a grandfather to be like my grandmother. The disappointment was deep.

Ruth, I'm sending you a photo taken at Ilha Bela [beach]. *I went with my group, in a van, both ways. We spent 4 wonderful days there. I only had 8 pictures left on the film roll that I didn't want to waste. The camera was with Rachel (remember her?) But she used them. Maybe I'll send you one from Ibirapuera. And you, when will you send me a photo? Express, eh? Ruth, I'm going to have lunch now.*

Parting, I wait for a long and quick response from you, with strong hugs from your friend with "saudades,"

Elana

São Paulo, August 19, 1967

Dear Udinha!

Unfortunately, I can't start like you, writing how much there is to tell you. For real, what I've been doing is studying, and for variation, studying some more. This minute (Saturday night) I'm surrounded by books and pamphlets, well organized. I'm enjoying it, it's nice to be organized, and so that's what I'm doing. My mother promised that if I enter university, we will go there in July 1968, and I'm coming so we can fight a little, because you can't do that via mail . . . a friendship has to have some little fights, don't you think? But seriously, are you on vacation in July? Yes, the photo I sent is recent. And you? do you have new ones developed? Very nice, your father is working, and you two [my mother and I] *are gallivanting, eh? Yoni thanks you for your wishes. He turned 21. I never thought that Esti would sit in front of the TV all day! She seemed an active girl who couldn't sit still. And Gabi? Strange. But they're doing well in school?*

...

Rachel is who we got to know in camp at Campos do Jordão. She was Ruth's friend, who you liked, and you slept in her bunk on the last night, because you didn't want to get painted [by toothpaste and shoe polish] *and her cabin had a key. Do you remember Tomi Grunwald? He liked Rachel at that camp. Well, Rachel also grew, and we met again. She's very nice. Do you remember her?* [Elana and Rachel are still friends well into their seventies.]

Miki is now a little lady, she turned 16. She lost weight, she left me behind. She's cute, and nice enough. And this is just my opinion, maybe she'd be someone interesting if it wasn't for her 2 crones (I'm sorry if I'm wrong, but that's my opinion) educating her to be like them. She is now dating Laszlo. He's in first year Engineering, and he's a nice guy. He lives here around the corner, on Barão de Limeira.

Ruth, if you came here, would you be able to get around and remember places? Regarding Miki and Gabi, I only know that she thought he liked her. But she likes George, his cousin. He's doing well and is in first year Engineering. We also have some subway projects. In Argentina I rode the subways.

Ah, I almost forgot. Do you remember Dr. Leonardo Berger? He was 54 years old. He died 2 weeks ago, heart attack. It was an unexpected and unbelievable news [he was our pediatrician]. *You know, the records you left me aren't helping. There are a lot of idiomatic expressions, and to understand the stories you must know the idioms.*

Are you studying something new on piano? I am doing the Ritual Fire Dance by M. Falla and studying Chopin. I feel like learning the violin. But that's for after university. Each and every minute now is precious. Right this minute, I am listening to the Russian Military Band singing "Tipperary" in English. Did I have this record when you were here? I love it and I don't get tired listening to it. I bought a record of Artur Rubinstein, with 6 Polonnaises of Chopin. Who is your favorite composer? Have you read something lately? And seen any good films? I really liked "The Russians Are Coming," a wonderful comedy.

Well, Rutinha, time passes quickly, and I fall behind. I still must answer another letter and then sleep. Tomorrow, I'll go to the Maccabi [Jewish sports club] *early to swim then will study in the afternoon.*

Do you go to a club there?

Regards to your parents, grandmother, Gabi, Esti, etc. and here goes a big hug from your nostalgic friend.

Elana

New York, August 1967

In the building where we moved to in the Bronx, where my grandmother lived, and where the Polish Halperns lived, there was a Romanian family who had also migrated to the US from Brazil: the Berkowitzes. Lewis, a dentist (without an American license yet), and Golda, a housewife, and maybe also a bookkeeper, had two children: thirteen-year-old Esti, and nineteen-year-old Gabe, known as Gabi. Elana had mentioned him before, sending him regards. I was interested in him, but not his sister. He was tall and handsome, with bad teeth, and perhaps some intellectual promise, and she was immature, silly, with dirty gummy teeth. Our friendship did not survive the residence at East 167th Street, so with no regrets, we went our separate ways. Elana had known the family in Brazil, where our paths never crossed. Gabe's cousin, George, who still lived in Brazil, became part of Elana's social circle. We overlapped in a strange way, leaving me on the outside of this Venn diagram. Any other almost-seventeen-year-old girl would have turned on the charms to trifle with this Gabe and chase after him with ease. I didn't; I was not like other seventeen-year-olds. Had I been in the company of Elana, with her intense interest in making friends, I think she would have encouraged me to look beyond the bad teeth and questionable intellect. As for Miki, she would have dated him and broken up with him within a month.

São Paulo, September 20, 1967

Dear Udi Udinha!

I was stupefied with your news. You prefer New York? Now you are closer to your aunt, too, right?

And school? Did classes start? Do you like it? No, this does not change our plans. The only thing that would change things is if I don't pass the Vestibular. You were not in "grade 13"? Your grandmother must be super happy!

Here the news is the same, just one thing we did not expect. My father has [deep vein] *thrombosis. Last Tuesday, he was walking in the street crossing Ave. São João when he felt as if they shot him in the leg. Now he needs to stay in bed for a month, with a lot of medicine. The leg is no longer swollen, but it's black and yellow, who knows. He's better and refuses to stay in bed.*

I haven't been able to study much. Mom is in the factory, and when someone visits (and someone is always visiting) I get to serve the coffee. I haven't been able to play the piano. I practiced in school.

Well, I hope all will go well, and that my father will be well in a month. [The piano was in the parents' room.] *I watched "Fahrenheit 451," and it was super. Loved it. No, I no longer use glasses, although I should. They are well kept in their case. You want to tell me that your glasses got stronger? Take care!*

Ah! Ruth, I still haven't thanked you for the presents, because first I wanted to see them. It's been a week since I went to the SNIF, and met with Mauro (he gained 12 kilos, if he goes on like this, I don't know . . .) and he said that you sent me something. He didn't bring it because he didn't know that we would meet (I go less often, lately) and he said he'd bring it home. He studies far away, in Sorocaba, so that he still hasn't brought it. I wanted to get it myself, but I don't know his address. If he doesn't bring it by Saturday, I will search for his address and go get it. In any event, Ruth, I thank you a lot.

It's noon. I'll go see if my mother wants me to come while she eats lunch.

Ruth, PLIS answer soon, OK?

And accept this sincere embrace from your friend, always,

Elana

PS I wait for photos. If possible, together with your parents. Demanding, eh? I'm shameless.

BAAI

New York, September 1967

Of course I preferred New York! I know I enumerated the various benefits of living near my grandmother, although I must not have mentioned how I thought the Bronx dreary and ugly. Blocks upon blocks of red-brick buildings of identical height, girdled in the metal carapace of fire escapes, was a view that did not elicit in me a romantic vision of New York. The monotonous buildings shrouded in grime, and vast procession of blocks unbroken by vegetation, was soul-numbing. But with a subway station nearby, Manhattan throbbing with its museums, theaters, restaurants, office buildings, shops, and architectural marvels was just a few subway stops away.

São Paulo, October 14, 1967

Dear Udinha!

Today is Saturday, a beautiful night, calm, when you feel like doing everything, but otherwise, doing nothing, because everything is impossible. Yom Kippur just ended. Did you fast? I didn't. Why? because at synagogue, I heard girls talk about boys, and vice versa, criticizing others, the matrons talking nonsense, and the men talking dollars. I prefer to eat, and for variety, to study. I studied all morning, then I had a Latin lesson and then Ana (a classmate) and I went to see "Blow Up," which I must confess I didn't understand very well. And now here I am writing to a friend who I miss, and in less than a year I WILL see because I WILL pass the Vestibular.

How are your parents? Grandmother? Give them my regards. Mauro still has not brought the doll and I'm angry. I met him at the SNIF last Friday for Kabbalat Shabbat, and he promised to bring this week. Nothing. Maybe tomorrow. I'm crazy to see her [the doll].

The Vestibular exams will take place in January and February depending on the subject. Of Classico [high school] *I am done, and in October, I finalize everything; the highest grade I still need is 8. . . . My grade in English is complete. I intend to close everything, and since I am not missing much, I won't go to class but will take advantage of studying at home.*

At the conservatory I got worse in piano, first because of the Vestibular prep and then because of my father who, praise be, is well and already returned to the factory. He works a little then lays down. He may go out of the house a little next week, but we're afraid. We're so used to seeing him at home all the time. My mother is very tired from work, and unfortunately, I can't help her. Yoni who has an excellent program, gets up at 4:30 a.m., goes rowing, then to class at 8, and returns around 6 p.m. He's real tall, robust, tanned, gorgeous. We fight less now.

How are your classes? What fortune having Hebrew class, don't you think? Next year I plan to organize my time better. I intend to do yoga, or rhythmic gym, or some sport, learn Hebrew and some seminars, dedicate more time to piano and studies in general. This year everything is upside-down. Full of surprises.

I lost some weight (amen) this month and my clothes need to be adjusted. But it's worth it.

Leni always asks about you and sends regards. Did I tell you I cut my hair short? I cut bangs, but no one at home liked it, so I comb it back. Do you know this joke: A man who used to go to the barber became bald. One day when he only had 3 strands of hair, he asks that one be cut to the right, one to the left and one back. When he had only two left, he said: half to each side. When he had only one left, he said: everything to the back.

Ruth, I really have nothing else to say but I want to continue.

. . .

I think that's enough [epigrams], *no? If you have any in English, I'll be delighted.*

Rutinha, write soon, don't delay, and send a photo, OK?

I end again, your friend who wants you very much,

Elana

New York, October 1967

Spending Yom Kippur studying, eating, and going out was not an anomaly. Elana and I were raised by secular Jews. Jewish holidays were observed with a nod and in the heart, but not in synagogue or in prayer. There's a moniker some Jews use, describing themselves as "culturally Jewish." That was not our case. We were Jewish, period. Our families were attached to a Zionist belief in a Homeland for Jews, and Elana and I were Sabras. Religious awakening, apart from our parents, came later for us. Our parents were not unusual: there were many survivors who found their way, even if it was for the short-term, to a secular homeland, where the religious were still a minority, and the orthodox did not yet wield a political influence. It was a different era.

In the Bronx, my one and only American high school year was a miserable one. If Canadian high school was monotonous but inoffensive, this New York high school was frenzied and rude. I don't remember the racial mix of students, but it seemed it was half Black and half white. There were plenty of Jews among the white students, the Bronx having been a mecca for Jewish immigrants in prior generations.

I did not befriend any Black students, because there was little interaction between groups, and I was reticent. The Black students seemed to have a good time in school, and some, just like many white students, didn't take studying seriously. I was envious of the evident bonds among the Black students. They were boisterous and sassy, energized and gregarious. Some were not prepared in classes, and the teachers seemed despondent. I remember a history teacher with weary eyes and a droning in his voice, probably thinking of retirement. He was getting older and seemed tired from his work and tired of the students. An econ teacher lectured into the ceiling, almost oblivious of the students in the room. Students who had any academic impulse made it to the honors classes, but they turned out to be mostly white. The discrepancy was due to either racial exclusion, lack of opportunity, or lack of effort. Education was designed by whites for whites, and the Black students grasped that. There were yet no Black studies topics or an honest disclosure and enlightened discourse on racism in education. The racial divide in those classes was clear. I did not spend time contemplating this disparity, I was only intent on passing through: one year of high school, and *I'm outta here!* Maybe that is what many Black students were thinking too.

The academic rigor of senior year was a travesty, and I missed the seriousness of my Canadian classes, but not Canada, of course. My incompetent counselor at Taft High School knew nothing about my previous education and didn't bother to inquire. I was not given any placement testing. She converted my grades, but to my disadvantage, and did not select me to attend any honors classes except French. It was soon obvious that Taft had no French honors class that would even fit my needs. Thus, I slipped though Honors French as the "genius" in the class, bored to tears. As a challenge, I took a Hebrew class and enjoyed relearning to read and write and pick up where I left off in 1958 as a second grader in Israel. It was a basic language class, and easy for me to manage.

In September 1967, I scarcely had three years of speaking English. My foreign accent was most likely faint, but perhaps it was obvious to some teachers, perplexing to others. With several languages behind me, I developed a talent for pronunciation. I started to speak English at the age of fourteen. But unlike Henry Kissinger, I did not retain my oral muscle memory for a mother tongue or for any subsequent language I acquired in daily speech. Maybe I had formed the Ruth's version of Esperanto speech—not one, not the other, but a mishmash. I recall people asking me if I was from the Midwest. Guessing Ruth's accent was a game, and it made me feel quietly smug observing their cluelessness. Inwardly, I felt superior, but outwardly elusive. I didn't like being an enigma, slowly and increasingly seething for quite a few more years. This feeling unfolded over the years into a rage I had to contain, and my cynicism eventually yielded some sardonic and evasive answers to these prying questions. I detested being asked where I was from, because the question came from people who were simply curious and naive. My insecurity allowed me to be intimidated by the inquisitive questions from the unsophisticated. This insecurity (and intense embarrassment about having moved so many times) can be attributed to the fact that I was different from my interrogators, because I was from somewhere else. Sometimes I assumed they knew my secret origins, although they didn't. Most likely, they were innocent questions posed out of curiosity, but they grated on me, nonetheless. Therefore, I would make up sarcastic answers, and my own evasiveness annoyed me, not to mention baffled my interlocutors.

For years I thought I was the only one feeling this way. Not so. In *A Beginner's Guide to America*, Roya Hakakian describes this common emotion.

However, with Elana, I could be myself. She understood where I came from.

São Paulo, November 1, 1967

Dear Udinha,

I'll take advantage that my mother is writing, and so I will too. We are sending the letter that your mother asked for. I hope it arrives and . . . good luck.

And you? Why don't you answer? Ah! News! Monday a telegram arrived from Africa saying that my grandfather wants to return. [Again!] *If he does that before July, it's goodbye to my parents' trip. My mother said that if they can't go, at least I will go if I get into university. But I'd prefer that we all go, don't you agree?*

It's already November. It seems like yesterday was first day of classes. And tomorrow is the last!

. . .

But that "saint" Vestibular is what's the drag. Whatever I study, seems like I must do more and know less. I am scared shitless, because a lot of castles will fall if I don't pass.

. . .

And you, are you studying a lot? It's already late, I must bathe, have dinner, go to the post office and to class. I'll go see if my mother already wrote the letter, OK? I talked a lot about me and about school. But what else do I have in my head now? I hope you do the same, talk a lot about yourself, your parents and your grandmother. Are you well in classes? and do you have friends?

Rutinha, I already must go, leaving you here with a strong and sincere embrace, from this real friend of always,

Elana

Let me see you! thank you. Write soon, eh?

São Paulo, November 16, 1967

Dear Udi-Udi!

Do you know what I have in front of me? OOKPIK! [A sealskin Inuit owl I purchased in Canada for Elana when I visited Expo '67.] *Yes, he's a good friend of mine and is always with me. Ruth, thanks for it, I love it, it's so cute and soft! And thank you for the scarf, too, I loved it, but I'm saving it. I'm afraid of using it, I'm going through the crisis of losing everything!*

Ruth, you're beautiful, it's true you haven't changed. I would recognize you anywhere now. Unfortunately, I don't have one, but soon I'll take a photo and you'll be the first to get it. Your grandmother seems younger every time. And your parents, how are they? My father is well now, only some small problems, seems like it's his stomach. Did your father start work? Is it going well? I wish him SUCCESS!

Ruth, go crack the trio for piano [a musical piece I don't remember], *because it's beautiful. I think one day when we get to play really well, it's almost a delight, and it won't matter what others like, and we'll hear ourselves play. Go strong! I am intending to study Anglo-Germanic letters. And . . . funny, I thought you'd do Engineering, but you have the same idea as I! Ha, ha, I liked hearing about Esti!* [Some gossip I don't remember.] *She didn't change a lot, eh? Does she still have ants in her pants? The epigram you sent was great. Send more. I already have 1011 (besides the ones I got recently). Some are super.*

About my visit there, as soon as I hear about my exams, I will start arranging the papers.

. . .

Ruth, see if you can send these photos back, they are Yoni's not mine, so excuse me, OK?

OK Udinha, it's getting late, and I didn't even practice today. Write a long letter soon, because it revives people to receive a letter! And here goes an immense embrace to this unforgettable little friend Udi, from her nostalgic

Elana

Regards to all!

"When it's the end of life, dying means to leave; when it's the beginning of life, leaving means dying." Victor Hugo

BAAI!

Why is your mother not writing? Did the declaration serve her needs?

São Paulo, December 18, 1967
Dearest Udinha,

I am absolutely confident that you forgive my delay, right? And if I relax, goodbye my visit to you. It's hard!

...

Truly, if I manage to pass this monstrous Vestibular, I'll be satisfied. But it's so hard. I give myself a 3% chance. But it doesn't cost to try.

...

I registered to the Vestibular of USP [University of São Paulo, the public U. and highest rated]. *It will take place the first 2 weeks of February. You know how hard this is for me, because I'm not one to study. Ah! and funny, we are taking classes at the Colégio Hebraico Brasileiro "Renascença." There were misunderstandings with some faculty societies, and they'd decided to get out of there. When I see you,*

I'll tell you more. [I didn't understand all the details.] *Ruth, if I pass, we will see each other in 6 or 7 months! Ah!*

Do you know who's getting married now on 12/24? Remember Flávia and her sister, Lola? She's getting married. I don't know if I told you, my grandfather is in Israel, and he wants to come back here [he could not get comfortable anywhere]. *My father is well, sometimes his leg gets swollen. My mother goes well, so is Yoni. He still doesn't know if he passed. I think he did.*

Yes, I have not only 1011 epigrams, but more. Send more, because I like them.

How is your new apartment? Congratulations! May it bring you good luck and happiness.

I haven't read anything, except for Portuguese literature.

...

It's worse, because I must analyze them, and it takes a long time. I think when I finish my exam you will hear my relief over there. I miss books from foreign authors, I prefer them. I also saw "A Man and A Woman." But here it was age 18 minimum. And there? Ah! I'm sending you a recent photo Yoni took. Do you like it? Don't forget what you promised me! [About returning it.]

...

And now Udinha, I will quit, because it's late, and I'm sleepy. Please don't delay, because when your letter comes, I revive. Write a lot, tell me about there, of everyone and everything.

Here I go, your friend,

Elana

P.S. Regards to your parents and grandmother, Gabi and Esti, and a special embrace for you.

New York, December 1967

A few months into my early experience as a student in New York City, I was not aware of the SATs; I didn't know what they were. One Friday, I was told to come next morning and bring two No. 2 pencils. I didn't know what a No. 2 pencil was, searched at home, luckily found some, and showed up with them the next morning. The proctor went over the rules. I unsealed a particular booklet for the first time in my life and took the test. I had never taken a multiple-choice test where you fill out little lozenges with a pencil. I was taking this for real, not for practice, and I was utterly clueless. No one explained it to me beforehand, because I was new to the country and new to the American education system which was not accommodating for foreigners (in addition, I had a lazy guidance counselor). This was a first and only go at entry to college. I was never told it could be taken multiple times. English was a foreign language to me a few years earlier. The testing system was still foreign to me. I was in the woods without maps or markers. But I'm a quick learner; I do well on the fly. I tackled this test the way I had tackled the many obstacles in my life until then, with resignation and endurance.

For decades I imagined that I barely broke 1,000 in a combined SAT score and buried the disappointment of my bad luck deep inside. One day, going through saved school documents, I came across my SAT score: it was a disgraceful combined score of 1,020. In 1967 the average score for college-bound females nationwide was 1,059. I did not understand how I pulled off a test at all without any practice or familiarization. English was my fifth language. At some point a few years earlier, I had stronger French skills.

I did not know how to advocate for myself by finding out if I could practice and retake the test; I was passive and submissive. I still feel the resentment over what happened and what I let happen about SAT testing. I've never worked it through, either with dismissive reasoning or rational defense. The truth is that wanting vindication is a complex and deep-seated need of mine that is beyond my reach, because the explanation lies in my being an outsider and a transient, with a personality of an uncompetitive underachiever. If I pay it no mind and find myself belonging to this life in this place, then it becomes irrelevant. But the feeling of belonging would be tenuous for the rest of my life. I am neither of here nor of there. I am deeply dissociated, even as I have learned to create a facade of having been absorbed—of belonging. The reality is that I never would be, and this has been my secret until now. The way I coped was to become an impostor. By the time I joined IBM as a Systems Engineer in my thirties, I had become a superb impostor. It was there, as an SE, that I shed the pretense and developed a glut of confidence. I'm not sure how I did it, maybe with my recurring burst of mettle.

Was I told I could take the SAT test again? No one told me, not even my inattentive guidance counselor. I did well enough to get into NYU, CUNY (before open admissions), and some other school this lackadaisical college counselor told me to apply to: Hofstra. I had never heard of it. But like Elana, I wanted to go to the free school, CUNY, as she did to USP (Universidade de São Paulo). We knew our parents had been poor, and neither of us wanted to be a burden to these people who would lay their life down for us and give us everything anyway. None of them finished high school because of the Holocaust, so it was imperative that we provide them with the satisfaction of seeing our achievement and success in higher education.

So far, our correspondence was mundane: school, grades, visits, short travels, benign parents, the intrigues of Miki's elders, our little dramas of death and loss. I didn't share the worst tragedy that affected me, my mother's delicate condition, and I downplayed the insubstantial parts of my life and my feelings of detachment and homelessness. In contrast to Elana's socially busy life, my attenuated one was a cause for insecurity. I was able to step outside myself and relate the outward activities of a teenage girl in my letters while needing to conceal her inner disruptions and lack of secure social attachments. For more than three years, my goal was to feign normality and suppress being different. In other words, I had succeeded in dissembling. I wanted to write Elana letters coming from a normal teenage girl sounding as normal as her letters sounded to me, and not as one who was now living in her fourth country and her fifth language. This may be trite, but I was adhering to the ploy "fake it till you make it." To succeed at blending in, I set a low bar for feeling happy; mine did not seem an indomitable spirit, just one that wanted to get by.

Had we not been so dedicated to each other, by this point, the correspondence would have ceased. To continue a mundane correspondence such as we had until now would have jeopardized the relationship. Something had to happen, and the coming year, our eighteenth, saw that development.

College Life, Political Upheavals, and Riots: The Year That Rocked the World

The coming year, 1968, was a year of intense correspondence between Elana and me. We were growing out of our adolescence and becoming young adults. It was a pivotal year for us as young women. It was a pivotal year in other respects, too, in America and in the world.

The tone of the letters changed. If they were ordinary and quotidian until then, a deeper self-awareness appears in the correspondence. The depth of sharing the tribulations of moving on academically was intensifying the letters in length and in tone. Elana's devotion remained steadfast, so much so that with four years having passed, instead of the expected cooling, the level of spiritedness between us seemed to be increasing.

She worked extremely hard to enter university. I did not. My last year (the 1967–68 twelfth grade school year) at William H. Taft High School in the Bronx was a joke. The school was academically below mediocre, and I was disenchanted and disheartened after having left a superior Canadian high school. And RVCI was hardly a star high school in Toronto! I felt my New York City education floundering in a wash of mediocrity and, worse, a student body that seemed not to care. I was happy to be in New York; I didn't think that I left the "good old days" behind. Out of the temporary friends I found at Taft HS, one stood out, and she is still my friend. A dark-haired, large-eyed, charming, intelligent, and striving student, with a biting sense of humor, Eve Weintraub, born and raised in New York, was a keeper. I always marveled at how she could quote literature. We entered Herbert H. Lehman College together in the fall of 1968.

Not only did Elana try to prove herself to me, but mostly she tried to do so for her parents. She *had* to get into university. Her wise mother dangled the promise of a trip to see me if she got in, and this provided Elana with more impetus to work and succeed. But let Elana's following letters describe how it was. Talk of coming to the United States for a visit runs through months of letters.

The year 1968 was a watershed year in the next phase of American twentieth-century history. In mine and Elana's too. It was the year we entered university, and we left adolescence behind. It was a pivotal year in the racial conflict in the United States and in the entrenchment in Vietnam.

Martin Luther King Jr. and Robert F. Kennedy were assassinated, the country seemed mad with fever, the conflict in Vietnam was quicksand, and the gulf between the national political ramparts was wide. Whenever I think of the election of 2016, which once again brought in an unlikely president with a minority of votes, the attempted coup by reactionary rabble rousers and their undemocratic inclinations in 2020, and all the ensuing emotional volatility that was forced to surface, I relive 1968.

Did our political surroundings affect us emotionally as friends? Elana was not political; she was always reluctant to express political opinions. But she didn't live in a vacuum and couldn't be completely neutral. Violence erupted in Brazil when the youth arose in demonstrations on university campuses, including Elana's campus at USP. These demonstrations were in opposition to the actions of the military dictatorship, such as extreme forms of abuse behind closed prison doors and the vanishing of many of the arrested. It was not only Argentina that had the *desaparecidos* (the left-wing sympathizers, arrested by the right-wing military dictatorship, who then disappeared without a trace), Brazil rounded them up too. Throwing captives out of a helicopter over water was not a hyperbole. Both the current president of Brazil, Luiz Inácio Lula da Silva, and the earlier president, Dilma Vana Rousseff, were left-wing revolutionaries who had been imprisoned and tortured by the right-wing military dictatorship in the late 1960s and early 1970s.

The student uprisings in São Paulo duplicated the student uprisings in Rio, New York, Mexico City, Paris, and elsewhere. In 1968, in general, youth was dedicated to expressing its views in real life, on the street, and without privately live-streaming activities with phone cameras. Demonstrations were more effective then; there was no pushback from social media awash in "alternate reality" and entrenched disinformation. But demonstrations were dangerous in a military state.

I did not participate in demonstrations in 1968. I was a new immigrant, and although I sympathized, I would not join my native peer group. The radical left failed to succeed back then, but it certainly moved the needle.

São Paulo, January 18, 1968

Dearest Udinha!

Seriously, you're gorgeous, beautiful. What is your secret? We loved the photo, thank you so much. If you have an extra one, I'll accept it, especially if it's all of you!

Yes, my dad got better, his hair has grayed a little, but what's important is that inside he's still the same prankster and understanding as ever. We are now in 1968. (Today I got a card from an ex-classmate! I'd like to know what this year will bring. Will we see each other? Nothing bad . . . but hope is waning, as far as exams, some passed and some to come. I had the Portuguese exam on the 15th at Makenzie [another private college].

. . .

Well, I haven't relaxed for a single moment. Now, if I deserve it, I pass, and if not . . . ay, it's not good to think about it!

. . .

My parents are going to the post office now, so I will hurry. I can't say more about Flávia, it's been a while. She gained a little, she's pretty. I also haven't seen Miki in a long time. She repeated the second term at the Alliance [Française] and *she has been dating for a year now. (Oh, boy!) What is she going to do, I have no idea. She changes her mind a lot, on the other hand, most of the time it coincides with what I do! Now she says she'll do literature. She's a cool young girl, between us, she's not like her elder ones! Soon she will have a brother, I think you knew her father remarried and had a little girl, and soon will have another.*

Yes, I already heard the record "Yerushalayim Shel Zahav," beautiful. The others, too. You're doing well collecting books, what else is better? Oh! I am taking lessons at the Renascença.

...

Ah! today I got a letter from my aunt, and it seems that she'll come here in mid-April. Udinha, I would love to talk to you some more, about the exams, how they went, how it sucks, but I'm overcome with sleepiness, and the post office will close. So, I leave you a big and tender embrace, here goes your friend who attempts to be the sincere and always,

Elana

PS Regards to your parents, grandmother, Esti and Gabi. How are they? And your cousin, aunt, uncle? You didn't write about them! Ciao!

São Paulo, February 29, 1968

Dear Udi-Udinha!

Seriously, I don't know how to thank you for the card, it was gorgeous, and so connected with our situation. Everything that I feel goes here: thank you very much, with a sincere embrace.

And Udi, imagine, something happened that I did not expect. I fought as much as I could, but I thought it seemed impossible: I got into university! So, consequently, you know that song? = "I'll see you in, in July —i.e. September" if everything goes well (for sure). [Elana anticipating her mother's promise for a trip to the US would come to fruition.]

Really, I admit, I was never one to study well, as you know. But I wasn't fooling, I swallowed 7 years' material in 2 months. I did not pass at Mackenzie [a private college], *and I was disappointed because the result came out before the others, and it was said that it was easier. But I continued. I started going to Maccabi every day with Rachel.*

...

One day, in Rio, our group was there at the beach. . . . We almost drowned; the lifeguards came. There was a woman with 2 children, she was very short and in a current, and she asked for help, since I was close. For me the water only reached my stomach, but for her beyond her chest. I held the girls, but I couldn't take a step. O, Ruth, it got worse, she needed air and then she sank. There was no danger for me, I was not nervous, and I know how to swim. When I noticed there were 4 lifeguards, I passed them the girls, and I got out alone. A huge crowd was watching us. We sat on the sand, and . . . it was then that I came to, got nervous and started to shake!

I took more photos in Rio, and I will send you some. I saw it get dark, and the lights turned on, by Pão de Açucar, it's very moving. I spent 4 wonderful days. Are you full? Holy Mary, it's time to say enough.

Don't think I am totally lazy, I already restarted to play the piano, beautiful music: Chopin's Polonnaise in C minor, Liszt Rhapsody #11, Études of Chopin, and Transcendental Études by Liszt, Villa Lobos' Impressions Seresteiras and Sertanejas, MacDowell's Polonnaise and Beethoven's Sonatas Op. 31 #2, etc. They're all hard! Classes start on the 4th. I will go see if it's in the morning or afternoon if I got into USP. I did not go to Alliance last year. This year, I still don't know yet if I will have time, piano comes first. Soon it's the contest for the Medal. I don't know if it's stressful at college, because I also intend to do sports.

Now it's for sure that I'll go there [USA]*. The question is when. If I go alone, then it's better in July, right? My parents still deciding if they will go or not. If they do, do you think it's better in July or December,*

January or February? Udi, please answer soon, and don't forget to give your sincere opinion, OK? Anyway, I will go to the Consulate to see if they can extend my passport [the Israeli one].

No, I did not laugh that you keep my photo in your wallet, because all of yours are in mine. You know, when you all left, we were crying, right? In the car, my father said, "You will see in 3 months you will forget each other, and writing won't last." HAHA! 3 months? 4 YEARS! Maybe it's natural to think this way because at 14 years, it's easy to separate and forget. But we have proved there are exceptions.

. . .

Miss Fleury sent me a [birthday] *card. I visit her occasionally and bring something. I owe her a lot, maybe 80% for getting into university. I won't take more lessons with her since I'll have them at school. Hey! This letter is becoming a romance!*

And your aunt, is she better? Did you go there? Congratulations to her, and your grandmother [birthdays]. *How is she? Is she still outgoing? And your parents? Is your cousin well? And you—does anyone "take you out"? Miki goes to her father's house almost every day. Soon she will have a brother, she already has a sister who is almost one year old. . . . And she's also going to the uncle's house who has 2 girls. Her mother is in New York* [actually, Elsa was in Miami] *if I'm not mistaken.*

From my writing you can see that I'm hurrying. It's already noon.

. . .

I part from you again, so I can write to you again soon, and so you will respond "soon" OK? I thank you so much, Ruth, seriously! Many regards to your parents and grandmother and a special sincere embrace from this true friend,

Elana

P.S. Are you still doing Israeli Dance?

Ciao!

PLIS [sic] *answer soon! And your mother, why doesn't she write?*

P.P.S. March 2, 1968

I went to the Consulate yesterday: "Do you want a passport? Then you must go to the army!" was their answer! I will have to find another way.

New York, February 1968

Elana was making pie-in-the-sky plans to come to New York. But she was not yet a Brazilian citizen, and therefore not in possession of a Brazilian passport. She had only an old Israeli passport. I was in the same predicament. At the time, the Israeli consulate would not issue or extend an expired passport unless we served in the Israeli army, which was compulsory for eighteen-year-old citizens.

Elana got into several colleges but was waiting for the result to come from her first choice, the free college. She was getting chattier in her letters. I wonder if I did too. She often mentions what I said, but in this case, two letters arrived and I'm not sure I responded both times, although I sent her birthday greetings, which she acknowledged. We weren't in sync like clockwork, but I made every effort to respond and write about what transpired in my life at the time. I was coasting through the end of senior year in high school.

São Paulo, April 5, 1968

Dear Udinha!

At last, the letter arrived. First, I ask you explain the business with your universities. You were already accepted, but you haven't finished your high school? Or you did. How is that? In any event, congratulations, and (I must say this to you) continue as diligent as you've been until now. Udi, it's been four years, and who would have said that we would be corresponding still, and about what topics?

PUCSP = Pontifica Universidade Católica de S. Paulo. [I had asked her what that meant.] *Yes, the results of USP came out March 4. I went to check, and I did not see my name. It didn't hurt much, since I was already matriculated in another, and besides, I didn't expect to be accepted anywhere, let alone USP. That was on a Monday. On Wednesday, I was at PUC in the middle of Religion class, and a girl came in late (we did the prep course together for 2 months). She sat behind me and said: "You got in." Me: "What?" She: "You passed." Me: "Where?" She: "At the Faculdade." Me: "I know, I am here." She: "No, at USP!"*

Udi, we had an ugly fight until she succeeded in making me buy the "Last Hour" where they published the list. It was true. I passed the "Modern Lit" at night. Among 500+ candidates they let in 27.

...

I dedicate the afternoon to music, at home or at the Conservatory. At night I have classes at university. For now, the classes have hardly started: there is either a strike, a march, or a demonstration, or a reunion, or the university closes. I don't know if by you there is news of what is going on in Brazil with the educational situation (and operational situation: perfect Dictatorship). There have been deaths, and I am afraid of what will happen today, because there will be a march and Costa do

Silva [dictator-president] *already declared that "ORDER WILL BE MAINTAINED!!!" They want and they provoke: repression.*

As for the passport, first, I am not naturalized. But I think dad is going ahead and we will succeed. But they do not want to go in July, they prefer the end of the year. Yes, I understand that July would be better, but . . . OK, nothing has been resolved yet.

And your aunt, how is she? Your parents, grandmother, Esti, Gabi, and you, Udi, what are you doing besides studying and playing piano? Tell me directly, eh?

Well, grandfather is in Israel, making foolishness, and he wants to return here, it seems.

You understood me well: Miki's mother, Senhora Elsa Schiff is in the U.S., I'm not sure where. It seems that the rest, that is the daughter, mother and father [grandparents] *will follow.*

Miki had a fight with Laszlo last Saturday and started dating Pali this Saturday. In other words, she took a week's "vacation." That's good, no? For whoever can and wants . . . Udi, tonight is the ball of "calouros." You are invited. Ah! how good that would be. Seriously, come here for about 6 hours from 10 p.m. to 4 a.m. I had my hair and nails done today. There is no need for jacket and tie, it's sporty. But no fooling, I'd love for you to be here. Seriously.

I am studying a Polonnaise in A Major (I am now listening to the record of Rubinstein), the Heroica by Lizst (Transcendental Édudes), Beethoven Apassionata, Black Keys Études of Chopin, Well-Tempered Clavier (Part II) of Bach and some others. Do you remember Dna. Clarinha (de Silveira)? I am studying with her.

April 6, 1968 [continued]

Ola Udinha!

Yesterday I stopped because I had to have dinner and get ready.

...

I arrived home at 5 a.m. I had to get up at 7 but couldn't until 9 a.m. At 10 a.m. I had Chorus and Analysis at the Conservatory. In the afternoon—wait a minute! Dona Maria de Carmo was talking about recorders, and she told our story. That one day "a little girl" appeared with a recorder, etc. and then a group playing the recorders was created. So, I showed her your [senior graduation] *photo. She couldn't believe it, she was so shaken. Really, she remembers you as a little girl, delicate and skinny etc. And now ... hm ... she wasn't convinced! You are beautiful! She sends you wishes for a happy Passover and many felicitations, etc.*

As I was saying, in the afternoon I played chess with Yoni.

April 7 [continued]

As you can see, this letter will go even under pretenses. Yesterday (I'm protesting) after losing to Yoni, I played the piano, then slept a little, and then went to Laszlo's house (Miki's ex) to give him an address he needed of a violin teacher. I was not going out at night because the previous night I came home at 5 a.m. ... Well, enough of the party.

Today I went with my parents to look for an apartment, but nothing turned out for sure. I did not go out this evening, because I THINK I should rest a little, since this week I didn't sleep enough.

Ah, Udi, Friday is Passover. Where are you doing Seder? At your home or here?? [Remembering the past.] *Well, we could do one day there and one day here. What good times! Ah, and after the dinner we'll go sleep, right?*

As for the trip, I'd go July, but my parents can't. We can all go in January (maybe not Yoni). It's a pity because I'm already restless, and crazy to be there to bother you! Ah, Udi, how wonderful it will be. I hope the year passes quickly. This week I'll visit Miss Margaret and bring her an Easter egg. It's been a while since I've seen her. She still doesn't know that I got into USP. Udi, I think you're already tired of all this nonsense. I'll leave a few epigrams, and give you a short Ciao, and a huge embrace full of "saudades," from the sincere friend,

Elana

And here go regards to your parents.

New York, April 1968

I received huge letters in early 1968, written over several days, the last one very upbeat, very playful, very relieved. It turned out that she got into her first college choice. It is amusing that Elana tries to understand how an American senior is accepted into college before graduating high school.

The differences in academic processes become apparent in the late spring of 1968, by which time I was accepted at Herbert H. Lehman College of CUNY. It was Lehman's first year as a separate entity from Hunter College. And I entered Lehman's first graduating class of 1972. I had applied to NYU, Hofstra, and Lehman College, my safe bet. I got into all three, but Lehman was free, and I didn't want my parents to incur any tuition costs. NYU would have been a dream for a city girl, but I did not receive a scholarship. So, I chose the free CUNY system.

Eva, my friend from senior year at Taft, also opted to attend Lehman, and so our friendship was going to grow in the next four years. She came from a modest family, like everyone who went to that school. She was smart and funny; she still is. I may have talked about her to Elana, and I certainly told Eva about Elana.

I also joined several Jewish girls in my senior year who belonged to an Israeli dance group. We practiced and performed. It made the year bearable. I finally was doing something that Elana talked about in her letters, joining clubs and performing ethnic dances. Even if I did this less intensely than Elana, it was still satisfying.

Just as she got into university and attending classes, the troubles started too.

São Paulo, May 10, 1968

Dearest Udinha!

I just received your letter. You delayed, yes. Well. Just so I can be different, I will not wait. Really, I don't have news.

...

Lately I've been going out very little, but last weekend I decided to go out. It was with Rachel and George (Gabi's cousin) who are dating, Laszlo, (Miki's ex-boyfriend, she's now dating Pali . . . no comment!!!) and me. We went to the Freshman Ball at the BioChem college, and mid-way George felt sick, so we had to take him to the hospital. It wasn't anything serious. He hardly eats and that day he was playing handball and got weak. He became pale and sweaty (in the cold) and could hardly walk. But the next day we went to the theatre "A Day in the Death of Joe Egg."

Sunday will be Mother's Day. I bought wool, and I asked a girl from our piano lessons to make my mother a sweater with her machine. It will be complex, and green. It's the first time I give her a present from my own earnings which makes me super content. Then I will ask her to make me a vest, a sweater etc. She charges more or less reasonably; the work is not expensive.

Udi-Udi, I don't doubt that it would be great for the two of us to tour New York etc., but nothing has yet been resolved. You know our "brave team," that is our team: CALM, MORE CALM [Elana's father's mantra]. *But with or without them, I will be there in January, and if we don't go in January, then I'll go next July. Just me. But it's sure (Amen) we will go in January.*

Ah, I imagine your situation at Passover because of Esti. But this didn't change your relationship with Phyllis, right? Maybe you can't make a more valid comment on education here and over there, but you know both places. I think it's not only "Papa's boys" who can go to university there; and besides high school and university you have more time to do other things and not get exhausted. [Generalizations about university life in the USA.] *USP is the best university here.*

. . .

But Udinha, I am happy. It's been 4 years, and we didn't dream we'd be corresponding and telling each other we are university students. Isn't it a marvel?

As for "what to do later" there's time. Profession, I already have, teaching piano. Next year, I'll have Practical and in 2 years will get the piano performance diploma. Financially I have no troubles. In addition, next year I can teach English or high school English or above, etc. What I want now is to learn. Most likely after I finish this faculdade, I will start another, or midway I'll switch to another [change majors]. *And thus forward. I've come to the conclusion that studying is really delightful when we learn something we like and are interested in.*

In my "Freshman Ball" (I liked the term!) [I translated calouro for her] *I went with Tomi, that guy that when we were little was wider than taller, but at the ball I stayed with my friends who are mostly good-looking. He found himself a girlfriend there, but it seems they already had a fight. Who knows. I danced the Freshman Waltz with a guy who's doing Economics in another faculdade but has friends in this one. I graduated high school with him.*

Udi, I ask you to write about your parents, your grandmother, you didn't say anything about how they are! I have to go already. I must be at USP at 1:30 p.m. and it's now 1:40 and I have to get dressed.

So, here's an embrace full of all the "saudades" and infinite friendship, from yours, always,

Elana

P.S. How about not waiting to write?

Regards to all of you, and Esti and Gabi

Continued in the same letter:

São Paulo, June 4, 1968

Ola, Udi-Udi! Sorry for the delay I am pressed for time, almost in outer space. Write soon, OK? An embrace, always Elana

New York, May 1968

Elana was as busy as a dreidel twirling at Hanukah. I was about to graduate from Taft HS in June. All I could feel was relief. Finally discharged from a school I disliked. The graduation ceremony, with us clad in a thin blue nylon gown and matching mortarboard, was a huge affair the size of a college graduating class, and it was held in a cavernous, old movie theater on the Grand Concourse in the Bronx. I had my yearbook signed by a few friends, but the only one I kept was Eva. My graduating photo was very glamorous, and I sent it to Elana. She comments on it in an earlier letter.

I was free. Free to face a summer living in a drab Bronx apartment building, but excited to go to Manhattan daily by subway. I was comfortable with living in NYC. I attended a typing class at a YMCA in Manhattan, and I felt pleased to be accomplishing something practical, anticipating having to type papers in college. I felt pleased, and not knowing any better, less than happy. Happiness must always be judged in relation to another frame of reference, and mine had been lonely and tedious so far.

New York City allowed an insecure immigrant like me to blend in and be anonymous in the city. A certain amount of tolerance and a certain amount of indifference is what the city offered, enabling a new resident to get lost under its protective cloak. This provided me with a paradoxical sense of security. I knew I was going to make this city my own. E. B. White has written, "On any person who desires such queer prizes, New York will bestow the gift of loneliness and the gift of privacy." What I hoped for from New York with this move was privacy, but not loneliness.

A spell of happiness appeared in my life that spring with a visit from my Toronto friend, Phyllis. She spent a week with me. She came with an agenda: Broadway shows and French and Swedish films: a play a day and at least one movie. Tom Stoppard's *Rosencrantz and Guildenstern Are Dead,* Ingmar Bergman's film *The Seventh Seal,* French delights like Catherine Deneuve in *Belle de Jour,* and museums. I was in Phyllis's cultural hands. She was "in the know"; I was the ingénue happy to be exposed to the exciting art and culture of the late 1960s. Phyllis's cultural background opened for me experiences in a city that was eventually to become my cultural mecca.

A few years earlier in Brazil, Miki was Elana's and my passport to popular musical entertainment that we could not have found on our own. Elana hardly ever followed cultural trends. I was not going to match Miki's popular culture erudition, but Phyllis took me by the hand and brought me up to date in a lively way.

São Paulo, June 24, 1968

Dear Udi-Udinha!

Four years this month. I no longer remember the day you left. Four years. So much has happened! I wonder if you had stayed here, we'd still be friends? Yesterday dad was saying, "We have to go visit Ergikét [Hungarian for little Elizabeth]. *Mom did not want to. Then he said: "It's time to visit Vikikét!"* [Little Victor, my father, in Hungarian. Ernö was missing him.] *Yes! Every saintly Saturday or Sunday, we used to meet. It was nice. We also knew how to fight, discuss, and importantly, BLABBER. Not bad.*

The photos are great, I loved your room, and mamma mia, you're not at a loss for book! But . . . why didn't you send me a picture of you?

. . .

On Saturday I went to the ball of the medical school, "June Fest" and really enjoyed it. Yesterday I stayed home (miracle!) studying. I'll go for lunch now. Ciao.

Ola, Udi, I'm back. It's already 3:20 p.m. I practiced the piano a bit, and now, here I am resting.

. . .

You will study Literature, right? Good. It's nice to know that in advance, and you'll go deep into it. It's enjoyable and interesting. I came to learn by myself, from books, etc., because the Philology professor is a parrot. I don't even attend his class. He says exactly what's in the book that he authored. There's no doubt that he's a good decoration. The one teaching Linguistics is very good. What she presents is not in the book, and she reveals her own research. She says there are ideas in books that we would not have a problem understanding. By the way, [the philosophy professor] *is Jewish.*

Inflation here just started! Student politics goes very poorly. There are many dead and lots of imprisoned students. The ugliest business is in Rio and here.

Last week the USP was transformed into a foundation. From next year on, there will be fees, and very good fees. [Includes the list of proposed fees.] *In university you only find 1% of students who are children of blue-collar workers. It's the elite that you find there. Now imagine what student body you'll have now that you will have to pay. That's why there are marches etc., and confusion mounts.*

Congratulations on your graduation! I would love to go congratulate you in person. So, don't reject a sincere embrace that goes via this letter, OK?

As for July, nothing is fixed. I'll go see if I can rent in Itanhaém. Even if he got it, it's Yoni who will go with friends. We'll see. I'm not dying to go. I have a lot to do here. There will be a piano interpretation at the "Pro-Arte," the education college; there are many pieces I need to observe and practice; study for school; help outside [in the apartment workshop]; *and go to Maccabi and have a good time.*

Yes, my parents continue to work as always. Yesterday I convinced them to see "Taming of The Shrew" with me.

...

If you came here, you would not recognize the place. They opened an avenue that now runs under an elevated road. It's nice. A lot of things changed in 4 years. Even we!! You think?

Ah, I forgot to tell you. The other day Dona Maria de Carmo came to the Conservatory and told me she had a dream about you. And with me, but only heard my voice. She said we were in a huge city, laughing, having a spree, and telling her "You see!!! ???"
[Here Elana copied a poem by Fernando Pessoa, a famous Portuguese poet, under the heteronym Ricardo Reis.]

Udi, once more I part saying so long, and asking you to respond soon and with a long letter.

Many regards to your parents, grandmother, Esti, Gabi, and from me to you, a big embrace from the one who has so much "saudades" for our times together, and for you,

Elana

PS Regards from my parents

New York, June 1968

This was an ugly summer in the American civic arena. Demonstrations were violent and cities burned. Minorities, students, and the disenfranchised took to the streets with a vengeance. A white, patrician society was in the throes of war with the progressive agenda of the 1960s. My private life as a spectator to this turmoil was uneventful, except for getting a license to drive, a trip to Toronto to see Judy, and waiting for my college life to begin.

São Paulo, August 14, 1968

Udi-Udinha!

Funny, I thought it was my turn to write and I almost started yesterday!

Udi, you gave me a fright with your letter. But now that your father came out OK, let's not lament. And the car, is it OK? What kind of car is it? And you, do you have a driver's license? I also want to get it, it would be so helpful, but I lack the courage and the time.

Today I'm really happy: your letter, plus we received a pretty telephone, it's light grey # 2207060 [her first house phone], *and today I start giving English lessons to a 12-year-old girl. She's my third student. The others are piano students who go slowly (age 4 and 6). Since my mother also gives me a weekly allowance, I earn about Cr$140.000,00 (old Cr$) per month. But today I spent about 30.000 on records, music, theatre ticket (a piece by Musset and Marivaux) and a book. No way. The more money you have, the quicker it's spent.*

Miki celebrates her birthday day after tomorrow, 17, right? I'll buy her a book. She's reading a lot of good things. Yes, Udi, probably we would have been very good friends, thinking about it, we had a lot in common and now even more so.

Dad started my naturalization. I went to the French Consulate to see what I have to do to get a scholarship to study piano there. First: Brazilian naturalization. Boom . . . Second: a good knowledge of the language. I'll go study and read a lot of French, and next year, I'll try for a scholarship. We'll see.

Once again you misunderstood: the university is still free (although it's true in August we still haven't had classes after the July break).

But they want to institute fees. The protests are against these fees and various other growing problems, becoming the reason we don't have classes at university. So, there's this big organizational mess. For me, it's not terrible, because I can dedicate more time for piano.

I got to know another young woman who is in 9th level piano and in 2nd level of virtuosity [professional performance] *in harmonica. We want to do a concert together at the end of the year: she on harmonica and me on piano, some together, and some individually. It's still a dream, but we won't stop planning it, and we want to make it a reality. I want to play Liszt Eroica, Villa Lobos Seresteiras Impressions, Chopin's Nocturn Op 48 #1, Rachmaninoff's Prelude, two Preludes and 2 Fugues by Bach from the Well-Tempered Clavier 2nd Vol., and O Sertanejo by Brasilio Itiberê.*

Together, maybe play Gypsy Arias, and something else we haven't picked yet. But maybe I'll change everything. My program to play for the final is now almost ready. I will finish by the end of the month. Then I'll dedicate my time for the concert, and "decorate" everything for the exam [cherry on top]. *Maybe all this decoration will become real, and I may win the 1968 State Governor's medal for piano. Udi, you must have noticed already. I am so enthusiastic about music.*

No, I did not go to Itanhaém, because I observed a class, "Chopiniana Interpretation" with Professor Jan Ekier, who came from Poland. It was 12 lessons or 4 hours each, but time flew so fast. It's there that I got to know Marie Claire and we became very animated friends. Now we're observing another class "Advanced Piano Interpretation" with Madalena Tagliaferro, a well-known pianist who has her own school, and spends more time in France than here. The last film I saw was "The Last" of Gorki. Next week I intend to see "Roda Vida" of Chico Buarque from Holland. Not "War and Peace," it hasn't come here yet.

Ah, you know I meet Antônio and Sueli a lot (remember? a good student of Dona Fausta's, who accompanied us on recorder with her at the piano) so we formed a pro-music group (first meeting) and it will be really interesting, for sure. I told you that Sueli has played twice at the Municipal Theatre, a Beethoven concert accompanying the symphony orchestra. She is now 14, cute, and is studying with Sousa Lima, who I hope to start with next year perhaps. Antônio is at the History faculdade and in Architecture. Old times, eh?

Udinha, it's almost time to go to class, and I must walk there, because there is a transit strike and it's far. So, I leave here a strong embrace for you, from your friend of yesterday, today and tomorrow.

Elana

PS Regards to you parents, to jealous Esti, and Gabi. How's your grandmother? You don't say anything.

BAAI! [in English] *ANSWER SOON!!!* [in Portuguese]

New York, August 1968

I thoroughly enjoyed getting these long letters from Elana, where she's as chatty as if we were sitting in her room catching up on the past week. Elana's letters were *schmoozy*. I now find it hard to cut and condense them. What was interesting to me can't be interesting to someone else who doesn't know her, or know her environment, or know all that we shared before we separated. And yet, it's hard to read these letters and not get to know her, because the letters reveal her motivations, her dreams, her fantasies, her humor, her indecisiveness, her concern for others (her family and my family, for example), while also revealing her classical musical education. And that education is universal, whether in Brazil, the United States, or China. As a result, I can't silence her enthusiasm.

I enrolled in classes at Lehman College in September. In the summer of 1968, it was split from Hunter College, no longer to be called "Hunter-in-the-Bronx." The traditional semi-Gothic buildings stood around a quad in a classic college fashion. It was built in the 1930s. Today it is about three times the size that I got to know from 1968 to 1972: Music Hall, Gillett, Carman, Shuster, Gymnasium, many sports fields, and parking lots I was to take advantage of starting my sophomore year, because I drove there. The campus may not even have been fenced off from the neighborhood. I found it was gated when seeing it again in 2012, out of curiosity and as a lark, in the company of André Aciman, a fellow French student from 1969 to 1972. But that did not make it look more exclusive. It was never an exclusive college, yet it provided a guaranteed higher education for ordinary residents of New York City, and figuratively a higher education too.

The first Lehman class had to attain certain academic requirements to enter: GPA, SAT, and references. The following year, the incoming class was the beneficiary of Open Enrollment. I was part of a class that felt jilted. We feared that the student quality of the next class would lessen and eventually taint our degree. However, that did not happen while I was there. My classmates were all smart and had strong academic credentials. The only difference between us and private university students, and even Ivy Leaguers, was that we were poor. CUNY, a very urban university system, attracted smart New Yorkers who had to continue living at home. It was practically free, after fees. Without dorms, there were no other expenses, except subway tokens and lunches some of us brought from home. Cheap coffee flowed steadily, and fragrant Danishes tempted us in the cafeteria. Although we lacked self-confidence, the level of education was as elevated as the one at exclusive private schools. Eventually, in one of my French literature classes we were scolded by Professor Ferber, who chastised us for wallowing in needless feelings of inferiority, being as smart as his former

Harvard students, he said, and learning the same things.

During freshman registration, I was asked if I would care to join the fencing group. I said no. Little did I understand the importance of unique sports in an academic career. I was asked to join the swim class (or team) and was given a test. I passed and I was told that I could get credit and sign out if I didn't want to compete. I wasn't competitive, so I bailed out of swimming too. If only I could have looked ahead!

In the first day of English class with Professor Appel, I made eye contact with several students, including Anka and Kenneth. They became friends. Yes, with me, but also with each other. They married in 1978 and are still married.

Except for Psychology and Communications 101 (required starter courses), classes were small and students did not need to crowd into auditoriums. My French and linguistics classes were intimate in size, and later, seminars for majoring students were practically private encounters with professors.

Lehman was a commuter school, meaning that everyone came in the morning, hung around, went to classes, and at the end of the last class went home, unless there was work to do in the library, or a tryst with a fellow student. Between classes, there was a specific table in the cafeteria in the Music building where we'd come and go, and there would always be someone at this table from our close group of friends: Eva and her English Lit cohorts, Charles Tobin and sometimes Gerry Dalgish, my linguistics cohorts, Anka and her Croatian friends plus her love interest, Ken, and on rare occasions, the elusive André. At the end of the day, I'd take the bus to the train station, ride to Tarrytown, New York, on the Hudson Line, and walk to the house from the station. By junior year I had a car, and I drove to school. I was lucky. The car was a used Buick Special my father fixed up and handed down to me when he got hold of another used car for himself. In his garage, there were opportunities to buy used cars that his clients no longer needed or cared to maintain. My father had taught me to drive as soon as I turned eighteen, and with a few refresher lessons from a driving school, I got my license before my freshman semester.

São Paulo, September 19, 1968

Dear Udi,

Happy birthday to you this dear date, with lots of happiness and many years. You are now an adult! Wisdom! Udi, I don't know why it's only on birthdays that we wish people happiness. But since it's like that, then we have to wish so much, to last 365 days. This will be a very significant year for you, right? at university, etc. I hope you will win in everything you fight for, that your life will see beautiful panoramas . . . and that you'll be happy, together with all those who you love.

I'm sorry for the delay, Udi, but this past 2 weeks were hell for me. I was going to send you a telegram on the 15th but seriously, it didn't work out. Ah, the letter was registered because I asked a friend to mail it from the post office that's close to her and she didn't know how, so she chose to send it registered. Yes, I wrote it Aug 14, but it was sent much later. Look at the envelope.

No problem, one day I'll explain to you in person about the university issues. I know that at this moment (2nd semester) professors are dropping weight around, throwing material, tests, and projects at us. Yoni is in 4th Medicine and there are 2 more (the 6th is the internship).

On the 27th I'm going to play Bach Prelude and Fugue 2nd Vol, in an audition. Do you like Bach? My favorite. The musical group we are forming will be officially registered next week. It's agreed in

5 departments that I will be a coordinator (extra-curricular), and Antônio and one more guy will be presidents. I'll tell you once what will happen, to get the gist of what's going on with this group. I would say that this business is really most interesting.

What a good vacation you had! Lucky! However, I don't understand "blind date" and what is a "double date"? How are the classes? What are the subjects? You like it?

...

I would love to go to you on vacation, but my naturalization is far from complete. And I don't know when it will be.

I learned machine stenography during the vacation, and if I don't have other plans, I'll work as a stenographer. I will visit Miss Margaret this week. OK, I'll send her regards from you. Last time I was there she tried to get a radio station in England. If I'm correct, her legs are a little better.

Udi, I am so hungry! Do you have something good and delicious there? Mmmm! Udi, I'm going to have dinner, because I have a test, and I can't be late. As for this delay, my wishes for your happiness are most sincere, and so accept this big embrace and a kiss, from your friend for always,

Elana

PS Do you have a photo of all of you? I'd love it if you send me one. Regards to your parents and grandmother.

New York, September 1968

In recounting my trip to Toronto in the summer, I wrote to Elana about blind dates and double dating, which were concepts Elana did not understand, and in her letter, she asked me to explain these customs. In Elana's social environment in Brazil, young people socialized in a group setting. Some paired off permanently, or long term, like her friends Rachel and George, and some paired off for a jiffy, like Miki and various young men she liked for a while. Someone unattached, like Elana, was part of a group and pairing was not necessary. As such, the social style was like double, triple, or odd man out dating—going out, going to shows, dances, parties, etc. And no one felt left out of it. The members or pairs in the group could unpair and re-pair without social constraint. Such groups, however, were the basis of establishing long-term bonds.

Even as I described dating to Elana, I knew I preferred her social environment to the stilted dating scene I had to endure. Nothing was worse for me than being out on a date with someone I barely knew, just to get to know him and find out that I'd rather be home. Or go on a blind date, and look at my watch for the time, anticipating going our separate ways.

My friend from Toronto, Judy, was a connoisseur of dating and loved the process. She dated frequently and widely, and she took it seriously. She had a very high tolerance for strangers and dance clubs, and each date was a ruthless test to find someone who would meet her standards: tall, educated, employed, Jewish, good-looking, and kind. She had no qualms with dispensing with anyone who failed her test. She visited me in Tarrytown, where I moved with my parents during my sophomore year, at age nineteen. She came with a boyfriend. She got all dressed up to go out Saturday night, but I could not give her advice on where to go dancing in suburban Westchester. She broke down in tears feeling sorry for herself and for her wasted Saturday night. I was perplexed. Going out Saturday night for me was an exception, not a rule. Judy was comfortable and self-confident in the presence of all men, I was not. I was still stinging from my terrorizing encounter in the elevator, and I feared unknown men.

São Paulo, November 5, 1968

Dear Udinha,

At last, a letter from you. And . . . photo! You're beautiful, on the one hand you look like you completely changed, on the other, that I saw you like that yesterday. I don't know why. How many years did your mother get younger? Thank you for the photo, Udi, at this moment I don't have any to send.

Yes, it's great to be a college student. And where you are, it must be better. You must be a good student, having opportunities and material to study.

*Yes, the meaning of faculdade here and there is different. Here faculdade is a university department. For example, the faculdade of literature at the University of São Paulo. My brother is in medicine at the same university. But I'm going to do the calculation for what we have learned this year: nothing * nothing = nothing.*

We counted the days of classes: 48 as of now. Including days when professors were not missing, we had 2 or 3 classes. At the beginning of last month, some sophomores were teaching in front of our building which is in front of Mackenzie on Rua Maria Antônia and has 3 departments: philosophy, social science and literature. That was in the morning. The Mackenzie-ites [more right-wing students] *thought that it was a lesson by the UNE Congress (National Student Union) and so they started to throw bricks, etc. at them. The sophomores then ran into the building we call Philosophy of M. Antônia. The university students already there together with the sophomores went out, the Mackenzie-ites provoked them, and they started to fight. There were many wounded from being burned by acid and hit by bricks etc. No police. The next day, when it was calm, I don't say that the Mackenzie-ites did it, but things started to be thrown out of Mackenzie, trying to interrupt announcements and posting of pamphlets in front of Philosophy.*

There were shots, hurtling stones from the street, acid, etc. and an upper-class student died. This started plus or minus in the middle of the day. When I got there at night, the situation was worse. They were throwing Molotov's from a tall building next to Mackenzie, and also setting gasoline cans on fire aiming at the Philosophy building. The firemen came in from another street and put out the fire at first. But of no use. Our building is worth nothing now. It's laid to waste. And the police did not want to intervene. They stayed out of it and . . . they did not help. One guy took a picture of the police giving arms to the people from Mackenzie. Our professors asked a battalion commander who was there to intervene, since there was now no one inside our building where everything was destroyed, library, museum, any material remaining, etc. He didn't.

Well, all this did not come just from Mackenzie students. But there are many people from the CCC (Hunt for Communists Command) who are anti USP students and staff. They took advantage of what happened to our building the next day. I don't understand and no one understands why they had to sack our building when there was no one there. Armed soldiers were surrounding Mackenzie, but USP was abandoned to the firemen. What does this mean? I guarantee that if the soldiers wanted to stop this, they would have in 2 minutes; but that was not their objective. Result: we have no classrooms. We were stopped by the order of the Governor for 10 days. We arranged space at the Cidade Universitária (in the Geography and History building) on Saturdays from 2 p.m. until 9:30 p.m. and Sundays, from 9 a.m. to 6:50 p.m. It is unbearable in this heat, I call it sadism. At times we can't stand it, so we go out for a round. The worst is that there were no tests during the year. The material accumulates and so do the tests and projects the professors are required to give, so they can submit final grades to the office. I don't know about final exams; I think even the professors don't know. We'll see. I don't know when classes will resume. But we've had enough, I know.

There are student uprisings in all of Brazil, and it's dangerous to be a student. They tried to form a VEE congress in the jungle, but they were all apprehended. 720 students caught hell in marches and demonstrations. And so, the situation for students here is horrific.

I succeeded in learning stenography in 28 hours, and I beat a record that was 57 w.p.m. in 35 hours: I did 58 w.p.m. in 28 hours. The teacher said I could have been faster if I had practiced at home. But at home I only read the lesson and closed the book. I then trained and reached 70 per minute. I stopped, so now I don't know how fast I am, I haven't used it. But it's easy.

During vacation, I want to do a course on Speed Reading, and to learn the guitar. Yoni already had his second guitar lesson yesterday.

Bach. It's wonderful. On Friday the 8th I will play a Prelude and a Fugue in audition. The exams are soon. I've already memorized the Prelude, a Symphonic Study and a Schumann Variation, and Chopin's 5th Study on Black Keys. I intend to memorize it all. I'm on my way. Udi, I must leave, will continue later.

November 6, 1968 [continued]

It's that dad gave me a ride to Jardim America. Last week our Theory professor assigned us a project we could do alone or in groups up to 5. I partnered with a guy. One day I couldn't meet, another day he couldn't meet, and even when we did meet, we couldn't get to practice. Then the professor said we must hand it in to his house by Tuesday. On Friday, we spent from 5 p.m. to 11 p.m. doing this damned project. And yesterday I handed it in!

That C, D, E, F, G, A, B are do, re, mi, fa, sol, la, si, I already knew. But I think it would cost me a lot to get used to that. We are studying Music History. Our group already exists. The inaugural concert was on Oct 27.

. . .

We invited the Madrigal das Arcadas to this inaugural concert. The auditorium was pretty good, so it seems we got off on the right foot. Its name is "The Society for New Advancement of Music."

I don't know it I told you, I am studying with Estrelinha Epstein. I had 2 lessons so far, and I like it. She gave a concert yesterday!

Ah, I did not finish answering your questions. Yes, we will only give concerts ourselves: individually and together, for example: piano for 4 hands, 2 pianos, solo piano, piano and harmonica, piano and violin, group of wind instruments, etc. and we'll invite people who can hold conferences, debates, etc. The members, you remember, are Sueli and Antônio. There are 3 directors and 5 department coordinators. My department is "internal activities."

What have you read? I am now reading The Brothers Karamazov, just started.

[Elana lists some epigrams.]

Udi, I'm going now to study piano. Write soon, tell me about all of you, about the college and about YOU!!

A big kiss from your friend of yesterday, today and especially, tomorrow. Elana

6 pages?? darn!

New York, November 1968

Why do I not remember what I was doing at the end of my first freshman semester? I was still living in the Bronx and family life was still the same. College life was interesting, professors were impressive, but there were no strong friendships yet. If my letters had survived Elana's many residential moves throughout her life, I would have the answer to my question. And yet, not remembering the four or eight weeks tells me there really was nothing outstanding to remember. I'm not repressing anything, because I was a contented freshman. My family included my grandmother living in the same building, and there were visit to and from Michigan. I probably wrote to Elana what she wrote to me: my courses, my piano pieces, my parents' plan to move to the suburbs. On the other hand, the drama that she describes taking place on her campus was a story that was to take place soon on American campuses. On the political stage, however, there was turmoil to come: Nixon was elected president in November.

São Paulo, December 19, 1968

Dear Udinha,

Eh, at last I am done. I'm calm, just as I like it. At the university, I passed 3 subjects, redoing one, and I still don't have the result of one more. I'm satisfied. I didn't expect as much. And I won't have to sacrifice anything during vacation. I am also done at the conservatory. My diploma will have an average of 8.8.

...

And so it is, if I had not played around since the beginning and studied instead, I would have achieved a 10.0 But no matter, it's a good lesson.

The commencement concert will be at the end of February or early March. I still don't know what I'll be playing. Now I want to prepare a concert with Marie Claire. I think I told you about her already. I met her at a Chopiniana class in July. We have a nice friendship. What brought us together was the interest in music, then we found things in common which keep up the friendship.

...

She's the one I will do a concert with, she'll play half, I'll play half, and the 4 hands: Guarani, and the Hungarian Rhapsody no. 2. For my program, I'll do Chopin 5th Etude opus 10 (black keys), Bach Fantasy in C minor, Villa Lobos Dance of the Black Indian, Beethoven Sonata opus 31 no. 2 (Tempest), or Mendelssohn First Concerto opus 25. What do you think?

In the meantime, I am studying with Estrelinha who gives me technical practice until I cry enough, and perfecting the fugues and preludes of Bach which I played at the audition. She also assigned Cirandinha of Vila Lobos and a Fantasy in C by Bach. The rest on my own. It's delightful. Maybe I'll play Liszt's Eroica. For sure I will be happy with this concert. I still don't know what I will do next year. Either stay with Epstein or go back to perfect my playing at the Conservatory of Marie Claire's. I still haven't decided, because I want to see what I achieve until then.

My grandfather is arriving tomorrow from Israel. Last Friday the 13th Marie Claire and I went to hotel Miami (Itanhaém—remember?) and we stayed until Sunday. Now I am resting.

December 24, 1968 [continued]

Ola, Udi-Udi!

I returned. From where? From every room and corner. I don't remember why I stopped writing. Now I read what I wrote. A lot changed [with her concert], *and I don't know how things remain, I'm thinking . . . But maybe tomorrow we will change the program again! OK. I've made up my mind for now, but I'm indecisive, maybe continue with my teacher, or go practice at another conservatory or go to Paris which is a musical center today. On Thursday I started to learn harmonica with Marie Claire, and I'm now on second level. In February we will try to advance classification to the 5th level. I am guessing your question!*

. . .

That's 17 hours of study per day. The rest for eating sleeping and relaxation. Udi, these are plans. Until today I have never done what I planned. Never. I am frustrated by this. But now I am really animated and . . . yay! Udi, I'd like to achieve something in life. Until now I have done nothing complete. I always go from here to there, from one school to another, from one class to another. What do I know? NOTHING! What have I done? Another nothing! And if this time I don't advance, then I fall. And I don't want to fall. So, the thing is to go forward, right?

Today I have a class with E. Epstein. On Friday she will perform at the Municipal Theatre. And she said I will participate in the competition in November, she assigned Handel's The Harmonious Blacksmith to me. Udi, Udinha, I'm content. Today is Christmas. Happy Christmas, then. I received . . . happiness, satisfaction. Have not achieved anything yet, but now I have decided on a laid-out plan. And WILL go until the end. But . . . I must be boring you with all this.

You—how are you? And college? and everyone there? What have you decided about Canada?

My grandfather arrived Friday, he's a mixed-up man. Rachel just called me. We'll to the movies to see "The Shoes of the Fisherman." Did you read it? did you like it? I liked the book. Until I return, Udi, one of THOSE embraces, from

Elana

December 25, 1968 [continued]

"*Oba!*" [a casual greeting like "Yo!"]

I think this letter will have to levitate. Yesterday, we arrived late at the film, so we saw "Histories of Edgar Allan Poe," by Fellini, not bad, very touching. Today I did not go out. I practiced piano and harmonica, read, and nothing else. Soon I'll go to sleep. Tomorrow is another day of vacation, so I want to sleep at least 8 hours a day. In January, I have to make progress with studying, because in February the group may go to Brasília, Salvador, Ouro Prêto, Cabo Frio and Rio. Would be great. Let's see how I stand until then. It's raining. It's Christmas.

And you, Udi, what are you doing besides studying? and music? tell me is there a good music campus there? And is college OK? If not, come here!! When you go back there you will find gold waiting for you.

. . . [Epigrams]

Udi, write soon. Don't do what I do. And give my regards to everyone. How's your grandmother? From you friend forever,

Elana

New York, December 1968

This had been a violent year: Martin Luther King Jr. and Robert Kennedy were assassinated, and the country convulsed with riots, anger, and demonstrations. The Vietnam War was very unpopular, triggering demonstrations. All was quiet on my college campus in the fall, my first semester at Lehman, although there were demonstrations at other colleges. The demonstrations during the Democratic National Convention in August had been traumatic to experience and to watch. These events shocked the country like a taser. And like a slap at the liberal youths who were fomenting—if not in revolt necessarily—for reform, Nixon, a less-than-charming Republican, won the presidency in the November election. The "adults" in the country (Nixon called them the silent majority) reasserted their belief in the "military-industrial complex," a term used daily that year as a mantra for the old order. It seemed like retribution for what happened in Chicago. Worse things were brewing that soon would break out on campuses. Elana's description of violence on São Paulo campuses was a sign that 1968 proved to be a watershed year. Youth demonstrated in other cities too: Paris, London, Stockholm, etc. There was a shift in the air. Hippies weren't just flower children; they wanted to mobilize. And Elana and I were caught amid these political events, and as outsiders, we watched these from the sidelines. I read her letters, ordinary and repetitive, and my responses were in a similar vein. But they did not contain the stories unfolding on American streets. I was a newcomer in New York and an unsophisticated campus denizen.

Love Interest: A Foreigner Navigating the Dating Scene

São Paulo, February 4, 1969

Dear Udi-Udi!

Congratulations! May all the best there is, come to this new home, and may only happiness reign in it. Yes, I can imagine how happy you all are now, having this house and being together indefinitely. And . . . appreciate it, because one of these days I will show up, you hear? Are you still on vacation? Even studies there seem to be pleasant! What car did you get?

You want to tell me that your cousin got struck by Cupid? And you, how is it with you in this regard?

Your grandmother will stay in the city—but in the same building? Why doesn't she move to a safer place? How is she? Why don't you write more about her? Is your mother working as a hairdresser?

Did you know that Miki took a hairdressing course here? But I don't think she finished it. Now she's working at "ManPower," a type of agency. They send her somewhere, and when she's done, they send her someplace else. She's well paid, about NC$9,00 a day (or more). It's by the hour. She does dactylography, a type of work. She's now seventeen and a half, and has been dating a guy for a year, and it looks like it's going well. I don't know what will happen when she moves there [to the USA]. *This is such a bummer. She's a splendid girl, inside. But . . . she's being so influenced by that grandmother. And she's without a mother which I think is irreplaceable. The grandmother and grandfather are getting along, now that the mother* [Elsa] *is not there. I no longer have that friendship with her, because more than once she's* *annoyed me, and I let it slide . . . and we're "just friends," like acquaintances. However, I would like her to be what she's inclined to be; not what others are making her become.*

My grandfather will stay here indefinitely. Yesterday he turned 76 "little" years. I think he's healthier than the four of us together! I'm still on vacation. But I study piano constantly.

. . .

Ah, the exams for the second semester are coming next. If you don't pass the final exam in December (1st exam = 1st semester), there's a second chance in February (2nd exam = 2nd semester). You forgot. It's always been that way, even in high school. But you never needed it—even the first exam! [I never failed.]

On Sunday we are going to Itanhaém for a week. How annoying, because it's just with my parents and my grandfather. There's still nothing to do there without friends. I think I'll stay 2 or 3 days and then return. I'll stay at Rachel's house. All this should be over by Wednesday, because I have the speed-reading class then.

What were the results of your exams? Udi, I think the news has now been exhausted. I am missing those times we had together. How would our friendship be, if you had stayed here? Would we have continued to get along? I think we would have. And you?

I'm sending you a picture taken 3 weeks ago in Guarujá. What do you think? Udinha, write soon, tell me about your move and everything there. A kiss, from your friend forever,

"Lembranças" to your parents and grandmother from me and from mine.

Elana

New York, February 1969

The week of a particularly heavy snowstorm, we moved from the Bronx apartment to a house my parents bought in Tarrytown, New York, on Miller Avenue. It was the first house my parents ever owned. Throughout our residence in the apartment building where she also lived, my grandmother had grounded my life from the time we moved to the city in 1967. She remained at that address for a few more years, and then moved to a larger apartment in the Bronx that she supported by renting out the bedrooms to Hungarian and Romanian émigrés.

My father's work consisted of maintaining a fleet of oil delivery trucks in Tarrytown that belonged to a decent, close-knit family. I considered them a decent family because they invited my parents to their son's wedding at Tavern on the Green, in Central Park, New York. This reflected not just on their decency; it was a sign of how they held the value of my father's work. They employed him until he ran his own truck-mechanics business, with their company as his major client. Eventually, he built his own garage a few blocks away in Tarrytown, taking in private cars instead of trucks, a physically easier job.

I recounted to Elana the move and the new life in a house in the suburbs while commuting to Lehman. These were all mundane facts, but Elana wanted to hear about my daily life, the way I wanted to read about hers. Our interest in each other was mutual, in comparing, contrasting, envying, and sympathizing with each other, and in describing our social life and city life, as we arrived at the end of our teen years, letting go of our adolescence. We wondered, in writing, about what the future was going to bring. And in each letter, she'd gossip about her friends, the ones I had known before, and the new ones she met, and all the members of her family. In return, I had to write to her about all the members of my family, not to mention all my new friends whom she had never met. And running through all this gossip, schmoozing, joking, and delineating, we shared our feelings by exchanging letters.

My life was collegiate: it entailed going to classes, studying, making friends. In concluding her letter, the big question Elana asks is: would we have remained friends? Yes, of course. Still missing each other—almost five years after parting. We expressed our dedication openly.

The letters seem endless and mundane. Without love, sex, intrigue (more exciting than Miki's story), or crisis, life provided us little to write about. And yet . . . we continued to write driven by some propulsive force that is visible only in hindsight: moving us to an escarpment—one that must be climbed or allowing the friendship to wither. At the end of our teen years, we managed to ride the boredom without falling prey to the scourges of this life stage. Our foundations were solid, and we knew this was just a passing stage in life leading us to concentrate on school, music, friends, family, and whatever pastimes were available in this era, as long as we concentrated on looking ahead. And we were fortunate: there was no toxic social media to bombard us with attention-grabbing malignancy. We were also lucky to be dorky.

São Paulo, March 18, 1969

Dear Udi-Udi!

I don't remember if I answered your last letter, but no matter, I just felt like writing to you now! It's a pleasant day, neither hot nor cold, with a blue sky. It's so pleasant. Sometimes we just don't know what to say about why it's so. Classes started 3/3. But we don't have room. They were getting barracks for us (plus or minus), but they were not ready, not by a long shot. If it starts after the blessed week [a religious holiday perhaps or cursing the school's incompetency] *it will be a miracle.*

You know, the restructuring was terrific. Everyone can choose 3 subjects: basic subjects (required), complementary and optional.

...

Does this make sense to you? It's a terrible confusion for us, and it took a while to understand. I took an English Culture pre-test and landed in 3rd year. Pity, because last year we hardly had classes in it, and by the end of the year I forgot a lot, otherwise I'd be ahead. Today is my first class (I'm late since it started on the 4th and I lost 2 weeks, I hope it won't be a drawback).

...

Estrelinha Epstein wants me to compete in November. I'm practicing and she's confident in me. But I am not. We'll see.

Udi, I think we're getting old! Imagine a girl (and a boy of course) from the group are getting married! She lives at R. Dna. Veridiana almost at the corner of your old house [apartment building]. *Whenever I go there, I remember our times together. And you know, all the friends are dating, going steady, or engaged. DUMMIES! Don't you think? And you? Did you also fall? Or who know, this is not falling, it's climbing the clouds. Who are you "in love" with? I'm not an angel, but I have my wings open, like a bird. There's flirting but nothing serious.*

...

But now I must go work. Write soon, and if possible, send a photo of all of you. How are your parents and grandmother? You don't write about them. Regards to all. And for you a truckload of kisses and hugs, from your friend forever,

Elana

PS I think I already wrote, but thanks so much for your birthday wishes and your words that translated how you feel.

Bai. Please [this time "please" is written correctly], *write soon with a lot of news.*

São Paulo, June 17, 1969

Dear Udi-Udi!

I just took advantage, and I'm thinking of you. And since the professor is filling a sausage [poor translation, i.e., BS'ing] *(or rather, killing the lesson) I'm writing to you on a notebook page.*

First of all, I mustn't forget to tell you this: Miki's grandmother keeps calling us to ask us for your address. When I go out with the group, Miki always asks. But one day, I was at home, and she called asking for your address, but I could no longer drag it out. I didn't want to, but I gave it to her, there was no other way. She's coming to Miami.

[I am sorry that I somehow made Elana afraid of sharing my address, because I don't remember I was avoiding Miki; there was no animosity between us.]

[The page is cut in half. On the other side is a letter to someone, perhaps to me, or just class notes, but the page is struck across with a pen.]

New York, June 1969

The fact that Miki's grandmother wanted my address was an innocent inquiry. Miki's stepfather had a relative who lived near my new home in Tarrytown. Miki was immigrating to join her mother in Miami, before moving to St. Thomas, the US Virgin Islands. She was not ready to share her plan to leave Brazil with Elana, so this may be the reason for being evasive, under the tutelage of Berta *neni*. Miki eventually came to visit me in Tarrytown in the summer of 1971, and I joined her at her relative's house for lunch. We did not maintain much contact after that visit. Elana would continue to fill me in about Miki's whereabouts or her endeavors.

The other side of the page is part of a letter but without an addressee. In this short page written in early June, she mentions that in her group she met a Czech boy she likes. He arrived in Brazil three or four months earlier. He was good-looking and was very *simpatico*. And with a test coming up, he was helping her with German that was not going well for her. She complains about not being presentable. She's falling behind in piano studies.

São Paulo, July 28, 1969

Dear Udi-Udi!

I won't come with the excuse of not having time to write, because I don't think it matters any more. We can always write, even if it's only two words! Yes, I already wrote you in school on a page from a yellow pad. I tried to write for at least 7 days. The letter is a complete joke, so, "here we go."

...

On 6/28 my aunt, uncle, and Philip, the older son, arrived in Rio. My parents and I went to greet them in Rio. They stayed at the Copacabana Palace Hotel! [A luxury hotel Elana's family would not indulge in.] *They forced us to stay there, too. On the 29th we returned. I had a test on the 30th. Yoni and I returned to Rio on the 1st. I stayed at the house of Ruth, an ex-friend from the Jewish clubs, and Yoni slept at the hotel in Philip's room. It was an awful getaway, since for my aunt and uncle, the only important thing to do was to see the commercial center, without wanting to know anything about sightseeing—nothing! I returned on the 5th, and they came here by plane on the 6th. At the end of another week, I returned to*

Rio for 3 days. It was because Rachel, her mother, sister, George (the boyfriend), and one more guy, Danko, were there. During these 3 days I had a wonderful time.

Wait, I hear the phone, and I think it's for me. No, mom didn't call me. Drats! [She was waiting for Danko's call.]

Udi, I want to tell you. Danko is Czech, and he arrived here about 5 months ago. Rachel's mother is friends with his aunt and uncle, therefore, he started to come out with our group. At first, we barely talked; our common language is Hungarian, and you know how poorly I speak it. Then things improved and we started talking more. We got along. A day after I arrived in Rio (the 6th) we started dating. I like him very much. I don't know where this will lead. Udi, I'm not planning on anything. For now, I feel wonderful with him, and I don't think it will end, because I think he likes me, too. But I've learned not to trust "the after." It's all so uncertain! Yesterday we went to Maccabi [the sports club] *together. It was wonderful. We even got suntanned. We are studying Portuguese, since he must take the Vestibular at the end of the year. In Czechoslovakia he was a freshman.*

July 29, 1969 [same letter continued]

Oba, Udi! [slang for Hiya!]

I stopped yesterday because he called, and he and George came to get me to go downtown. They had some things to take care of and I had to have my eyeglass lenses replaced.

...

But as I was saying yesterday, he was in the first year of university and had to stop, in order to enlist in the army for two years. When he went home for about a 2-month break, he "came" here. [What Elana is saying, he skipped university, skipped the army, and escaped out of the country—it was right after the Prague Spring.]

Udi, I feel so content with him. I'm still on vacation until August 4. I must help a lot at the factory [the glove workshop], *because it's winter and the orders have surpassed what my mother can make alone. I am studying piano, and I go walking.*

You know, our friend Miki is engaged (not officially, she says).

...

My second semester will be tough.

...

I got into English Culture in April after having left it for a year (there were no classes in 1968 [due to student uprisings]). *I thought the 3rd level very easy, with nothing new, and very boring. That's why I want to do 4th and 5th levels in one year. Well. Five hours of piano, and college (which is getting intense this year). In addition, I have a piano student, and possibly a student of English. And maybe I'll also practice swimming. I started today, but when classes are on, I'll only go when I have time.*

I'm sleepy, and it's only 9 p.m. I'll go sleep so I can get up at 6 a.m. tomorrow.

Udi, what did you think of the moon? Marvelous! You were all probably so happy there! We now have a television (it's at the other apartment), but I watched at Rachel's apartment.

OK, Udi. I must stop, and I ask you not to delay, because it's my fault I have not had news from you in a long time and I miss it. Write about you, about everyone, and regards to all.

One of those hugs from your friend,

Elana

New York, July 1969

Elana was in love! Danko appeared in her group. There was no need to be set up for a blind date. No six degrees of separation: one person knows another person who knows another relative . . . and pairs get together.

Danko skipped university and army service in Czechoslovakia when the Soviet Union and the Soviet Bloc invaded the country in August 1968, after Alexander Dubček's attempt to liberalize the country in what was called the Prague Spring. Danko followed in the footsteps of other relatives who came to Brazil. His parents and brother remained at home, and communist restrictions prevented them from traveling for many years; in turn, he could not risk going home to visit afterward. Therefore, in the coming decades, his family, when allowed, would meet him in Hungary. Eventually, they could get visitor exit permits. Danko came from Komarno, halfway between Bratislava, Slovakia, and Budapest, Hungary. It's the reason he speaks Hungarian fluently, which allowed the two of them to become friends quickly within their group. And it's the language he and Elana speak among themselves even today.

It is hard to fathom, when I look back at historical events, that anything else was occurring besides the murderous Vietnam War. But life continued like an eight-track tape. What was awesome in July 1969 was that human beings landed on the moon. Elana and other Brazilians were figuratively also over the moon about this feat. The fact that American astronauts walked on the moon highlighted all the pride Americans felt about their know-how and advancement in science and engineering. The moon landing prompted all the envy and awe felt by the rest of the semifree world (excluding communist countries that distorted international news or who had their own space program, like the Russians). Brazil was a dictatorship, but news from the outside world was not censored, allowing Elana and family to watch the moon landing on a TV at a friend's house.

Brazil's population has strong nationalist feelings. I always felt that Brazilians have had a love/hate relationship with the United States: loving the culture (to emulate when no one is looking, especially when one had extra money to spend) and hating the culture, because Brazilians believe theirs is superior. They view the United States as a modern imperialist country, and they resent it. Even so, they envied American strength and leadership in the democratic West. And yet Brazil hadn't managed to maintain a democracy for long in the twentieth century, even as the country's strength and wealth had grown exponentially since the 1960s. Still, if you ask an American who is Alberto Santos-Dumont, you'll get a blank stare; if you ask a Brazilian who are the Wright Brothers, you'll get a denial that they invented flying airplanes (i.e., planes heavier than air). Brazilians' most powerful competitive urge had been to have access to basic products. While America was producing high-quality products, anywhere from cars and other industrial products, coveted personal items and clothing, pharmaceuticals and medical treatments, Brazil was producing copies of almost everything, but of lesser quality. Made in the USA was not a right-wing slogan at the turn of the twentieth century; it epitomized products a Brazilian wanted to buy but couldn't. For a while, Brazilian nationalism prevented American cars from being imported, to boost the nascent Brazilian auto industry. But as a status symbol, nothing beat a Chevrolet or Cadillac, even with their whopping import tariffs. All this, of course, has changed dramatically since I moved away.

I also felt that pride during the moon landing. It was so easy to like being an American. If you separated the social (and some political) aspects of American life from national standing, the economy, scientific development and progress, nothing could beat the corporate wealth, the academic openness, the infrastructure, and scientific research of this country. I did not take my college education for granted; I was grateful, although I hated being the outsider. I could understand why my father wanted to come to the United States and drag his family from country to country to achieve that goal: five years in Brazil plus three years in Canada—eight years of waiting. My mother paid dearly for it, and so did my father when my mother succumbed to schizophrenia. Hands down, though, if you were a wanderer or an exile and wanted to land somewhere, you landed in the United States. What Americans who want to selfishly close their borders out of xenophobia don't understand in the twenty-first century is what a shining light it has been for the stateless (such as me) and the persecuted (my father). Uprooting a family from one country to move to another is a very difficult thing to do, which means that only the most motivated do it.

The ongoing saga of Elana's relationship with Miki as described in this letter had long before turned into a soap opera. The threesome friendship, in various levels of earnestness, continued for decades. One way or another, we couldn't let it go or let it die, because we (and our families) were tied together during our most formative years. Elana and I, especially Elana, pulled that friendship on by hook or by crook. Mostly, it was via Elana's admirable forbearance throughout the rest of Miki's life. I remained on the periphery, friends with Miki for the rest of her life, because of Elana.

São Paulo, August 14, 1969

Dearest Udi-Udi!

You must have received my letter yesterday, I held on to it, with all the disorder in my room (we changed furniture) I don't know where my writing pad went, the letter, my notebook, plus I couldn't find your address [the predigital age]. *I had to call Miki, and she gave it to me.* [What irony!] *Not her, her grandmother, since Miki went to Santos.*

After going to Maccabi with Danko, the post-office was next. But when we saw the bus, we ran. The letter stayed with him, and he sent it. The fault of this delay is mine. Your letter arrived more than a month ago. Udi, you know, your letter made me very surprised, dumbfounded, and moved. Until today you only wrote news, and not ideas, opinions or plans. I was so pleased. Udi, your news that you may come here has turned our family around. My parents are ultra happy, and I already started thinking of trips we'd take. As for me, as you know, I want to see you so much.

Right now, I'm at Maccabi, sunbathing, writing to you, waiting for gymnastics. On the way here, I was thinking: how about a trip together, maybe to Europe? Do you see a possibility? Do you think it'd be worth us thinking about it? On Wednesday I went to see how I can get naturalized. I can't wait for Daddy anymore. He doesn't take the initiative, and I want to be done with it. It seems it won't be hard, and it can be done in 6 months. [It actually took years.] *I did not seek a dispatcher. I'll do it alone.* [She eventually had to get a dispatcher.]

I was pleased that you seek more independence. But Udi, always take care to show your gratitude to your parents and remember what you mean to them. I don't think of "escaping," that was childish. But I do everything to be free, so that they understand that I know what I want, how and why. It's hard. They take everything badly, but that's normal. There will always be tension between generations. In my opinion it's easier for children to understand their parents than vice versa. [Of course that is not always true.] *Udi, this is a difficult subject to discuss in letters. I hope we'll have better opportunities to talk. But seriously, do you agree? I didn't understand very well what you wrote: do you intend to leave home after college? How? Alone? Or . . .*

[Going away to college was anathema in Brazil; one lived at home and attended classes locally. Some years later, students from well-to-do families, or recipients of scholarships, attended college in the United States. For the most serious students, graduate school opened the world.]

I spent some nice days in July. But we had a little to-do with my little aunt (!!!) I will write about it in another letter. I am going to learn to drive; I don't know when. But I will. Yoni already drives and has a car. Day before yesterday he turned 22. His girlfriend turns 20 tomorrow. On Sunday we'll have a little gathering at his house for the two of them. We wanted to do it Saturday, but he had to intern at night.

Udi, don't complain about the distance to your aunt. It was worse before. You weren't even able to visit! But how is your grandmother? Now that you'll have a driver's license will you go get her? Your father must be very pleased, and you, too, right? Has he opened his garage?

You did well in your exams! (Although that's not news, right?) Here I am ashamed to write my grades, they were awful. With English and English Culture, I manage. Will complete the 4th level at the end of the year, and the 5th, Allah willing, in June next year. [The reference to Allah was a twist on the Brazilian custom to always say "God willing," that is, "se Deus quizer," with every wish for the future.]

The professor arrived. "Bai."

8/15/69 [continued]

Hello Udi!

Only now can I get back to the letter. It's a quarter past midnight. I returned from college, and here I am in bed with a glass of milk and a piece of cake (so I won't lose my "figure"!!!) I still want to study a little German. Tomorrow, I have an audio-visual in Spanish, then return at noon, then I go to Maccabi [pool club] *where I have gym at 2 p.m. In the evening it's the birthday celebration of our little friend, Miki. We bought her PJs and housecoat set (Rachel, George, Danko and I together).*

Udi, I'm so sleepy. I'll study till 1 a.m. (even then there's a radio program "Midnight Concert"). Write soon, I'd like our correspondence to be frequent now; write a lot, about you all, and give all my regards.

To you Udi, affectionate hugs, from your friend who misses you,

Elana

PS would love to get a photo from there! Thanks . . .

New York, August 1969

I started to write to Elana about visiting her the following year. This was still an early plan, and she and her parents were very happy. She was not reserved; a hint from me became a reality for her, even though there were challenges to overcome. At the same time, she still dreamed of us traveling somewhere outside Brazil, even though she did not have a passport. Elana's enthusiasm was boundless; it was outside rational boundaries.

This summer I worked in the office of the GM plant in Tarrytown, filing invoices when nothing was computerized yet. The summer that Americans walked on the moon, and almost five hundred thousand young people descended on Woodstock, created this American cultural bookend of 1969. I did not go to Woodstock, although I had college friends who went. When I heard what it was like, and how awful it was to try to leave at the end of the weekend, that's if you had a ride, I knew I made the right decision to avoid going, giving in to my timidity, and my queasiness with hippies. Even after a year of college, I could not transform into a hippie—they were too alien to me. I was still trying to get a sense of who Americans were. I was not one of them yet, still trying to find out where I fit.

São Paulo, August 18, 1969

Dear Udi-Udi!

First, I want to wish you a happy birthday, and everything good that you wish for. And that before we turn 20, we will meet. I think it will be hard to go from 1's to 2's. [From nineteen to twenties.] *Udi, apologies for the delay, of wishes for your birthday, and a Shanah Tovah wishes to all of you. These past weeks have been very busy. After English class today I stole away, wanting to send you a telegram. I wrote it, and I got sidetracked. I didn't know how much it would cost. So, I'm sending it enclosed here.*

I won't start saying a lot, because I'm standing here at the post office. I want to do it here, because if I write it at home, it will take more days to mail it, and my "shamefulness" won't do.

Udi, I sent you 2 letters and there hasn't been an answer. I hope you're not mad at me at what I wrote. And if you are, tell me, OK? I'll stop here, again wishing you happiness and a successful 5730 [the new Jewish year]. *I started with my "left foot," but who knows, will I follow with my "right"?*

A hug from your eternal friend who misses you,

Elana

PS Regards to everyone and Shanah Tovah

[A letter from me must have been lost or delayed.]

São Paulo, September 29, 1969

"Dearissima" Udinha!

[A portmanteau word, of English "dear" and the Portuguese suffix for "most" in the feminine gender. A *Portenglish*?]

"I also have just got your letter." [She writes this in English.] *(This is to start writing like you did!)*

And you know, I am so content. Don't know what, but your letter woke something in me. I was worried about the delay. But it arrived, let's go ahead.

It's 4:30 p.m. and I have very little time to write. I have a German test tomorrow, and I need a good grade, since the last ones were 5.5 and 4.0: bad, bad. And this evening I can't skip the class. Tomorrow morning, I have English class, Education Psychology in the afternoon.

The matter is to pass the night (awake). And worse still, I woke up today with a bad cold that bothers me.

Udi, I am super happy with your decision, and I am sure that here or in Europe, we will have wonderful travels together. [I was aware of her mix-up with my planned visit and her wish to go to Europe.]

9/30
I could not continue yesterday. I return now. I am lying about 9/30. It's already 10/2. Past midnight.

I got a 10 in Educational Psych, but the German test went poorly. It's awful I did not open the Psych book, and I studied the German quite a bit!!! I don't know why it happens to me, if I study, it goes badly, and vice versa. But enough of complaining. The business is to study for next time.

Udi, I understand completely what's going on between you and your parents. I give you credit and admire your decision. [I wonder what I told her!] *But Udi, remember, you're a university student, your parents were not. You're in a phase now of surpassing their education. Analyze the period they lived through, and what you live through. They have lived for only you, now more than ever. And they know that any moment you will escape them. Udi, put yourself in their place. More in your mother's place. I think most of your troubles are not with her, right? You are right, I respect that. But it would be easier for you to understand your mother's attitudes than she yours. You know how difficult it is for her suddenly not to be needed in going with you to buy clothes. These are little things, but for her they're enormous, thoughts she harbored and calculated ever since you've existed.*

Udi, if I tell you this it's because I remember your parents, and the attention and love they had for you. I would love to be talking to you in person now. But . . . can't . . . but will, eh?! What I tried to say, but didn't express clearly, is this: adhere to your independence, your ideals, opinions, personality. But don't flaunt it at home, because without intention, you're offending your parents. Yes, show your independence. But show that they continue to be your parents, and that you accept everything, and you owe them your independence.

Udi, it's easy to talk; I talk, but act completely differently. Here, too, I have the daily fights for the littlest thing that only I could avoid. Udi, gaining independence and being independent are two different things. Our parents are not helping either in action or thoughts for us to gain it. And if we already experience it, they're offended. I just re-read what I wrote and I'm not sure I expressed what I wanted to.

Now I'll go sleep, because it's 1 a.m. and I have English at 8.

Ah! tomorrow I start tutoring at a Vocational high school, 4th year.

"Bai" Udi, I'm dying to sleep. I already turned off the light, but remembered your letter, and felt like writing. But now: xxxx . . . "Bai" until tomorrow!

Hi, 10/1!

Udi, just to finish from yesterday: can you imagine what it is like for a mother and father to notice their child does not need them? Udi, I'm saying all this without knowing all your problems with them. I imagine I know. Maybe I am completely wrong, and if yes, don't take it the wrong way.

Changing subject:
When dad woke me up this morning I was ill disposed. I decided not to go to English class. I got up and practiced piano until now, stopping at every musical interval to blow my little nose (pfoo!!)

Udi, I am preparing a mini concert with my friend Marie Claire. And now that you will come, I'll see if the concert can take place when you come in July. That way, my first concert (if you can call it a concert, in any event), will be dedicated on my part to you.

As for Miki, it's been a while since I saw her, last time was at Danko's birthday, 9/7. I think she's still engaged (I don't know if the engagement is official, or an understanding between them. When they first appeared with a ring, they said it wasn't official, but this has been a while.)

...

Miki is going to Miami, Florida, to join her newly married mother (at the end of '69 or early '70).

His name is really Kaplan Danko. He's 23 years old. His Portuguese is now better, he goes to the Roosevelt [school]. *We only talk in Hungarian, and when I hear him in Portuguese, I split my pants. He will not take the Vestibular yet this year. He's working in an electronics lab, and he wants to bring his parents here. That's far away, since he'd have to support their trip and life here; it would be very expensive. But he will succeed, because he wants to. He came here via Vienna. On 10/6 it will be 3 months that we're dating.*

Udi, I'm afraid. It has never worked out for me. And if this ended now, I . . . I don't know, I don't want it to happen, because I really like him. Every day is an expectation for another day. I know what I want (more or less). Profession, I have—piano teacher. I'm not saying that this will turn out excellently, but it will be enough to live on. You know I don't desire a lot. In the future I'll teach English (besides, I'm starting today), maybe even Portuguese (although I doubt it because I don't love it), and German. I am studying calmly, because I don't have a career choice hanging over me. And when I'm fixed for income, that is, when I think I'm making enough, maybe I'll start studying Psychology or Education. As you can see, Udi, I am already earning a little (in truth almost nothing), and I'm studying, and I intend to do this until . . . who knows.

As for you, I think when you finish college you will have a career. You're not sure that you'll want to teach; why not? Teach Linguistics, since you like it so much! In the meantime, do research, and . . . I don't know, Udi, I think that with what we studied, especially you, it will allow for doing a lot of things. Small things that you like (I say small things because teaching is not necessarily full time), and you can study something else, and so on. In this respect, I'm optimistic, maybe too optimistic. Maybe one day I'll stumble. Maybe not.

Yes, my phone is 2207060. I will find out how much it will cost to call there [USA]. *If it works, OK? Danko's parents will call him on the 25th from Czechoslovakia. It will be about $40 for 10 minutes (If I'm correct).* [A large sum in 1969.] *And Czechoslovakia is far!*

. . .

You didn't write anything about your grandmother. How is she? And your aunt, etc.? I will stop here (only 6 pages!!!!) [handwritten] *it will soon be midnight, and I want to study a bit more. Udi, write quickly, and think hard. Tell me if I was wrong in what I wrote.*

A fond embrace, your friend always,

Elana

PS Do you have some photos? I'd like to see you. Right now, I don't have any, maybe soon. "Bai." Write soon!

New York, October 1969

Who needs a therapist when she has a friend like Elana who sounds like a (rather inexperienced) therapist? The irony is that my struggle for independence from my parents was not that different from hers. I know she bickered with her parents when they were strict. She admits it, but she stepped out of the role of a fellow nineteen-year-old and wrote to me like a very conservative and old-fashioned advice columnist who lived in another cultural milieu. I chafed at living at home with my parents. They stifled me with their neediness and their solitariness. They had few friends and few interests, and my father was constantly at work. They lived a quiet suburban life, and I felt trapped by it. I longed for more excitement. I longed to be living on my own, but I was too timid and still afraid of the world. Of all the ironies: I had seen more of the world than anyone else in my college class, but I had not yet learned to turn this fact into a strength and build self-confidence. I knew I needed to study full-time and not delay my graduation. By living at home, I did not have to get a job and cause this delay. I simply told myself to wait for graduation and manage my impatience. So, I poured my frustrations in the letters I wrote to Elana. Our letters, hers and mine, were full of contemplations about the future as adults, even if they sounded naive. I knew my future was going to be living away from my parents. I wanted to go away for graduate school, and that meant leaving home permanently. That was an "American" way. To Elana, that was incongruous: she couldn't fathom that I'd be living on my own away from my parents. For now, this was just a chink in our understanding of each other.

São Paulo, November 2, 1969

Dear Udi-Udi!

I received your letter day before yesterday, and I started to answer at night in bed. Result: I fell asleep on top of it. The past two weeks have been horrible. From 7:30 a.m. to 2 a.m. no stopping in running from here to there, to classes, giving lessons, preparing for lessons, studying. I should not have started to tutor just now, at the end of a hard year. It was a mistake, but at the same time the experience was worth it. We must take advantage of opportunities when they come. I give English lessons at a 4th year vocational high school. That's 8 classes a week to students who are behind. It's hard. They are horrible uncontrollable pests. But it goes, one way or another.

Yes, you are right about the phone, it would be silly, but an attractive idea. [Calling?] *Giving it serious thought, July is only 9 months away. Do you think we'll speak in Portuguese? And why not English? Yes, both. We'll find a way for you to remember Portuguese, and for me to improve English. Udi, will you really come here? We will really be seeing and talking with each other? And the dolls? I don't know where mine is. Ah yes, it's in a bag on top of the armoire. Udi, I'm so happy.*

You are right it's easier to pass Ed Psych than a language. I think I flunked German. Don't know yet. But most likely. I understood everything, and if I had the page in front of me now, I could teach it to a third person. But I had so much to do that I was not able to memorize and assimilate. It's a pity. One more thing to fall behind on.

Danko is here. Just finished writing home, and I think he's leaving it's already 10:30 p.m. I'll go downstairs, then come right back up.

November 3, 1969 [continued]

Yesterday my parents wanted to take some things to Yoni's house, so we gave Danko a ride. When we returned, I suddenly got very sleepy. This morning, after English, I went to the college to see about German. I flunked. And along with me, 100 others. I got a 4.5. Other departments allow at least a repeat, but not this one. I'll see next year how many will fight to get in (the freshmen and the repeating students). I don't know how I'll tell my mom.

Udi, I was really surprised at what you wrote. I didn't think the problem was with your father. I don't know what to say. I remember he used to like to argue. I remember it well. But my memory of you is about the two of you, arm in arm walking and talking, you asking him questions and he answering. And now I can't imagine you arguing.

So, did you finally choose Hebrew or Swahili? I would like to learn to read and write Hebrew. I am starting to have trouble speaking it.

Udi, I'd like to do so many things. And I start doing too many things at once. I look back, and what did I do? Nothing! Udi, really, I'm not being modest, it's true! Until today I don't play anything on piano the right way. English, I think I should know more after 10 years. College, I didn't take anything seriously, I managed to pass but learned nothing. I study. I am very superficial; I have not delved into anything. Now it's beginning to hurt. During vacation, I feel like staying home and trying to recover. It's time. I have written exams on the 18th and 19th and orals on the 4th and 12th. I think vacation will start on December 5th. A month from now. Hallelujah. Udi, I know my fear is nonsense. But it won't be the first time that I stumble. He [Danko] *gets upset when he notices I'm insecure. It doesn't matter what he says, I hope time will make this go away. You know, Udi, the better you have it, the more you fear losing it. On the 6th it will be 4 months that we are dating. When we reached 3 months, I asked if we'd reach 4, and then I asked if we'd reach 5. With summer coming, I'll start going to Maccabi (I stopped last month) and practice swimming. We'll take a photo together and I'll send it to you. If you have one, send me, too, and of your parents.*

Udi it's 1:35 p.m. and I must go give a lesson. Write soon, send lots of news which I wait for. A hug from your friend of yesterday, today (more than ever) and tomorrow.

Elana

PS Regards to your parents from me and my parents.

New York, November 1969

Sometimes, our letters caused misunderstandings due to language differences: my letters written in English, and hers in Portuguese. Elana was under the impression that I wrote of my problems with my mother (it's possible I didn't write clearly enough). It wasn't so; it was about my difference with my father and my need to live away from home. It could have been prevented by attending a university where students live on campus. By sophomore year, going to an urban commuter school posed this problem for me: living at home. Eventually I got a nice used car from my father—wasn't I an ingrate?—and I spent more time on campus with friends. I also had access to some cash from my father for buying lunch, books, and other personal needs. Looking back, I was fortunate; it wasn't so awful. I wasn't wise enough to deal with life at home. Elana pulled me back from the brink of frustration and impetuous rebellion.

[Postcard] *São Paulo 11/25/6*

On Saturday 11/22 I was going by the post-office and wanted to send you a card. I bought one, wrote it, and forgot your address . . . just remembered 34!! But I know your address by heart! Udi, I am during exams and start vacation on 12/5. Here everything is OK, I wait for your letters. I don't know when I'll go by the post office again, but I'll send this card soon. Udi, I wait for July as never before, and I already bought the music for the concert (recital). Do you have a preference? If yes, write me the title. A huge hug from your Elana

São Paulo, December 18, 1969

Dear Udi-Udi,

Funny, in the past I answered your letters because they came. I liked it, but didn't feel much. Now, I miss them, and you have no idea how happy I am when they arrive. Maybe because in the past we only wrote about day-to-day routines: "here everything is OK, this is what I read, this is what I saw, this is where I went, ciao." Sometimes it was different. But now, at great cost (and after so much time) we started to write about ourselves, about things we feel, and about our thoughts. I think it must have been hard because of the age when we separated. An age when we just stopped playing with dolls, and didn't know whether to leave them behind, and we started to notice other things. I say "we," I speak for myself, at least that's how I feel. Now that we have other objectives, and the world is different, everything is different, but it's hard via letters to remain the same, to see how things are not how they were. But I think we succeeded, and it was you who opened up first. Sometimes I wonder how it would be had you stayed here, if I would feel the same way about you, the way I feel now. And now I ask myself how things will be when we're together next year, will we be able to speak wholeheartedly. I know it will be wonderful. I just wait for the day to arrive.

Do you remember that we sometimes argued? We'd be sitting a long time without resolving or talking. But now it won't be like this. Udi I am blabbing, ahead of time. But one thing is for sure: I am eagerly waiting for the day you arrive.

Tomorrow (it was going to be today, but ex-president Costa e Silva decided to die today), dad is going to the office to arrange for my emancipation (giving me the legal rights of 21 even without them getting me citizenship), and the following week I will bring all my papers to the dispatcher and take care of my own naturalization. Hallelujah!! This is after imploring my father for two years.

I also start my driving lessons tomorrow. That way we will be able to go every which way, South or North. Udi, seriously, I don't know any place, and depending on how long you will be here, we'll be able to do a lot. I also want to know how long you'll stay because of the recital. I know . . . it's still early. You know, sometimes I think and become so excited that I feel it's going to be tomorrow. In July '71 I hope to go there. No: I will go. There, we'll have no obstructions!

Udi, what have you thought about Europe? Do you think anything is possible now? Or maybe better to leave it for later? Do you have a chance to get a scholarship to go to France? Or Germany? Any place? Or 1/2 a scholarship?

How is it going at college? And piano? You haven't written to say what your favorite piece is. I am really on vacation. Udi I never expected so much from vacation, not even when I was preparing for the Vestibulares. And I never felt on vacation. But at the end of this year, I paid for a lot of things, I can't bear it. For the first time I failed, worse, I failed at something I was doing that should not have failed at: 1st piano, 2nd English, 3rd German, 4th Portuguese material. Just and just. Maybe it was piano and English tutoring that got in my way. Now on vacation I sleep about 8 hours a day, and I'm playing piano 2.5 hours and will increase little by little, following a rigorous schedule.

Udi, I'm going out with my mother. If I return, will continue today, if not, then tomorrow.

"Bai" Elana

Hi, Udi! it's almost midnight, I'm writing in bed, above my cover. I went with my mother to the house of a lady who sells clothes. (The Midnight Concert is about to start on the radio. Eldorado station, until 1 a.m. and I love the program.)

...

Don't worry about the winter. The beach is possible at times. Udi, before you come, I will maybe ask you to bring me some records, but there's time. I will buy a tape recorder, I think it's better than records, and more practical.

Udi, really, my writing changed. I don't know why. Yours has not changed. I also have all the letters, since your first one. It would be neat if you brought all the letters, and we read everything at one time. What do you think? I think we'd laugh a lot.

[The first time that reading the letters was mentioned between us!]

Udi, this is the last page in the pad, so I must stop. I hope you will answer soon, and you know during vacation it's easier to write, talk, tell. My mother wants to write (it's only been a few years!!) and I'll see she does it this time.

A huge hug, from this friend who wishes you the happiest 1970 and ... that in the middle of it we will meet.

Kisses,

Elana

PS regards to your parents and grandmother, and happy birthday to your mother.

I was already in bed and remembered to tell you. Flávia got married and is expecting a baby. 4th month, how about it? Yára also, and I think she already had the baby.

New York, December 1969

We were no longer adolescents. The tone and content of our letters transformed from the mundane and ordinary to revelatory. Elana liked to analyze every letter I wrote. She shared her life with me, with her opinions, and I did the same. But Elana often changed her mind from the beginning sentence to the end of her thought. She was brave and impetuous; I was timid and steadfast. I was a killjoy compared with Elana's irrational exuberance, and yet, that was not the tone I took in my letters. Mostly, I deferred to her expansiveness.

Some of Elana's nineteen-year-old friends started getting married and having children. I did not know anyone in my school or in my social environment who was married, let alone had children. The fact that two of her girlfriends were becoming mothers at nineteen was disagreeable to me, because it showed me that my mother's teen marriage and pregnancy was not out of the ordinary. I just believed it was. I considered my mother a child raising a child, luckily with the help of her own mother. I wanted to break that cycle, and a college education and an advanced degree, in my opinion, were the way to do that.

This seemed to be a diverging social difference between the two cultures we were living in. That's not to say pregnant nineteen-year-old Americans, married or not, were rare; it's simply to say in my environment, I didn't know any. I only knew young women in my college. I had known Flávia when I lived in Brazil, but not well, and had no opinion about her life. All I remember is that her parents may have divorced, and she was living with an older sister. Education was not a priority in Flávia's family. By contrast, Elana's parents drove their children to study hard. It seemed to be all dependent on the parents' expectations.

For Elana and me, the expectations set by our parents were paramount: to get a higher education and to establish a career. Elana's plan was to be a piano or English teacher. And yet, her brother aspired to a medical career, and nothing stood in his way: no social encumbrances or any intellectual barriers whatsoever. What were Elana's barriers? Maybe her parents did not expect as much from a daughter as they did from a son (Vera used to express her wish for Yoni to become a doctor). Her only barrier was mostly ruled by her personality and her priorities. Yoni was unwavering in his focus. Elana was now in love, and even piano playing was getting in the way.

As a new decade was dawning, Elana's future was cast. Mine was not. At least, I believed my possibilities were limitless, albeit mysterious. And as time unfolded and I immersed myself in feminist literature, I was ready to ride the feminist wave. That's not where Elana was heading. My interest in feminism was a departure from our shared interest. We were beginning to diverge due to our cultural and educational environments without being aware of it for the time being.

Elana mentions that Brazilian president Artur da Costa e Silva died. He was the second military dictator after the coup of 1964. He was replaced by Emílio Médici, and his authoritarian military dictatorship continued until 1974. The right wing's grip on a dead democracy continued. Elana never expressed an opinion about the form of government that ruled Brazil for more than a decade. She did not care to discuss "politics" or history in the making, and so we did not. I doubt I shared with her my deep dislike of the new president, Richard Nixon. I doubt I shared with her my strong conviction that the war in Vietnam was a deadly mistake. I doubt I shared with her how the country was divided by pro- and antiwar sentiments. We wrote frequently, she more than I, and we wrote personal and confiding letters about our activities, the people close to us, our feelings and our dreams.

In her long letters that she wrote over several days, sometimes falling asleep as she wrote, Elana bemoaned the fact that she failed several classes and needed to retake them. But she was also busy with teaching piano, English, taking gymnastics, or harmonica, or starting a musical ensemble, or countless other endeavors, while dating someone she was in love with and participating in their social scene. Her life was full.

First Reunion: Testing the Limits of Friendship

São Paulo, January 1970

Dear Udi-Udi!

I was sure I already sent a letter. I got the pad to write to Rachel, and there was yours still not sent.

First, best wishes for 1970 to be a year full of happiness, pleasure, prosperity for you and yours, and this year that will also be our reunion. Amen.

Udi, what did you do during the holidays?

I'm alone, because my parents went with Yoni to Guarujá [beach town]. *He will spend a week there with his fiancée, Tzipora, and her parents! Since there was no room in their car, with him having a leg too badly injured to go by bus, my father decided to take him. Danko was going to go with me, but since I stayed behind yesterday, I decided it wasn't worth going there, so my mother went instead. Danko will arrive here soon, and we'll go out, don't know where.*

Miki left today: Miami. We did not go to the airport, with no lift, or driver.

Danko arrived. I'll stop now, and I hope you don't follow my example. Write and send soon!

Udi, a big hug from your friend forever,

Elana

PS Regards to your parents and grandmother

"Szerbusz" Danko [written by him in Hungarian].

Postcard:

Itanhaém [beach town] *1/11/70*

We are in Itanhaém, swung by the town where I bought this card. Do you remember? We were scared out of our wits of those gray bugs. Now I'm no longer scared. But I'm afraid of falling. I went there with Danko yesterday. But the "bed" [a place at the rocks] *was occupied! It's full of tourists here. I've been here since the 7th, with my parents and grandfather. Danko came Friday night. Soon we'll go to Guarujá to get Yoni. They will all return to SP because vacation is over for them, and I'll stay with Yoni's girlfriend at her place. I'll mail this from Guarujá because the PO is closed today. Waiting for your letter.*

A big hug, Elana

New York, January 1970

January is summertime in Brazil. The city of São Paulo is not that close to the coast, but outings for beach vacations were common when we lived there and thereafter. Beaches were a means of escape from the stifling, immense metropolis, and Elana mentions many beaches in her letters. Some I knew and some were new to me since leaving in 1964. The old beaches we used to visit were no longer as pristine in 1970. The exotic and unpopulated beaches we used to go to in the state of São Paulo were outliers and barely inhabited then, but that eventually changed after I left.

In New York, we found beaches for daytime jaunts on Long Island, such as Jones Beach. In Brazil these were not daytime jaunts. One had to stay in a hotel or be a guest at someone's beach-town apartment.

While Elana was on summer vacation that included many beach visits, NYC was plunged into winter. The Christmas of 1969, like other years, we drove to Michigan to celebrate with my relatives. Gitta would put up a Christmas tree, and on the evening of the 24th we'd exchange presents. There was no Menorah anywhere in sight.

Gitta and Egon, my aunt and uncle, did not live Jewish lives in Michigan. And my cousin, Jack, had not been bar mitzvahed. Not only did they keep their religion hidden, but they didn't celebrate privately either. They landed in Michigan after immigrating to the United States in the late 1950s, when immigration quotas for German-born and other northern European petitioners were generous. My uncle was born in Germany (actually, in Prussia) and his brother, Heinz, had become an American citizen and worked as an engineer at Ford headquarters in Dearborn. Therefore, Heinz was able to provide Egon and his family with an immigrant sponsorship. Heinz was aware of the rampant antisemitism at Ford, a racism that pervaded the company from Mr. Ford downward into the ranks. In Ford's publication, *The Dearborn Independent,* Ford blamed Jews for everything that ailed the country and its culture. In 1938 Ford was the recipient of the Grand Cross of the German Eagle given by the Nazi regime. Nevertheless, Heinz helped his brother to adapt to American life but extracted a promise from Egon to keep his religion under wraps to protect his career, and my uncle was happy to oblige. Heinz, passing as Christian in public, denied ever being half-Jewish. With his history as a Jew hiding in a Berlin cellar from 1941 to 1945, while his father was shipped to Auschwitz and gassed, he was helped by a Righteous Gentile. It's conceivable this affected him psychologically. He died by suicide in 1983, leaving a former German wife and their son, and an American wife and young daughter.

São Paulo, January 27, 1970

Dear Udi,

Every day your arrival seems more real, concrete, true, and the expectations increasing. I received your letter today, and there was a fight at home. I doubt we'll go to Europe. Udi, since July of 1968 I've been asking my father to have my passport arranged, and my naturalization is a prerequisite. I've asked this from time to time until Sept '69 when I started to implore every day. Did you arrange it? No. Until now he'd always say: Tomorrow. Now he says "today." Soon he'll say, "yesterday," but I don't see papers or anything. In the end, this summer there's less than 1% chance of going. I'd like to. But thinking it through, there's only one month before classes start again, as you remember.

Udi, it seems to me that for both of us there's another 2 or 3 years to finish college. In '70, you come here, in '71 I will go there, then we can think about studying abroad together. Let's take advantage of visiting and studying, and time will not stand still. These are just words, a lot of things can happen before, to help us go earlier or later. We'll talk about it when you come. I hope it will be decided at my house by end of February whether we go to Europe or not.

But if it doesn't work, there is a lot to do here. I got my license. I had 11 lessons and took the test on Jan 22. I passed and today I'll go pick up my license. Won't have to rent a car, dad has one and Yoni another. One of them will be available. But there's another problem. Will my parents let the two of us travel alone? Well, I don't want to discuss this with them for now, I'll wait, with the approach of your arrival their excitement will grow, and as a result there will be more concessions. Either way, we'll manage. Or I will arrange with the group, or Yoni, who knows. We'll find a way, I am positive.

...

I am at Rachel's house now. Did I already tell you she went to London to learn English? Well, before the course was over, there was a widespread flu epidemic and she's very susceptible. So, her parents left earlier and went to meet her in Zurich. Her mother started to refurbish their bedroom and had to quit in the middle. She asked me to come by often to check up on the housekeeper. I come every afternoon, I study, read, or . . . write. It's nice and peaceful here. Rachel's aunt comes by here in the morning, and George comes by in the evening.

Speaking of George, I don't know that they're going there [NYC]. *I think you're mistaken. Maybe it's someone else. Udi, yes, there are classes in August, but that won't prevent us from going out. Usually at the beginning of the semester there's little work, no tests, and nothing that would keep me at home. But we would only be able to leave the city on weekends. Udi, now I thought about this: maybe in July we'd go South: Uruguay, Argentina? OK. First, I have to check at home. I always have ideas, and then I doubt them myself.*

...

How is your course in Portuguese? Do you understand better? I'm sure you do. It's just about getting used to hearing it.

...

How are your parents and your grandmother? You never write about them. Udi, I'm going to ask you to bring me tapes (mini cassette). I'll write which songs in the next letter. I've heard them, they're old, but I love them.

Now I'll finish, because I have another letter to write and it's 5:10 p.m. Afterwards I'll go with Danko to Miki's "fiancé." Danko wants to go to the same college and will ask Peter for a "hand."

Udi, write soon and don't forget a photo you promised.

Here goes a huge hug, from your friend of yesterday, today and tomorrow who has her eyes and head in July.

Elana

New York, January 1970

In the last part of 1969, we started talking about a reunion in earnest, meaning that I would plan a trip to go visit her in São Paulo. Unlike the constant talk of her coming to visit me, which was always just talk, because she was still not naturalized and had no Brazilian passport, my intention was to fly to Brazil during my 1970 summer break from college and her winter season. Our vacations would overlap in July. It seems obvious that she also conflated my visit to Brazil with her enthusiastic wish to go visit Europe or other South American countries. To become a citizen and be eligible for a passport, she gave up on waiting for her father to get the paperwork done. In parallel, an American citizenship is what I wanted. It takes five years of residence in the United States to apply, and I knew this was on my agenda for 1972.

São Paulo, Undated 1970

Dear Udi,

I'm in the middle of Portuguese class and I don't understand a thing, since I missed the last 2 classes. Before I explain why I want to apologize, 1st because I haven't written, or answered your letter of birthday congratulations, and 2nd for waiting so long and making you worry. But Udi, so many things happen at once, I barely have time to breathe.

...

This month I started classes with Miss Margaret. She is well and very anxious to see you. She has a student who wants to know about Canada, he has a bar (here known as Hamburger, with a place to sit, drink and listen to music). You probably know what that is, since here everything is copied from there. Udi . . . no. I'll tell you later, otherwise I won't be able to write more.

How are your papers? Are there any problems? I hope not. A month from now I will be counting the days. I'm doing everything to be completely free in July. As for August, I thought this, we could leave São Paulo in July (e.g. Bahia, Brasília, North, South . . . we'll see what interests you) and in August we can see São Paulo. There are a lot of new museums. If I have a lesson maybe you'd be interested in coming with me, even at college they don't know who's a student and who's not. If this doesn't interest you, there are many things to do at home and elsewhere. You will not have lack of company. But I hope to have 3/4 time free in August. What I mean is that I want you to stay through August, or as your classes permit. Udi, if you have any ideas in mind, tell me.

...

[Continued on March 14]

I had to stop writing yesterday. Today classes end at 9 p.m. I must go to the post office, and to the telegraph office. Imagine I sent a telex to my aunt in South Africa, which arrived in 32 hours. I was so nervous and in a hurry that I did not pay attention.

I told you that my grandfather returned here, right? OK, last Thursday, that is, 2 weeks ago, he started to feel chest pain. They did an EKG and other exams, but everything seemed right. He didn't feel bad. Thursday he felt bad, and the doctor came and did an EKG immediately: everything OK. Two hours later, he felt unwell when I arrived from school (he was sleeping at Duque de Caxias). Only my mother and I were at home with him. He soon got better. When my dad returned home, he got worse, and my dad called Yoni at the other apartment. They came, and my brother got worried, and did everything he could. He sent my dad to buy injections, and called for an ambulance from the Hospital where Yoni works. They couldn't send one. So, Yoni and my dad carried the old man down the stairs in a chair [the elevator was too small]*, and my father drove the car onto the sidewalk, and they took him to the hospital. He got better and Yoni said he may return home the next day. On Friday he had another attack and an embolism, and on Saturday evening he died. It was all so unexpected and so quick, that today it seems like it happened a year ago. We visited him at the hospital, he was in a shared room in the ICU. I sent a telex to my aunt on Friday (we had already sent a telex warning her), and she called Saturday morning. We wanted to know if she wanted to come to the funeral. The telex arrived on Tuesday!*

Last month, it was dad who played with us. He had labyrinthitis, and he has very high blood pressure.

Udi, it's late and I still want to write to Miki. Write a lot and soon. Don't be like me, Udi, because it's awful waiting. I'm sorry I did it. Regards to all, from your friend of always, who wants to see you soon,

The "saudosa" Elana

New York, February–March 1970

Elana was not as upset about losing her grandfather as she had been when her grandmother died. Relatively speaking, he was young, in his late seventies. Elana seemed less attached to him. As she recounts in her letters, he went back and forth between South Africa, Brazil, and Israel, and was not comfortable for long anywhere, while he made everyone else uncomfortable with him. There might be another side to the story, there always is, but I could only see him as she described his vagabond life. Perhaps he was adrift, a Holocaust survivor aging and widowed. Without his wife he was a lost soul, finally dying in the proximity of his kind daughter, Vera.

In most letters Elana asked about Magda, my grandmother, a woman who was a very important part of my life. In 1970 she was fifty-seven years old, and still young. The loss of relatives was yet a long way in the future for me. I had very young, healthy parents, a young aunt, a cousin the same age as I, and most significantly, I had this young grandmother nearby. She was the anchor of the family. She and her two daughters, my mother, Edith, and my aunt, Gitta, were a matriarchal threesome. I enjoyed being in this midst, even if I took them for granted, although I knew very few families that were so grounded and lucky. Having a young grandmother made me different from my contemporaries whose grandmothers were distant, disregarded, disregarding, senile, or dead. For that reason, and for the fact that my mother was psychologically fragile, the three maternal figures in my life condensed into a compounded, triumvirate entity that kept me psychologically grounded and safe.

Elana loved old people, and she still does. I don't think her grandfather was an exception, but he upended the equilibrium in her immediate family for several years, so she was not effusive when he died.

São Paulo, May 18, 1970

Dear Udi,

The lesson ended sooner today, and so I have a free hour. I should be practicing. I practiced this morning. But I don't feel like doing anything. I was at Danko's house yesterday.

...

What do you think of the photo?

Ah, I don't know what to do. You know, Udi, ever since I started dating Danko, we meet every day. I don't think there have been even 10 days we missed meeting. Sometimes it's just to say hello, or meeting at the bus stop, on his way home. But... we meet. And today? No! He didn't even go to work, he had to help the uncle. And I feel like a cheap fool. But let it be.

This will be a tough week. I must submit work in Brazilian literature on the 25th. I hate working on literature. I like to study the language, read and comment. But under no circumstance do I like literary work. I flunked this last year. I like the theory, but not to put it to use.

You know the Hungarian Quartet is here, and I would love to go. But they only perform in the evening when I have class. They're staying till the 30th. Maybe one of these days I'll skip classes. They are very good; they say they're the best in the world interpreting Beethoven.

Udi, I'm scared about piano. I'm not sure my pieces will be ready. I'm studying, but they're hard. The Lower is scheduled for the 12th. The idea of this exam drives me mad. Sometimes the instructor gives tests in class, announces who failed, I've reached 70% and I've even "achieved" 40%! It's as if he's playing with luck instead of knowledge.

Udi, now I must go. I think my father will give me a lift. I hate that bus. They're crowded and on top of that those men have no shame. Sometimes when I get off the bus, I am in such a rage, I could cry. Is it the same way in New York?

Udi, write soon! How are your parents? Why doesn't your mother write? Tell her not to mind that my mother doesn't write. She already knows her!

Udi, write about how the documents for the trip are coming along. And here goes a huge hug from your friend who waits for you impatiently, and for always.

Elana

São Paulo, May 31, 1970

Dear Udi-Udi!

I opened your letter here at the table and Danko seeing "Nanica" said he will also call me that. I got mad at him and told him no one can call me that but you. He told me to write to you that I am being bad, that it's much worse than when you were here before, and he's happy you're coming, expecting you'll have advice on what he should do with me, to "educate" me, because he just can't stand it any longer. And he sends regards.

Do you see? What am I going to do with him? Udi, it's all a game! In reality, I talk so much about your arrival, about you and about us, that he's caught my contagious anxiety. We are all waiting for you. And that your letter will say "I will arrive on . . ." Udi, I will put a rubber hat on so when I read that, so I won't bang my head. It's soon, but it seems like an eternity. Udi, tell them in the office [Brazil consulate] *you're coming 2 weeks before, and insist! They can't impede our reunion!*

On June 12, I have an English exam. I don't think I'll pass. The course is short and I'm ill-prepared. If I pass it will be by luck. German is going well; I got a 9 and a 9.5. I now have a piano student for a July competition.

Udi, when I wrote about my grandfather, I was calm. I wrote a few days after it happened, and it may have seemed I was not emotional. But that's not so. It was so unexpected, so quick, but we were prepared and expecting it, so it didn't shock us. But we miss him and his little quirks. We always fought, but inside we always liked each other. I was much more affected when my grandmother died. Maybe because of the distance. Or because of her coming visit.

I know well how the situation is at college. We had this happening in '68 and '69. This year seems like it's going normally. But there's always something happening everywhere. I hate politics, even if I seem disconnected and disinterested. But I don't like it, and as much as I try reading about politics, I can't connect.

Udi, you seem to be preparing to speak Portuguese. But we will speak English, too, right? You'll teach me a lot, OK? I am not giving English lessons at school; I just don't have time. My parents and Yoni are doing well. Yesterday we went to the Municipal Theatre to see the Hungarian Quartet. Unbelievable! They played Beethoven, marvelously. Tomorrow Cziffra Györgyi will play, but we can't go, I must return a project.

...

I'm passing by the TV and it's Russia v. Mexico via satellite. Danko is rooting for Mexico today, but he's sure Czechoslovakia will win. We'll see. Udi, one more month and you'll be here!

Do you have a place you want to go see or something you want to do? Write all about it soon!

My mother got your mother's letter. She also misses our gatherings, our feasts and holidays. Now they're always home, reading or talking. Udi I've got to go home, it's late. Write a lot! When, where, how, everything! Even if I don't write.

I'm going to drop this letter off at the post office. "Lembranças" to everyone, tell your parents not to worry about you, my parents will watch out for you like they do for me.

Ciao, Udi, with THAT embrace from your friend who awaits anxiously for you.

Elana

WRITE A LOT!

Szerbusz [Hello/goodbye in Hungarian written by Danko.]

New York, May 1970

What was going on in American colleges: sit-ins!

American campuses were paralyzed with antiwar demonstrations. This letter was received right after the Kent State massacre. Many classes were canceled. The frenzy of student uprisings affected even my college, Lehman, a commuter school that could not ward off the sentiment that energized the well-to-do students at Columbia University, for example, and that erupted on most American live-in college campuses.

A twenty-year-old in bell-bottom jeans, tie-dyed shirt, bandana holding back long greasy hair, and beads around the neck, could be an affluent Columbia student or a working-class Lehman College student. The antiwar sentiment cut across all social classes, not just those cutting sociology classes. I did not wear a tie-dyed shirt, or bell-bottoms, and I didn't demonstrate. I was a new immigrant and not yet a citizen. Although I hated the rationale for sending troops there, and the thought of the gruesome fighting in Vietnam that was broadcast on nightly news, I felt somewhat removed from it and not encumbered to demonstrate. It was not my turn to make a political statement, I was still learning about American politics. I tried to attend classes, whatever classes were still in session, given by professors who felt guilty drawing a salary and not showing up.

Unlike Elana, I was interested in politics. I was fascinated by history, knowing I was living through such history in the making. I paid attention and I wanted to learn. I followed TV broadcasts, newspapers, the civic movements, and the parties. I leaned Democratic, because I thought Democrats had a kinder social conscience. At the time, Republicans supported corporate citizens and the rich, not working citizens. When Barry Goldwater was running for president spurting fired-up conservatism, covert and sometimes overt racism, I felt repelled by his demeanor and his ideology. The openly racist George Wallace was also running for president as an Independent, and he sounded evil. I was relieved when Goldwater lost. And when Hubert Humphrey lost to Nixon in 1968, I flinched about the future. I also cringed watching the demonstrations at the Democratic Convention in Chicago and the police actions that turned so violent. I could be a Green Card–holding immigrant and be interested in politics and elections, but I could not yet vote, so I thought I had no compelling reason to demonstrate and cut classes. In May 1970, the voting age was twenty-one, so most of my classmates could not vote either. The Twenty-Sixth Amendment that lowered the voting age from twenty-one to eighteen was passed the following summer, in July 1971.

While there was much turmoil on campus, I was deeply grateful to be attending college for about $250 per semester. I was grateful not to have to rely on my parents for full tuition—which they would have gladly paid—but mostly, for not having to be indebted to them. Put another way, I just did not want to cost my parents anything, and I didn't want to rely on their support. In short, I wanted no more than what my parents had already given, and they had given me a lot: I was showered with unquestionable love, and attentive fulfillment of all my minuscule needs. That's not to say I was ungrateful. I wished them to have more for themselves. But oh, how wrong I was! Giving was their raison d'être, and wrenching that away was to wound them deeply.

On another topic, when Elana mentions her rage when riding the buses in São Paulo at the men who have no shame, I sympathized. I'm not sure whether I wrote back saying that was not a major problem in NYC. Occasionally it was, but not to the extent it occurred in Brazil. There were other more concealed threats, especially in workplaces, and the solution for those hazards were years in the future and never resolved to women's satisfaction, either regarding sexual harassment or pay parity.

São Paulo, June 8, 1970

Dearest Udi-Udi!

"Yes, it was a very good work!"

Just received your letter. I can't believe it. It's just too marvelous. It's too good. It took a long time!

Udi, I can't even think straight. Can you imagine it? I am going to see you! We will be speaking to each other and see each other! Doesn't it seem like a lie? Spectacular! Udi, when are you arriving? Don't wait until July. The minute you get the visa, jump on an airplane! I will be free a week from now. The faster you come, the better. Even today or tomorrow! What's this story about visiting your aunt, when? for how long?

Udi, when I arrived from English class I asked the super if a letter came. No. I came upstairs and in 10 minutes the letter arrived. I re-read it aloud for my parents, and they all had goosebumps. I could hardly finish reading the letter. Udi, write soon! better yet . .. arrive soon! I think we will stay at the other apartment (a block away). It's nicer. Ah! you didn't say how long you can stay. Udi, it's going to be wonderful. I can hardly wait.

On Friday 6/12 and Tuesday 6/16 I have English exams. I think you know it: the University of Cambridge Lower Certificate in English. It's for a language diploma. The exam is from Cambridge, and they mark it there. It's hard, they expect a lot.

...

Ah, what do you think of soccer? If Brazil wins, I hope you will be here to see the partying. Yesterday they won against England and mass transit stopped. Everyone went crazy, even happier than during Carnaval.

Udi, I like Danko, don't you doubt it. I can't remember what I wrote to you to make you doubt it. Sometimes we argue. But I am the intolerant one, and I don't relent. We will talk about all this, OK? But don't think I no longer like him. I like him more than before. He's not perfect, has faults, big and small (like me), but what I like is that he tells me my faults and I tell him his. On 7/6 it will be 1 year that we've been dating. It's a record for me! He wants to study English. I'll send him the "English for Today" collection and maybe a dictionary, too.

I already wrote you a letter and I'll send it together with this one. Mom asked me to thank you for your condolences [for Vera's father] *and will write after the 12th. Until then she has a lot of work.*

We now have a TV. It was broken in the other apartment, but here we have a good one. Don't think that the only objective here is money. Everyone thinks that. Ah, talking about your grandmother, the other day I saw the man she dated, Dezsö Borgos. He gave us his number, so you'll call him here. He's 78 [my grandmother was fifty-seven in 1970], *and seems maximum 60.*

Danko loves old people. He likes the old as much as children. Udi, write soon, if possible, come already. Send a telegram, we wait for you any day any time. Seriously, I want you to arrive immediately. It won't be a bother here, even if you come in June, you can come to the college with me, maybe it will interest you.

Ah, I remember, Udi, bring clothing for summer, also. Last year at this time it was cold, but now I am wearing a light sleeveless dress. And as you remember, our days have 4 seasons. Udi, now I will really stop. It's already 1:40 p.m. and time to study. I expect news soon, preferably a telegram saying you're already coming.

I send "lembranças" to your parents, and don't forget to say my mother will write soon.

A hug, a kiss and a . . . immediately!

Your friend,

Elana

New York, June 1970

It is interesting that Elana mentions soccer. It was the summer of the World Cup, and Brazil was on the cusp of winning the "Copa."

Neither of us were avid soccer fans, nor fans of any other sports, for that matter. However, it is hard to live in Brazil and not be exposed to soccer fever. It is a game I still like and prefer to football or baseball. Neither of these American games have aroused my interest; after decades, I still don't understand their rules.

The foremost topic of our letters in mid-1970 was my upcoming visit to Brazil. Our suspenseful anticipation of a reunion was felt with unrestrained excitement and a whole lot of impatience for the obstacles in our way, including the uncertain plans we were tossing between us regarding what to do during the visit, or even the length of the visit.

Elana warned me to bring summer clothes in addition to winter. In truth, it turned out to be very cold, and I did not have the right clothing for July in São Paulo. Feeling the cold there, I had to buy a suit to wear to keep warm. The summer clothes came in handy when we traveled to northern Brazil.

My grandmother remained single after she cast Ziggi off when she found him dallying with a German woman in early 1964. She was fifty-one then and a very desirable woman, always vivacious, full of life, and a magnet for men. Just before we left, she met Dezsö Borgos, who courted her, but she told me he was too old for her. I didn't understand, the age difference didn't seem so wide to me then, although looking back, yes, he was twenty-one years her senior. But he was so debonair! He dressed in an impeccable style, he was gentle, unassuming, soft-spoken, but not timid. And he had money. I found him attractive (I was fourteen) and a perfect catch for my grandmother. This made me a clueless matchmaker. Instead, by 1968, my grandmother found another Hungarian man, who was the opposite of Borgos: crude, provincial, ugly in a rustic way, and he was also not Jewish. But she claimed they got married (thankfully they just pretended to). It didn't last long. She also discarded him; unlike Borgos, he was after money and a woman who'd support him. I hope he failed in cleaning my grandmother out, because she was savvy and had prior experience with dependent men.

São Paulo, June 13, 1970

Dear Udi,

My mother is going to the post-office, and I'll take advantage to send you a letter, too. Don't find it too strange, but I'm writing on my knees. Danko is sitting at my side.

Yesterday was my oral Lower Cambridge test, and it was so-so. Tuesday is the written, and then we'll see. They say it's very demanding, more than the orals. 1/4 who took the test yesterday are doing it for the second time. Can only take it a second time, if a person passed the other.

Udi, why don't we hear from you? When are you arriving? Mom is already making room in the closet in the other apartment. Yesterday Danko's uncle arrived from Czechoslovakia. I only saw him for a few instants.

...

Send a telegram right away, because we are waiting for you, and I want to SEE you when I talk to you. Lots of hugs from Elana, and this from the comic: [Danko's signature.]

São Paulo, June 22, 1970

Dear Udi-Udi!

Hell, I thought we'd be together already! Unbelievable, this bureaucracy. Isn't there something to do to make things go more smoothly? You said there's a short time, but it's discouraging! Udi, I was so disappointed. I thought we will not get more letters, just a telegram, and you. And now there is time to exchange several letters. The second week of July will arrive. Haleluya.

Udi, I was talking to my parents about going to Bahia, and north, to Recife. I have a friend there who will accommodate us. He stayed with us when he came south. I think I told you: Izinho. There are 2 brothers, and their parents seem sweet. But—there is always a but—my parents are telling me they can't agree, because the distance is too great, and they're responsible, and . . . and . . . and . . . whatever you want to fill in here. What do you think? What do your parents think? I did not argue a lot with my parents, because I wait to hear your opinion so I can argue better with them. And I thought it would be better for you to talk with your parents first, and then the 2 of us will talk to mine. If your parents don't allow us to go, maybe my parents will have a way, but who knows. Write to me about your opinion and your parents'.

You must have already gone to visit your aunt and uncle. How are they? and your cousin? You continue to get along well? How did you pass the time there?

Udi, I don't know where we'll stay. It looks like there's a buyer for the other apartment. I don't know if they'll accept just anything, I hope not. But it doesn't matter, because in my room (do you remember it?) two will fit comfortably. If he sells that apartment, my father will make a room here outside [by the entry of the apartment] *one way or another. Even now, Yoni sleeps where my parents used to be, I sleep in my room and my parents up front. My father cleaned out the corner near the entrance, and it's looking nice. There's a table, a sofa, chairs and the telephone. A little living room. So, if the apartment sells, we will be comfortable here anyway.*

...

Today I would have had a test for Brazilian literature, but not knowing if they'd call a holiday (because of the COPA) it was postponed [on June 21, 1970, Brazil won against Mexico].

Did you follow the games? It's a perfect Carnaval here, a mixture of holiday and celebrations. Even before the game in the interior, and on Saturday, all the cars were decorated with green, yellow and blue flags, everyone yelling The Cup is Ours! Brazil's third World Cup and so on. Imagine the hoopla when Brasil actually won. The noise was deafening. Mass transit was impossible, and the population went absolutely crazy. Impossible to describe. The sky was full of balloons, and planes were making pirouettes. It sounded like the whole of Brasil was declaring victory.

Udi, please don't worry about health and getting sick, and don't apologize. Apologize for what? This business of arranging travel documents is always like that. Sometimes it gets done in a week and at other times in years. You can only insist and sit on their head. Can I help from here? Mom says maybe a letter of invitation from us will help. What do you mean by writing Rx? You wrote: "How about that for Rx?"

The weather is great for now. I hope it continues like this. But even when it's cold here, for you it will be nothing, I think. [An impression about northern winters.]

As for presents, Udi, please, don't worry, believe me, you are the biggest present that you can bring. Nothing will satisfy me more than that. Maybe Yoni asks for something. He's not here now, so I'll ask him later. Your mom asked if we need razorblades. Last year my aunt brought so many that we still have enough for a few years! And now they have good ones here.

As for money, dad says bring money not traveler's checks. I'm writing this, because I don't know when mom can write, she's very busy. Udi, I will now put a period on this line, because I must study. Write soon, and if you can, send a telegram, which might be useless, if we know the date the time and airline via mail.

Excuse my errors and write soon. Here goes a big hug and kiss from your friend who can hardly stand keeping her arms down, because they want to rise and hug you.

Elana

PS "Lembranças" to your parents and your grandmother.

New York, June 1970

I do not remember anything about encountering bureaucratic problems for international travel. I repressed that memory. Were Elana's comments about this topic in anticipation generated by her excitement, or were there bureaucratic roadblocks I had to overcome in New York? I can't remember.

In 1970, I had a Green Card, which conveys a permanent US resident status, but I did not have American citizenship or an American passport yet. Brazil may have required a visitor entry visa, which would have compelled me to go to the Brazilian consulate in New York. I don't know what document I must have submitted. Did I get an Israeli passport in the meantime? Doubtful, because I did not serve in the army. I do have an Israeli passport, but how I got it occurred later in 1974. There were alternate papers for travel and for visas, sometimes called *laissez passer* documents, but I don't remember having those. We encountered the same problem when we had traveled from Toronto to Detroit before we got our Green Cards in 1967. Once we moved to New York from Canada, we experienced the welcomed relief that the Green Card provides the holder. But tourist visas, if required, need a document to be stamped in, and it's usually a passport. Perhaps this is the bureaucratic process that I described to Elana in my letters.

I know that my classes would have ended in early June, the end of my sophomore year at Lehman College. I think I must have flown to Michigan after the semester ended to visit my cousin and his family, but that was something I did frequently with my parents. My mother loved to visit her sister near Ann Arbor. We used to drive there, which my father liked doing, or I flew to Detroit when I went alone.

It was hard to fathom international travel, even in a modern 1970, one year after the first moon landing of the Eagle, while Apollo 11 circled above the moon. Today, we access an app on our phone and book a flight in seconds. In 1970, I used a travel agent my mother was friendly with in Tarrytown, New York, to book the flight.

I have made few comments about Elana's letters, because each described a frenzy of expectations and anxiety, eagerness, and suspense. I was excited too. And nervous about my first international trip alone. But it was Elana who expressed her feeling with such unrestraint and with such abandon. It was a childlike trait, and in a way, Elana was the forever child, and I was forever the grizzly. She lit me up, her fire kept my excitement alive.

Elana described in this letter the Carnaval atmosphere of winning the Copa in 1970. Brazil eats and breathes soccer. It could have been similar in the summer of 2022; however, Brazil lost the World Cup to England in the final. Over fifty years had passed since it had won the Copa, and that's a long time to wait for another win. The disappointment in 2022 must have been intense. Not just losing in soccer, but at the end of a very contentious Brazilian election that mimicked American elections in 2020: a political nightmare replete with fake news, allegedly stolen elections, violent attacks on democratic institutions, and a frenzy of misinformation spread on social media and consumed by enraged or unsophisticated people.

This was the last letter before I arrived in São Paulo in the Southern Hemisphere's winter of July 1970.

São Paulo, August 22, 1970

Dear Udi,

Funny, it's just like before: just letters. It seems you were here for just a tiny second, a quick glance. And now, it's just college, English, piano, students. No Bahia, no emotions. Udi, you say that you loved everything, and you're happy. Udi, I know that I failed in many ways and with some you were displeased, and some didn't go right. I also know that after a trip like this, only the best memories remain, even if there were obstacles. Udi, I ask you to please tell me how I let you down, because at the time, you shut down your thoughts. Now, from far away, it may be easier to be critical, and for me to accept it. And vice versa.

For me, Udi, we are exactly as we used to be. I felt about you as I did 6 years before. With the difference of being conscious of facts that I did not know before. The same friendship . . . the same disagreements. But even a rose has thorns. And we are roses (!)

Udi, I really hope you had a good time, despite some regrets. That was my intention. And I ask you to really write what you think. Rest assured I will answer. This you know, right? But let us go on. When did school start? Are you free? And piano, did you give your teacher the music yet? For me, everything started and very intensively. Work upon work and many tests.

. . .

Ah, do you know the card I said I wrote last week . . . it's here! Together with a letter I was sending to Miki. Remember? I was wondering why she wasn't writing! I left them in the German book, and I only noticed during the first class. We are having fun with the "stuff" [things I brought]. *You are too much! Thank you.*

Is your grandmother's sister there for a visit or to live? I will do what you asked about Mr. Borgos. And with that I'll send you film. We are now going to the PO, and I await an answer.

A hug as big as an elephant, from your friend,

Elana

PS "Lembranças" to your parents and grandmother.

Regards—Danko [in Hungarian]

New York, August 1970

This is what I admire about Elana, a trait that I lack: the ability to admit shortcoming and ask for an honest appraisal and critique in order to improve.

As much as we were stupefyingly anxious about meeting again after six years, the obvious reality, as Elana explains so well in this letter I got after returning home, is that we were still the same. If we had arguments before 1964, then we had arguments in 1970.

However, we are very different from each other. Elana is slow and deliberate. I am quick and resolute. She dawdles; I jump ahead. She weighs all possibilities; I instinctively pick a course of action. I don't think I'm impetuous. Some people would say that I am, it's just that I analyze a situation and see different outcomes quickly. Elana will take forever to buy something, mulling it over and over and weighing pros and cons, price, and emotional need. I either buy something or quickly decide it's not worth it or I don't really need it. I think quickly (not always correctly); Elana thinks slowly (sometimes paralyzingly so). I get ready in a jiffy. Elana packs and repacks as if every item were precious and should never have a crease. I am always on time (not so as I age), and Elana is always late. I also have a keen sense of direction (a trait I inherited from my father), while many people don't—maybe I was a migrating bird in another life? I assert myself when it's a question of which direction to take, and sometimes my companions will dissent, Elana being one of the skeptics.

None of this should have been a surprise to us, but it was. I tend to give the impression I have an attitude. I don't mean to show this posture. I've been told that all my feelings and thoughts are written on my face. I don't seem to be able to dissemble in appearance; I am a terrible actress. If Elana was late, I bet I said something, or I tapped my toes and crossed my arms, or lost my smile. And yet none of this was of any consequence, and I was never bothered for long. We had a stupendous trip. The months of Elana agonizing about this, that, and the other thing was of no concern in the final analysis. Everything worked out, even as she agonized about every decision.

Did I arrive with some expectations? Yes, I did, I arrived with an American mentality: two twenty-year-old women could get a car and drive around the United States; two twenty-year-olds could make travel plans and follow them. That was naive on my part.

I stayed at Elana's parents' apartment, sharing her bedroom, while Yoni was in the other room, and her parents in the newly organized entry room. My being there disrupted their living arrangement. Ernö would under no circumstance allow us to take a car and drive to northern Brazil! My parents had no input into my trip, and Elana's worries about what they allowed or did not allow was a moot point. I was independent minded. Was I more so than Elana? That was a shocking revelation. Perhaps I was a twenty-year-old American college student simply and unequivocally of her own mind.

I went back to a country regulated by patriarchy and authority (Brazil had a military dictatorship with a junta ruling for the sixth year), and the fear of allowing women to travel by themselves was deeply felt. With enlightened, but overprotective, Jewish immigrant parents who survived the Holocaust, Elana and I were not to go off on our own, as per her parents. She was terribly disappointed. I went with the flow. It was not up to me to be mad at them. I just wanted to manage in the context of Brazilian mores. I figured if Elana ever came to see me in the United States, we'd be free as birds. I accepted my hosts' terms.

And so miraculously we found a way out. Or as they say in Portuguese, we found a "geito" (solution). We signed up for a bus tour to Bahia. And we had a blast.

If I wrote to Elana that I had a good time, I meant it, even if she didn't believe me. She dwelled on the rough patches; I dwelled on the fun it was to see parts of Brazil I had not seen before, such as São Salvador de Bahia, the historic and very quaint colonial capital of the state of Bahia. With the food, the sights, the Capoeira performances, the exposure to the religious practices of the descendants of African slaves, it was beyond exotic, but authentic, in an age before mass tourism. Traveling with Elana was a dream come true, and with other agreeable people in the group that was a bonus. We did have a good time. But as Elana ruminated after the fact, I basked in the travel afterglow.

We bickered over our differences (as I expressed above), but they were not important differences. Elana is incredibly sensitive and wanted to talk about it, as in an exit interview. Of course, I am also sensitive to differences and show impatience, followed by being reticent for about an hour or two, but then I forget all about it and its importance vanishes in my mind. Then in a spiral, Elana is sensitive to my temporary closure, granted, one of my bad traits. But after going silent and stewing a little, I then forget it and am back on track.

Bahian food, with deep African roots, is exotic, spicy, and has complex flavors imparted by the oil of *dendê* (red palm oil) used in cooking by the local women wearing colorful clothing and head wraps. The vision of these authentic women was spoiled by the films with Carmen Miranda (she was Portuguese, not Brazilian) who wore ridiculous getups with fruits on her head. In Bahia, I was introduced to the delicious *moquequa*, a fish stew. At one point after a wonderfully spicy lunch, I had diarrhea and felt very sick (not because of the spices, but because of the local water). Elana seemed very attentive, sympathetic, and patient. Or at least that's how I remember it. More about it in the next letter.

I had a camera with me, and I took a lot of wonderful pictures. Everywhere I turned, the sights were a photographer's dream. The numerous small Baroque churches, with exteriors painted blue and white, had interiors dripping in gold that could take your breath away. When I put them in an album, I was able to look at them and relive the trip for a long time. I've always been organized that way. It's another difference between Elana and me. I save, organize, and remember how to access things. The story of the photos and the negatives required for making prints was an ongoing saga between us for several more years. I never got the negatives back for years. I should check if I did get them, since I still have all my developed negative filmstrips. Elana loses track of things, including my letters. This is not a criticism. Maybe I'm the one who has an obsessive compulsion to organize things, and I know it drives some people to piqued distraction. For example, some find my stashing everything in its rightful place a useless endeavor to be despised, because things stashed away become invisible.

São Paulo, September 20, 1970

Dear Udi-Udi,

First of all, rest assured: everything is OK the film negatives arrived.

Udi, I know I should have written this a long time ago, believe me, last Sunday, I sent you a greeting card (I hope you received it) which Danko took to the PO. And imagine, I forgot to say in it two words: negatives arrived. I remembered about it too late, and I ask you forgive me, Udi.

The negatives that I had with me will be mailed today. In the last letter, the envelope was too small, and they didn't fit. I already gave that photo to Borgos. Before leaving, he went to the toilet, and . . . when entering there afterwards I found the envelope he forgot. We laughed a lot. In 5 minutes, he returned to claim the envelope with the photo.

Udi, your last letter made me so happy. First, because of the contents. Second, because of the time I read it. I arranged a new English conversation student, and I had just returned from the first lesson. I was tense because she's a 19-year-old and was knowledgeable, and I don't speak English fluently. Aside from this, September was awful.

...

Yesterday the weather was so nice that we took advantage: we went to Maccabi. And today I got up at 10:15! But now, enough. I now write to you, then have lunch and then will take studying seriously. Piano is a little neglected, unfortunately. Ah, what did your teacher think about your music? [I brought home sheet music of Brazilian composers, such as Heitor Villa-Lobos, to study with my piano teacher.]

Udi, as for the topic of your last letter, you know, you moved me. I didn't know that's how you felt. I won't be gentle or fool you. You know how it is or it's not. And you know me well. Yes, Udi, I tried very hard to make you feel good, but many times, I went amiss. Even if I didn't want to, I was momentarily forced to, and for this I ask forgiveness. Udi, it's not just you who feels bad when you're disappointed. I am too. And maybe that's why we sometimes have the disagreeableness between us. But Udi, as the poets say, every rose has its thorns, and so does friendship.

You know, Udi, when thinking it though, the fact that we show disappointment, shows that we actually care. Sometimes we don't like something, or don't want to do something, but we do it, why? to seem gentle, good, etc. Yes. And if we don't do it, then we confide in our companion, and expect her to understand. Udi, what was missing between us was a little maturity in the friendship. It's been 6 years since we've known each other well and we understood each other's nature. But now the rhythm of our friendship did not change. But time and distance made us ignorant of our attitudes and ideas that we have gained since then.

Udi, if I tried to make you feel well, it was not out of gentility or goodness, or even duty. No. Never. Udi, I wanted so much, for so long before we'd meet, that we'd spend time together (and Udi believe me, I am now pleased, I am not disillusioned), and what I really did (and still do) was spontaneous and not calculated.

September 22, 1970 [continued]

I had to stop. I'm just returning now. To continue what I was saying, you know, it's been years since I had such a vacation like this. For now, I was free, completely free, without compromises (even the one that took me half a day) and I had desired for anything, i.e. everything (nothing = everything, right?) I wanted for you to take me, for you to tell me what to do. That is, I wanted to do what you wanted to do. Not out of gentility. For carefree relaxation, Udi. Because in reality, I had no preference for anything in particular.

Udi, you said that "you practically forced this trip." Never, Udi. I wanted this trip so much. Very much. I don't repent anything. Everything was perfect. And please take out of your head the idea that we did something bad to my father. He's better than ever. Where did you get this idea? Yes, he and even my mother had headaches. In the end, look at where we went and what distance! But my father finally has nothing wrong, amen! In addition, they're satisfied now and are pleased that everything went well. You ask if there was a way to avoid any of this. It wasn't about us avoiding something, my father had no problem at all! And second, I think everything came out the best possible way for all of us, except for Dankochko, but that was unforeseen, and finally, everything came out well and good.

Udi, my parents were not "against the trip." They were against us being alone, which in the end, you and I have to understand. Parents will be parents, from one century to another. You saw how once we decided to go with a tour group, they were less concerned. Otherwise, their hesitation, that's normal and ordinary here. Even when it's about minor and easy things, or unimportant, the uncertainty, the disequilibrium is always present. So, no, no, we should not have backed out. I don't say that out of selfishness. In the end we caused no one any harm.

Udi, as for the fact of being sick, don't apologize. It's the same with me, at least this time I got luckier than you, and I didn't catch anything. Maybe this time you were a little weaker, and were more affected, but in the end, you didn't ruin anything for me. Only my reaction seemed to be impatient, nervous, obstructive, wanting to discuss things. I know I am like you, and it's hard to look in the mirror. But this wasn't consciously done. Instead of helping you, I was showing that I wasn't happy with you getting sick. Let's not be modest, you have, had and always will have, just like me, and like everyone else, (in different degrees) your caprices. What was missing was for me to be understanding, patient, and who knows . . . You understand, right?

Udi, I don't know why, but not just when you were here, the whole first semester, I've been like this. You saw it: I argue with everyone, and especially with Dankochko. All it took was for him to open his mouth and BOOM, I blew up. You know that time in the taxi? That hurts me to this day. This never happened before. It's a terrible sensation. But now everything is OK. We hardly argue, and if we do, it's in friendly terms, finally arriving at an understanding.

When you had that conversation with my mother, Udi, I wanted you to tell me, and so it irritated me a lot. Yes, I recognize it, I know my parents' opinion of him. I know more than they say. I know they find him incapable, without initiative, conformist, and accommodating. I know all this, but I wanted you to tell me. Maybe you heard something else. I would have felt better about it. But now it no longer matters. If you thought you shouldn't talk then, you have your reasons. Now that I've unloaded about this topic, I'll desist. Udi, I know Danko very well. I know he's weak in some respects. But Udi, I really like him. I would not be able to leave him. I don't know what it is, but something pulls me to him, but everything is clear. I'm not blind. I know the weaknesses, the faults, and his foibles. But Udi, am I looking for a companion or for support? Oh no. At least a companion. That's all. Nothing else. He is honest, good, factual, and I don't know. I love him. Why do I study? because I don't want a husband to support me completely. I work for my clothing, shoes, and other whims. I will help. I'm studying a subject that will allow me to work even with 10 children. Udi, I'm sure of one thing. I will always be independent. I won't have a husband to be dependent on as a first objective. I will continue to study and work, that will be compatible with housework. Maybe my parents don't understand this; they don't have confidence in me? That hurts. But the day I can prove it will come soon. Maybe in less than a year. I can't do that here in my parents' house. I adore them, I don't blame them for anything. I was born different, with different tastes and different impulses. Not with different ideas. I wouldn't want to be educated differently. I'll give it a go. Maybe there is a little less understanding on their part for some of my attitudes, and some aspects of my character. I grew up always hesitating, always fearing doing something wrong, uncertain. Maybe I did not demonstrate enough sufficiency for them to notice. They don't understand me in that respect, they're not psychologists. But it didn't faze me. I see it in myself, and I try to change internally. If they don't see this side, I understood them, they had more important things to do. I am grateful to them, and I understand why they found me at fault in many aspects. It hurts to think I cannot yet comfort them; this has been happening for years. But soon everything will fall into place. They deserve comfort and peace. The fear they have when their children enter life on their own (not marriage per se, but studies, expertise, etc.)

Udi, I said too much about myself. I must turn to us. I don't think we have reasons to apologize for, or to be sorry for, or to defend any slights. Everything including misunderstandings, will serve to be more intimate and mutual.

I now have to go. I need to see Miss Fleury. She called me yesterday; she saw in a magazine that a student was looking for a piano teacher who spoke English or French. I called first. It's an 8.5-year-old girl. I'll go there tomorrow. Two things I like that joined up: piano and English. I hope it goes well. I spoke to the mother in English on the telephone.

I take 2 lessons a week with Miss Fleury. If not, it won't improve. Either a person jumps on a language, or . . . In my next letter, I want to ask you a few questions about studying there. Don't forget to write about it so I won't forget, OK? Now I have to run.

Udi, I hope you got my greeting card. In it, and here, I wish you a thousand congratulations, for everything good and pleasant, as your wish, will come true. We have arrived at our 20th! They say a lot happens in this decade. I see you already have a car. That is fantastic! Take care, and . . . brrrr . . . good luck in your life!

Udi, a huge embrace, from this crazy friend of yours, who wants to be a real friend, and wants you to consider her so, because she wants you so much as a friend.

Elana

PS Greetings to your parents, "lembranças" to all, from them and from me.

New York, September 1970

Oh, my heaven's wonder, what just happened? We just left childhood behind. Suddenly we're adults. Naive, but all grown up.

Another round of letters between us reveals that we're still deconstructing the trip, how things happened and how we treated each other. We saw things differently as they were happening in July, but we tried to put our differences in perspective after the trip was over and I was back home. For example, the candor that Elana expressed and the understanding she felt for my deferential letter regarding her parents; what we were allowed to do or not; how it affected her parents; how regretful I became after the trip regarding our travel agenda, and her parents' constraints, that is, whether it was wise of them to let us travel by ourselves and where, so on and so forth. These were issues we were trying to iron out. The long view from decades hence made this a minor incident, but at the time it was major. Unfortunately, in September 1970, we didn't have binoculars to look ahead, but after the trip, we used a microscope to look back. I preferred to use binoculars to look back.

Elana's "psychological analysis" letter was intense. She deconstructs me and herself and restructures our friendship in even stronger terms.

If this friendship wasn't meant to be, it would have died at this point. Six years of anticipating, and finally reuniting, which could have ripped up the friendship of any other two girls, did the opposite. This is the point where the friendship solidified forever. We worked at making it so via our correspondence.

Elana reveals between the lines that she and Danko will marry. Yes, her parents objected to him at first, but little did they know . . . and maybe would never know, especially Vera, who would not live to see the result of the match they made. Ernö lived longer and grew to love and respect his son-in-law, and was taken under the wing of the young man who would become very successful for the next fifty years.

São Paulo, September 27, 1970

Dear Udi-Udi,

It's 12:52 a.m., but don't wonder, I must stay up until 2 a.m. to take a medicine. I have an awful gingivitis infection. It's in the wisdom tooth, that's been out for a while, but the gums did not heal, there's a little piece of tooth left. Like this: [a drawing]. *Well, I think the tooth grew out recently, but I didn't feel it and I must have bitten down on it like a piece of meat! The little bugger gave me an inflammation and pain.*

. . .

It's 1 a.m. and I have an hour, I will bear it. And you can understand this letter, right?

Udi, you must have started college already. How is it going? What is your routine? What is new, and what opportunities does the car bring you? (Aside from comfort and "a life"?) Must be a marvel.

It seems Miki is in college, in psychology. She hasn't written to me about it, it was her grandmother who told us.

Ach! Hell! I don't know about these teeth! It's the first time my teeth hurt. Or rather, anything in my mouth. And imagine, I, Elana, can't eat properly! Doesn't matter, right? Maybe it will be for the better.

Changing the subject, Udi, as much as each of my 32 teeth have a history, I'd like to tell you something and to ask you something.

Udi, I decided I can speak English. Did I tell you I passed the Lower? Don't yet know the grade. OK. What's missing is correct pronunciation, practice, idiomatic expressions, and daily speech habits. I could learn it all here, I wouldn't be the first one to do so. But you know, it's a pain to study here, and gain so little, with little value. I could do this in 3 or 6 months in the US or England. I don't mean culture. That I could complete in a year. In reality, to speak like you, like an English speaker.

This is also a problem with German, but that's not so urgent, I still have more grammar to learn.

What I'm thinking about, is to go 6 or 8 months to England and 6 months to Germany. But do I have to say it? Is this stupid? Yes, but you have to understand me. No. One thing is clear. For this to happen, I would leave tomorrow. What they say in Brasil, "Se Deus quiser" [God willing]. *Opportunity is opportunity. If we wait for a second chance, it's a second chance. The first will be lost and all else with it. Overseas I'd also like to specialize in education, music and language.*

...

What I'd like to ask you is, are there possibilities to go there? Is there a school that would meet what I want, and if there was, could I have some job there? What kind of life do you think I could make, as independent as possible, most modest as possible in relation to everything: language, practice, education and music. Udi, I am not running now, just in search of information. There's plenty of time.

You know the one thing that's not a problem is the travel. I could go, dad would pay for my travel, study, living (maybe I am wrong). I wouldn't want to accept it all. But if that's the problem, why not? But it's not. They are little doubts, what to do first, what ends first, where to start first. I want to do all this and not be sorry in the future. I want to be sure, do everything as it should be and at the right time. OK, I think you understand, since most likely you've thought about it, and we've touched on this subject.

Today, Sept 27, was dad's 51st birthday. I bought him a pair of shoes. I hope he likes them. On Wednesday we were invited to dinner at Tzipora's house. A family dinner. Imagine what a large family, since on the bus to Bahia we met 8 family members! and they also invited Danko. I was really pleased, because I would not want to leave him all alone for Rosh Hashanah. The person most surprised is my mother.

Udi what do you say about home? your parents? your grandmother, aunt and cousin? and you? Write me a lot. Now I will go to sleep, it's already 1:45 a.m. I'm taking the meds; I can't stand keeping my eyes open. Good night. You must be wandering though high dreams. Udi, one of the hugs from your little friend, Elana

PS Thank you for bearing with this blabbing until now!

New York, September 1970

Elana was flying on painkillers! Most of her letter did not make sense, although it was obvious she wanted to study overseas—United States, Germany, France—with vague goals to learn English, or German, or music.

I was back at Lehman starting my junior year, and intensifying my double majors, linguistics and French literature. I developed a close friendship with two other linguistics students, Tobin and Dalgish, and we formed the trio of the only students that started in that track, so we had very close access to our professors and went on to graduate together in 1972. We had a few extraordinary professors who inspired us, among them Professor Garcia and Professor Rafael. It was a special time being the darlings of the new department.

São Paulo, November 8, 1970

Dear Udi-Udi,

I have to answer both your letters. One I tried to start when I received it (Oct 17), in Boqueirão, where we went. I did not finish it, and now I couldn't continue it. So, I'm starting again.

I am not in great shape to write to you at this point. You have been writing to me well and with friendliness. Your letters are a little different, and I'm thankful. I always like your correspondence, but since our meeting in July, I think it united us further in a way. After 6 years, people hardly know each other, and couldn't write with such liberty.

Udi, I thank you for writing the penultimate letter, I'm sincerely grateful. I've already thought about this idea of "independence," but superficially and abstractly. Probably I would not have arrived at what you opened my eyes to. It doesn't seem important; in reality it is very important. It's not just about Danko but in relation to everyone in my life.

You know, the fact that I am like this, proves my self-interest. My inclination to be authoritarian, and my lack of confidence with everyone. And if you think hard about the times when we've been friends and played together, you'd probably see a reflection of all this clearly. But it's very hard to get out of this rut. There would be a need for resolve and I'm irresolute.

Udi, I already sent you the film that you left here. Did it arrive? The negatives you mailed have not been developed yet. I will have them developed in December or January. Is it OK?

How is the "Congada" [musical piece by a Brazilian composer] *going? I think you will play it sooner than me. My poor piano is lonely. Maybe I will be able to play more during vacation. How is college going?*

Udi, you made me very excited with your last letter (Nov. 4). It's just that I don't know what to do.

I still have exams, German on the 20th, English on the 3rd. Then I'll go to the consulates to ask for information on all types of studies and opportunities in the US, England and Germany. [She keeps going farther afield.] *I might decide to go there* [USA]. *I'd like you to find out more about these music schools. That is when, and if, you have time. Maybe it would be just as easy for me to get information here. Let me try first to do as much as I can, and the rest, I'll ask of help.*

I've been emancipated [legal dissociation from parents]. *Now I'm being registered, and on the 20th it will be ready. On the 23rd I can start my naturalization.*

And thank you for writing about living accommodations. I would be grateful, but before I need many other things. You have to see the difficulty and the inconvenience for your parents. But please don't talk about it yet, first we'll see where, when, how and why I'm going. There would not be a problem with my parents, I know. But with Danko it will be hard. But I'm sure he'd understand. He'll have to understand.

November 9, 1970

Udi, I interrupted yesterday because Lewis and Kati (remember them who are engaged?) called for us to come see the apartment they rented. They're getting married Dec 26. George and Danko will be witnesses. (Ahhh! Who would fulfill this for me?) [She also wanted to get married.]

Udi, I don't think you know yet, Miki's grandmother died in October. It was sad. The old couple was getting along well lately and preparing to go to Miami now in November. On Rosh Hashanah he came here, he was crying, he said this wasn't a life, etc. One evening I called her, and we talked a little. She asked about you and she said she was proud of Miki for taking psychology, asked me to visit her, and asked me to forget the things that happened in the past. This moved me, so I decided I'd visit her once in a while. The same week she died (cardiac arrest) I was thinking of bringing her chocolates or flowers. She did not give me a chance. The old man was in shock. He had lunch here one time, and I thought he felt well. Last week a letter came from Miami. From him! Surprise on top of surprise. He went and returned. I didn't hear much of the conversation. Said they're all well there, but that life there is a tremendous race. He is registered to live there and can return. But I doubt he'll want to go back to Miami.

Udi, and your car? How are you driving? Does it help? Take care, OK? And the other car, did your father fix it? Don't let him work so much! And your mom? I believe she's depressed about your grandmother's attitude. [Perhaps about the new beau.] *But it's all about life, as they say, even if we don't accept it. But I keep a very different image of your grandmother.*

...

You know, I sent Miki a little earth from the burial with a lady going to Miami. It looks like Miki will come here in June.

I arranged a job at home: to call companies and to make appointments, and if I succeed, I earn Cr$20 for it. In 7 hours, I made Cr$120 (24 dollars!) I had a little luck, if this continues, alleluia!

Ah Udi, you ask my sizes. I can imagine what for (!!!) this reveals everything. But if you want to send me something, send a book, and this, on condition that you tell me the price. I have a student for piano and English. I sometimes have trouble with musical terms. So, I need a book on Elementary Music in English. You know, theory. Do you think you can send it? If not, no worries.

Udi, now I must go. Reply quickly, OK?

"Lembraças" to everyone there and to you.

A huge embrace from your friend forever,

Elana

New York, November 1970

Elana's meaning of emancipation was a legal one, in order to apply for citizenship on her own before turning twenty-one, gain a Brazilian passport, and travel. Her letters are full of dreams of studying abroad any way she could, but papers were a prerequisite.

I was writing to her about my need to be independent of my parents. I lived at home while going to college, but by this time, I was more impatient. I was going through a period where everything my father did and said rubbed me the wrong way. For years I kept leaning further toward liberal views and away from his conservative point of view. Politically, maybe he supported Nelson Rockefeller as governor of New York state, I don't know. Even Elana mentions her parents were conservative, but she related to them by being sympathetic, and by understanding how their views originated. I was not as agreeable in my differences with my father. And so, I sat in classes fuming and raging and trying to plot how to extract myself from these circumstances. My parents supported me, paying my small tuition and modest college living expenses. I wanted to be out of the house, and I could hardly wait till graduation and a move somewhere else. It barely registered in me that I was picking up the mores of a college-age American young woman. Without realizing it, I was plainly assimilating.

I saw Elana was choosing a way out—through marriage. She vehemently objected to my characterization of feminist independence. For the time being, though, she was following along the same path: studying so she'd have a means of support, and as she said, not have to rely on a husband. In the meantime, she was also very deferential to her parents' need to protect her.

As life progressed, Elana ended up helping in her husband's business and did not become a piano or English teacher. Being single for many more years, I was to chase a career and live alone, to be living the *Mary Tyler Moore Show* (it first aired in September 1970). The only difference is that in 1970 I was restless and itching to be in my 1977 shoes so I could be living like Mary Tyler Moore's character.

These were the Nixon years: the age of moon exploration and the grinding Vietnam War. We were living incongruously between the lofty and the debased. In our letters, we only paid attention to our dreams.

São Paulo, December 7, 1970

Udi, Udinha,

Do you see? I can't even tell the date. Time flies and I can't catch up. I am going crazy. Imagine it. Last week Danko told me that the husband of Lenke neni sent word that there's a liquid at her house for me.

[This was regarding a bottle of shampoo I sent her via a visitor to New York who subsequently used the shampoo and never gave her the bottle.]

You know, Udi, it's not that I need shampoo at all . . . but to lose respect for things of others? What is this? These old people who talk about the young ones being perverted, uneducated, and shameless. Udi I still have some hope. That this is a joke. I wanted to go get it now, but Danko said the old man was going to bring it to the office. They work at the same company. And the two of them including my father said it's best if I don't go there. That's right. If I went, and in front of her I saw that she used it, I'd throw it in her face. Don't misunderstand me, Udi, it's not the shampoo, I'd do it even if it was a piece of rusted hook. But we'll wait. Maybe they have a sense of humor.

Udi, I thank you so much, even after all this complaining. You shouldn't have bothered. I didn't even know she went, I just found out yesterday. I was disappointed because I didn't have the chance to send you something, not even the little spoon you forgot here. But it's safe with me, OK?

She *showed us pictures from there, and you were all together including John. Everything you wrote me in the last letter surprised me and made me happy. What do you think of him? Are you still friends? Don't misunderstand me, I'm not implying anything. It's just that I was happy you met. That's all. Anyway, send him Good-Bye and regards.*

Udi how are you? What are you doing? Maybe you are also on vacation, right? How will you spend it? . . . you already have a car; how do you take advantage of it?

. . .

Udi, I so want us to meet again. Now! I don't want to wait. Ah, my nonsense. I don't know what to do, where to go. Now I will collect all the information during my break. I hope the result will be US, New York. Would be marvelous. But there's more.

What will I do with Dankochko? Udi, I'm not afraid of losing him. We have confidence in each other. But you know the first time I left him alone something terrible happened, and again, the second time (in July). He said he is certain if I went away, something would happen again. And I don't want anything to happen to him. You know, we're saving a lot lately. His salary doubled and more was promised. We need him to earn more, plus what I make which is not consistent. When we reach that income, AHHH!!

São Paulo, December 14, 1970 [mailed together]

Dear Udi Udi,

I don't know why I stopped last week, but it goes to and fro, and here I am. As for the shampoo, nothing still. The results for English come out the 21st. In January, I'll try for the Michigan Certificate. I am now on break. The first semester I have Brazilian Literature. I am passing my time arranging closets, playing, reading and working with my 2 students. I make my calls for the company. It's going well.

And don't laugh, you know what I started on Thursday? Ballet! Don't laugh! Do you know what it is? Jose Leon has a dance school here at the corner. Ballet is also exercise, so it's really convenient, and really close.

And you, what are you doing? your parents, your grandmother, how are they? Udi, write soon, don't do like I do.

My father is working too much at the station. Spends the day there. [Ernö invested in a gas station.] *I already experimented with the*

Polaroid, but they don't come out well. I'll try more, and when I succeed, I'll send you a photo in each letter. But you also must send photos. Udi here's a big hug from your

Elana

New York, December 1970

This is the second or third time that I sent Elana something, via a traveler, and she didn't receive it. It was not possible to mail a package, because the Brazilian postal system was rife with theft. DHL got its start only in 1969. Instead, it was customary to send something with someone who was traveling: to meet them and to hand them the package.

Was she too busy to pick it up? Didn't the traveler have the compunction to drop it off?

Do these people make promises they just can't keep? Tomorrow and tomorrow? *Amanhã*?

Always *amanhã*.

This characteristic of Brazilians, even immigrants who become Brazilian, is a trait that was prevalent in daily living, and it made me flinch. Elana was angry because she wanted my gift. Not the shampoo, but the gesture, the object I handled and picked for her that she would then use. She loved receiving gifts and was a grateful recipient; it was a pleasure to send her gifts. That is why in many letters she enumerated every article she got from overseas, from her aunt, from her mother, from Miki, from me.

When I arrived in July, my big gift for Elana and her family was a Polaroid camera and extra film cartridges, which was the photographic rage in the States at the time. She and her family were in ecstasy for such a modern marvel. But I don't remember later receiving a Polaroid photo from her; maybe there was one or two.

The reason I sent her the negatives taken in Bahia is that they were lighter to mail than the developed copies would have been. In hindsight, I should have developed a second set and mailed the heavy package to her. I was being too miserly. It would have avoided the long wait for their return.

The comical saga of exchanging photos, or having photos developed in the age of 35 mm film cameras, continued and was another one of the frustrating experiences between us. She didn't have a camera and occasionally borrowed Yoni's camera, or she relied on others to take pictures.

With a 35 mm film cartridge, it can be a long time until the twenty-four or thirty-six frames are filled, the cartridge removed and taken to a camera shop. This whole process came to a standstill with Elana and her companions, either Yoni, Danko, or a friend. Months and months would go by before she had something to send, and I would be waiting anxiously to receive a new photo of her.

I went to the camera shop frequently. I always had another roll developed and always had photos to send. I loved my camera, I loved photography, which was a hobby I acquired from my father. He had a Kodak Retina II (made in Germany) that he purchased in Israel in 1958 when we were about to emigrate. This is the fixed lens camera that took photos of us on the ship and on shore excursions in Dakar, Senegal, and it is the camera used to take pictures of us all, well dressed, on weekends, visiting the parks in and around São Paulo. My father was a little more than a casual, and a little less than an avid, photographer. The developed prints came quickly after exposure—he made sure of it. I followed his example. He wanted to teach me about photography: exposure, light metering, balancing speed and aperture, and how to load a roll of film. I listened with half an ear.

How did he know all those things? My father was always full of knowledge of things that didn't seem to be in his purview, and he could explain them. He showed a deep understanding of history, including expressing his interest in and absorption of Zionist history. It is the reason he was so eager for Aliyah in 1945–47. I remember his deep dislike of the British for abrogating their prior stand and closing the entry in Mandated Palestine to Jews in 1939. Had they not . . . many would have survived. I am sure he knew who Nahum Sokolow was, a Zionist leader many Jews currently are not familiar with (he was president of the World Zionist Congress before and after Chaim Weizmann, and he was also president of the Jewish Agency). For someone who was dyslexic, I never understood or appreciated how my father absorbed so much historical information. He was not a reader; there were no libraries for him to access, no Google or AI. He was a sponge, and it made me wonder at the source, the external evidence, of what he siphoned into his mind. People in general had an opinion of him as intelligent and knowledgeable, even if he did not have a full secondary education, interrupted by the Holocaust, and for the lack of opportunities, never completed. His attitude was not great, because he knew that he was knowledgeable, and he could not abide the ignorant. I suspect he was always resentful about the curtailed fate of his formal education. He spoke about wanting but not having an opportunity to get an engineering degree from the Technion. He was smart, but he was not humble.

In any event, photography was one of his interests that rubbed off on me.

As for the car mechanics he taught me, it did not rub off. But I did learn from him how to replace a tire, which I had to do on the side of a highway one day, and wave off men who stopped to help, shaking their head that a twenty-two-year-old woman could jack up a car, loosen the bolts, replace the wheel, and so on. And of course, there was that used Mustang he told me would be mine when I was twenty if I came for lessons on how to take the engine apart, clean, and rebuild it. Nothing in life made him happier than having me in his garage. So, under his supervision, I had taken apart and reassembled the engine of that 1967 Ford Mustang. Later, instead of that Mustang, which was difficult to drive, he passed on to me his Buick Special, a sweet car. I did not become a mechanic like my father, and never again tinkered under the hood of an engine, except the checkups he taught me to perform for the oil, transmission fluid, brake fluid, radiator water level, windshield fluid, poking of the belts, and so forth. Photography interested me more.

Today we can upload a photo or share a photo via WhatsApp in an instant. What a world of difference! The outdated mechanics of photography of 1970 filled paragraphs of protestations in the letters between Elana and me. But photographs were important. We were becoming young women, and we wanted to see each other in addition to reading about each other.

I read the old letters and smile. We've come a long, long way.

Letters 1971 to 1982

Young Adults: A Common Past Diverges

São Paulo, February 19, 1971

Dear Udi-Udi,

What's the matter? Why don't you write? Every day when the bell rings at the time the super comes up to bring our letters, I run . . . but nothing for me. Why?

Udi, I have so much to tell you. But first before I forget, I must tell you what I should have said before right away after sending my last letter. Right after, I got your shampoo (3/4 full), and I thank you so much. It's already all gone, and it can be seen with my hair! I think if I was going there, I'd come back with a suitcase full of the shampoo bottles.

Udi, I don't know how it's going to be in July. My naturalization is in the works (in Rio already) and the dispatcher said that the fact that I'm a student, and single, and that my parents have already naturalized, it will help, perhaps by April or May. But the trip depends on a lot of things. But I think it will work out. Do you still want me to come?

Udi, I will tell you what you will be the first to know, and that now my parents know: I am engaged! I told them and Dankochko came to speak with my parents yesterday, but Miki's grandfather came, then Yoni and Tzipora also came (unexpectedly form Guarujá), and so he couldn't speak to my parents. Tomorrow he will talk to them. But there won't be a problem. I'm a little disappointed, not because of Danko, but because of me. It's mostly about my father. He repeats, "Is it serious? Want to tell me that I will lose my daughter?" I am not a good daughter as I should be, but I will be a better one afterwards. A lot of things changed lately. I think my parents will change their mind and start liking him.

...

We will get engaged on my birthday (officially with family). I told my parents that you already know about it and have seen the rings. Unfortunately, his parents are not here, but we will call them on Saturday the 27th. Just to open a bottle of champagne. Udi, I am happy, not just because I'm engaged—I already was—but because my parents are accepting him as my choice, and they even seem pleased. I couldn't have expected anything better from them. Who said Dankochko didn't reveal who he is? OK Udi, enough of this, but you know, I have "Szajmenés" [blabbermouth in Hungarian].

Udi, what are you doing? Going to school? Have you decided what will follow college? What do you do in your spare time? and the car, does it help? And John, have you seen him? How is he? And your parents? and your grandmother? and your aunt? Udi please write, it's horrible not knowing anything from there!

...

Boy! I'm writing like a rocket, faster than I could talk!

Udi, you know, I feel sorry for Miki. She left a fiancé here (who apparently doesn't want her any longer). She went to her mother and a new "father" and now she's alone. Her mother and Marvin moved to the Virgin Islands, and she's living with a friend [in Florida]. *I may be wrong, but I think Miki is suffering. A lot. She stopped writing to anyone, including her "parents." She has 2 mothers, 2 fathers, a grandfather, uncles and she's alone! Her grandfather is thinking of going to California to join some family and is taking lessons with Miss Fleury. When she tells me how it's going, I almost wet my pants from laughing, but she says he's a good student. Rachel and Danko are also taking classes with Miss Fleury.*

Udi, I tried taking pictures with the Polaroid but they're no good. Maybe it's the battery. After the Vestibular, I'll take it to a shop to get some instructions on how to use it, the instruction manual is not enough. Then every letter will have a photo with it, OK?

Ah, after Carnaval, one of these days I will take your negatives to have them developed. You're already mad at me, right? I'm sorry, Udi, but one time I'm low on money, another I forget, or lose track of time. But now I will do it.

Udi, I just ask you to write to me soon, even if it's just a card. Tell me how you are, and that everything is OK. Is it cold there? Here we're broiling and we can't move. Udi, give everyone "lembranças," and for you a huge embrace, from your forever friend,

Elana

PS Again, thank you for the shampoo, and I apologize for all the confusion!

New York, February 1971

Engaged! Apparently, I knew that when I visited her in July, when they showed me their rings. It was a pleasure to see her so much in love. She was so young! Engaged at the age of twenty-one! That was so hard for me to fathom.

I did not even have a boyfriend. And John, whom Elana mentions in this letter, was not a boyfriend. He was working on a doctorate in computer sciences at Cornell. I soon lost track of him, shamefully, because I found him unattractive, and even his superior intellect, gentleness, and kindness could not move me. I was truly naive.

My school day revolved around a table in the Lehman College cafeteria where I and a group of friends would come and go and alight like butterflies on a puddle, to-and-fro the business of collecting class sustenance. It was gratifying; I enjoyed the friends I made at Lehman. The intellectual atmosphere hummed at Lehman, and the surrounding cultural climate of New York City sated us with an intellectual nourishment we did not get at home. None of my friends had college-educated parents or professional parents: all of us came from hardworking, dedicated, and honest families, working class, first- or second-generation immigrants, some Jewish and some not. There was not a rich or upper-class family among us. We were a kaleidoscope of flittering escapees metamorphosing into a generation of professionals.

Since I am still friends with many of those at that cafeteria table, I know all have succeeded, and none abandoned their ties to the families that launched them, before slowly their elders died away.

The one characteristic that runs through me, my friends in New York, and Elana in Brazil is that we were devoted to parents who had nurtured us each in their own way, but always because they worked to give their offspring a stepping stone, dismissing their own needs. Was that a coincidence? It could have been; maybe I chose friends who had deep roots and strong bonds. It was not until graduate school and after that I met mavericks, the eccentric and loner rebels. In other words, even throughout college, I was sheltered. I know my parents were in awe of me. They understood nothing of a college education, except that it was a ticket for a better future. Sadly, within just a couple of years, I realized my mother was living vicariously through me, until to my horror, she wanted to be embedded in my life like a parasitoid wasp. But I refused to be a host or die in the process, even if it meant shrugging her off, devoted to her or not. But that was a story for the future. I'm just trying here to recognize the earliest evidence of that swerve, as she showed a deepening and unhealthy attachment to me. Her overprotectiveness was understandable but not desirable. Because she was a Holocaust survivor who lived through persecution and a precarious existence, her psychological need to protect her young was to be expected. The fierceness of it was common among other survivors who had children when the war ended and the persecution subsided. As a mother of only one surviving child, having lost two others, she was doubly traumatized.

Despite this devotion to parents, the need to break away from them was a real propulsive force in me.

As for Miki, per this letter, I knew very little about her tribulations. I know soon after this time she joined her mother and new stepfather in St. John, the US Virgin Islands, where she attended a community college for a short time studying hospitality services. Not long after, she flew to London to live with her stepfather's mother, and her future was secured. At a luncheon given by the lady, Miki met a scion of a family that owned an international business. They married not much later than Elana.

Miki's calling in life, eventually, was to be the wife of this London businessman. She filled that role to perfection. She was the perfect hostess, the doting partner, the loving mother, the generous volunteer, and the ultimate art connoisseur. She filled the shoes her mother dreamed for her. Whether she was happy, I do not know. On the other hand, Elana was happy as a wife, mother, and business assistant of her husband. Elana did not aspire to enter high society; Miki reveled in it. I didn't have much detail, since Miki and I did not correspond often. We met a few times over the years, however, and eventually, with computer access, we emailed one another on our birthdays and Rosh Hashanah, the Jewish new year.

I was the one left single. I had to prove my feminist gumption and pursue my chosen path, leaving the old standards behind, while my girlfriends embraced them.

São Paulo, June 5, 1971

Dear Udi-Udi,

I no longer understand anything. You told me that my last letter was in February. Since then, I sent two more. The last one was "registered" and if it didn't arrive, I have to go complain. Udi, I understand the situation you were in, and I hope that things have improved. What are you going to do this coming semester? How much more before you graduate college? What kind of work are you going to do at the library?

Udi, I think my trip to see you is water under the bridge. The dispatcher said that my passport, i.e. my naturalization, will only be ready in August (IF!!) I call him every week, but he tells me my name has not appeared in the daily record, and there's nothing he can do. I arranged my schedule, so I'd be free in July if this came about. If it is ready by the 15th–20th of June, something could still be arranged.

Udi I am also in a funk, but my reaction is different from you. I am burdened by everything; June has been terrible. Full of tests, work, lessons, private students, piano. Really, this is nerve-wracking.

Udi, sometimes I wonder if I'm not doing everything wrong, and it fills me with such despair. I would like to be different, to do things as they should be done, and not be as impressionable as I am. You know, the best definition of myself? Rotten.

Your grades were excellent. About programming, have patience. Not everything is easy for everyone, and everyone is not always interested in the same thing. Your health is more important than "computer programming." And don't forget, it's proven that no one can grow and survive without help from colleagues. As a result, don't avoid help from others.

Here everything is going well. My father has the flu (in other words 90% in S.P. have it), but it doesn't stop him from working every day. Yoni is doing a lot of interning, and it's obvious to me he wants to earn a very good living. My mother, as always, is sitting by her machine [sewing] *all day long. Danko has a lot of work and studies, and so all of us are carrying on living.*

...

As you can see, I don't have much news, even though I write as if there was. It's not for lack of interest, because all week I wait for Saturday afternoon so I can write to you. I think it lacks style, though.

Udi, I'm asking you to write soon, since June is the last month of the semester. Write a lot, and believe it, your letters, good or bad, bring me such comfort. Give "lembranças" to everyone, from everyone here and for you, an extra special embrace from your friend who would like to be right next to you.

Elana

New York, June 1971

The lively and perky friend who sustained me though years of lonely solitude in my new countries has now slid into a self-doubt I had never seen in her before.

It was my turn to cheer her up. She was facing the rigors of too many classes and activities, while in anticipation of her new life with Danko. There didn't seem to be any external issues. Was she slipping into depression? That was something I struggled with, but not Elana. I had never seen her depressed. This was a far cry from the exhilaration of a year before with the expectation of my visit.

It seemed we were both in a funk, as she stated. I must have complained about my life at home, and the tension I felt between me and my parents, the frustrations about struggling with a computer programming class, and the rigors of the previous junior semester in school, but I don't remember any of it well. I know I went to Cornell in the spring, where John was doing postgraduate work in computer engineering, and I asked him to help me with Fortran programming that was setting me back in grades.

The tension I felt at home with my father was intense, but it was my fault. I came to think, "I didn't like him." But he didn't change, I changed. And I was too immature to know how to deal with this. In hindsight, these feelings were driven by my need to leave home, and I felt trapped by another year of waiting. Not being the impetuous, running-away kind, I believed in laying out a plan first: to move to graduate school after Lehman. I just had to wait it out, and as much as possible, to live my life outside of home—where I only slept.

In the summer of 1971, I landed a well-paid internship at a local public library and my mood improved. How lucky was I! Not to wait on tables, not to punch a cash register, or perform other menial and minimum wage jobs, the ones frequently had by college juniors without internships. Or, for that matter, to perform office filing at the GM Tarrytown plant office. The staff at the library was kind and engaging; I learned to catalog books and eventually to help at the children's section. It went so well that the children's librarian asked me to work part-time after the internship was over, including returning the following summer. Somehow, I'd convinced the program directors that I was interested in getting a master's in library science. I should have considered it and become a librarian, but I didn't, because languages interested me more. The staff at the library didn't care that I did not apply to an MLA program. And so, after school, I spent my days at the Greenburgh Public Library for another year.

São Paulo, July 8, 1971

Dear Udi-Udi,

Udi, I so much want to be with you now. You can't imagine the cesspool I'm in. My classes ended July 2. On the 5th I went with Marie Claire to Itanhaém and returned yesterday. Today I went to check my English Culture grade to see if I passed: no! I flunked. And so, I started to think: what is it that I do right? What have I done so far that's right? I can see the answer is Nothing. It's true, Udi, my life passed for a disorganized fugue. I look for where I made a mistake, at what time in my life did I get lost, but I don't find it. It's horrendous. I can't think straight. I can't get the ideas in my head organized. And why? Udi, I try to be sincere with myself, and I am. Even so, I can't see where I went wrong. Sometimes I think I should go to a psychologist. But I'm afraid. I'm afraid of getting into even greater confusion, and not improving things. Most people tell me I'm doing too much. It's not true. Do you remember, when you were here, I didn't even do half of what you did, and I was 5 times worse off! Most certainly, if I did only one thing, it would be the same. I can only arrive at one conclusion: I am incapable. The more I try to prove otherwise, I don't succeed.

You know, Udi, the only good thing that happened to me in my life is Danko. Udi, forgive me for being so disconsolate. I delayed writing you, and when I write, the letter comes out like this. I couldn't help it, Udi. You know, I almost succeeded to travel to see you. If I had more energy, I would have. Imagine how I am if I don't have the energy for that!

Udi, how are you, your parents and everyone? What are you doing? what is your work schedule? what do you do there? Udi, I want to ask you one more thing. What do you think is the chance of me going there in December? Maybe I'll earn a stipend for Germany in January, and first I'd like to go by and see you.

Yoni's naturalization is ready, and mine will lag another month or so.

Yoni is getting married in September! It will be on a Thursday, don't know which yet.

Udi, I can't write straight. I wrote all this because I want to receive news from you, and so I have to write first. Please, write soon and send good news, and a really long letter, OK?

Many, many kisses, Udi, from your crazy friend,

Elana

"Lembranças" to your parents, and ask your mother to write us, too!

New York, July 1971

Elana started to mention her depression in the previous letter, and in this one, it is full-blown. She is despondent and deeply self-critical. And yet, she had this ability to share her fears and doubts with me and to analyze what was troubling her.

In 1971 we did not go to see psychologists, and certainly not in 1959. I was not taken to therapy when I was nine and almost catatonic. My mother did not go to a therapist when she was reeling from the grief of giving birth to a full-term dead baby (pardon this contradiction, but a woman induced to go through labor to deliver a baby no longer alive is how it's done), for the second time in her life. And Elana was afraid at the time to go to a psychologist and unearth more confusion. However, decades later, Elana didn't hesitate to see a therapist with her family, when she found that her children needed psychological support.

My summer was going well at the library. I socialized with my friends from Lehman. Since I lived in the suburbs, I could host them at my parents' modest house, which they called the Zelig château. Some of them had summer jobs, others did not. We were a generation lucky enough to have few expenses aside from going to the movies or the theater before such entertainment became outrageously expensive. A runaway inflation had not yet started.

São Paulo, August 10, 1971

Dear Udi-Udi,

Eh, let's talk. Sit here, get comfortable, feel at home. Do you want some cookies? There are some in that cabinet, take what you'd like. Good. Now, what can you tell me? What have you been doing? Besides working, of course.

Udi, I think you must have received the letter I sent in July. But I have to admit, I don't remember what I wrote in it, so I'm capable of repeating myself. You know, when the semester started, I was looking for a notebook, and when I found it, I also found some letters you sent me. The one in which there was a photo, and the one that I am late in thanking you, asking for more photos. How are your parents?

You know, that letter arrived during exams, so I read it, and I forgot it inside the notebook. Ah, Udi, what a horrible month July was! Bah!

Did I already tell you I failed Culture? I have to repeat the advanced 6th. But I can't. This semester I will also have lessons with Miss Fleury, since it's not worth being mediocre in Culture. When USP ends, I will retake Culture, and I'll be finished in a year. I will do the intensive 6th and 7th in each semester. I passed well at both USP and at the Music Academy. Amen. The Academy makes me excited because of the teachers. I am beginning to notice what music really is! During July holidays I didn't do anything, that is, I rested a lot. I am in good spirits to start the second semester.

So . . . you are at graduation's door. For me it will take two more years in one and 3 in the other [subjects] *plus a year in Culture. That is, if I don't start something else. No, no, I think that's enough. I'll start more, but first I'll finish this.*

Ah, Udi, do you know who's getting married? The . . . wait . . . wait . . . it's on September 9. It's . . . Yoni! Well, maybe it's not a surprise [she already told me] *because I forget if I wrote this already. This was decided in July. What do you think? The invitations are not ready yet. But here between us, I found them ugly* [description including a sketch]. *Well, you'll see it when you receive it in the mail. This is just my opinion. Maybe you'll like it.*

Ah, Udi, I want to marry soon. You know Danko changed work. He left that company, where he started at 400 and increased to 900 [Brazilian cruzeiros]. *But he couldn't continue because the IBM machines did not arrive. So now he's working as a salesman and this first month he reached 2,000. See the difference? He said if this continues, we can get married at the end of September. But I doubt it. It would be too good. Anyway, it will be for sure by December, and we will get married a day after I return* [Elana is fantasizing again].

I'd like you to find out about an English course. I could leave in December until the end of February, beginning of March. That's if I don't go to Germany. If I go, then I will pass by NY before, or after, to see you. [The marriage date seems forgotten.]

I also want you to tell me if I came for that whole time would that be an inconvenience and be in your way. Udi, all of this, as usual, is not for sure. I am undecided, and I'd like you to help me. I just know that I want to travel, and I want to see you. My papers are almost ready, and by then they will be ready. Let me plan, but I won't start until I hear your opinion.

Are you playing? What? I'm doing a lot of technique and learning Haydn's Sonata no. 42, Bach-Siloti Prelude for organ in Sol major, Bach Prelude and Fugue X volume 1, and Study 139 of Bela Bartok. Now I will start taking others. My teacher is excellent, and imagine, in each cycle, one of his students is always chosen to be Classified. [Graduate level?] *That's really rare.*

Udi, I have to stop, I have to go to class. Please reply soon, really soon, and tell me what you're doing, what you think of my ideas, and tell me if you have other ideas.

A big kiss and a tight embrace, from your forever friend

Elana

New York, August 1971

Elana's blue cloud had lifted. And once again she is recounting doing more than seems plausible. But she begs me to give her my opinion. How can anyone be such an optimist, and have such pie-in-the-sky plans? In one paragraph she says she will marry soon, in the other she wants to come to NYC then to Germany, but nothing has been finalized or made concrete. She was so energetic, so indecisive.

I don't know what I wrote to her. As I look back, she's her usual self in this letter, taking on more than she can muster. Her impulses are driven with a passionate force. Her studies at university seem endless, her move from one conservatory to another seeking a musical diploma in addition to her language diploma, while taking on young students is breathtaking, but perilous to her academic success. Elana did not have the single-minded focus of Yoni; that is the reason he finished his medical training and was already doing his residency, while she plows though class after class sometimes passing, sometimes not. Elana is smart. She could focus, but she focused on too much at once. Yoni was unwavering and resolute, without the social distractions, but Elana's focus was sporadic. Maybe she was always full of hope and never seeing obstacles, even the obvious one?

What did I tell her? Today I would have pointed out the inconsistencies of doing two things at once. In comparison to Elana, I was always too cautious and too practical, even to the point of being too timid to charge ahead: my path had to be planned and laid out, although when it came to choices, I was impetuously decisive.

I usually did not take classes in summer. But in the summer of 1971, I had taken a Swahili class taught by a former Peace Corps instructor. He used a successful and effective language-learning process I've always felt was the key to learning a language: immersion. It involved role-playing and oral repetitions between actively engaged conversation partners. There was a textbook, but we didn't study the text, we practiced the role of verbal exchanges. The purpose for this Swahili class was for me to pick up another non-Indo-European language for my major. My department chairman suggested that I add Swahili to my Hungarian and to my Fortran (a computer programming language). After all, he said about the latter, it's also a language, and it's not Indo-European! (Hungarian is also a non-Indo-European language; it's Finno-Ugric, part of the Uralic language group.) This was my seventh language. I was always keen on learning a new one. Fortuitously, despite my love for linguistics and French-language studies, it is this introduction to a computer language that launched my working career in 1977.

Elana's next letter reveals a surprise for me.

São Paulo, August 11, 1971

Hey Udi,

Here I am again. I wrote you a letter on Saturday which fell into the water [figuratively]. *Yesterday I wrote you another, which I am sending here, and now I received your letter, so I am finishing it. Udi you are amazing, and you cannot imagine how I adored your words. They truly comforted me, even though I started to feel more settled. I think internally there is only one success that will calm me.*

Danko just called me from S. José de Rio Preto. He went there yesterday at 5:30 a.m. and will only return on Friday night. You have no idea how I miss him. Even I didn't think I'd ever feel this way. I wake up sometimes at night, and I feel concerned. There is no cause for this, yesterday he called me at 11 p.m. and today at noon. He's well, and these 2 days he earned 600 Cruzeiros. At Ecel he would have worked two months for this.

Eh Udi, I want to get married. I keep getting crazier over it. It is he who is saner and has more expectations for better conditions to be married, so he wants to wait. Bah, for me, I'd live in a hole somewhere, but we'd be together. OK, this will happen (Amen.) Udi, I'll tell you what I do now.

...

What do you think? I think I got it well balanced this time. These past two weeks were great. Let's see how it progresses. As you can see, I only let go of Culture. I don't have the courage to take on more. And this is temporary.

But Udi, why give up piano? Don't do that! Every once in a while—please play! I am so grateful for what you wrote and what you said. You were awesome to me. You made me feel so good.

The invitations for Yoni's wedding are ready. He brought them last night. They turned out a little better than I expected. I think they will be sent tomorrow.

I will end here since I must have lunch then leave. Please always write to me, and a lot. Maybe in four months we will see each other! Udi, here goes a trunkful of embraces. Watch out!! It almost hit you. OK, kisses from your "saudosa amiga" Elana

PS What happened with John? You don't write about him. If you see him, send "lembranças."

New York, August 1971

I was so relieved! Elana received the letter where I must have comforted her and told her of my support and faith in her work. For all she had done for me just being herself without effort or artifice, lifting me up for years, it was a relief that I did the right thing and was able to send her comforting words she wanted to hear.

We did not talk on the phone; that was impossible due to cost. As seen in these wordy letters, we could not talk with just a few sentences! On the back of one letter, she added the comment

"So many words and nothing written!" These letters were the only means we had to comfort each other.

My summer break was ending, and senior year was about to start. I did not end my piano studies with Ms. Fishman; those lessons continued until graduation. I continued to work part-time at the library. I started to lose track of John; my pastimes were with Lehman friends.

São Paulo, August 15, 1971

Dear Udi-Udi, Edith and Victor,

Edith néni, a mamám nem ir, mert sókat szaladgál. De én meg igertem hogy közelbe fog írni, es kérem hogy írjanak nekünk. Most be fejezem, sok sok czókokal mindenkinek. Szerettetel, Elana
[Edith *neni*, my mother can't write because she's running around. But she promised she would write soon, and I ask you to write to us soon. In closing, sending lots of kisses to everyone.]

Yes . . . this happened. Who would have thought that little boy would marry? Well, we are super happy. We would be even happier if you all were here with us participating in our happiness, with the newlyweds, and their future babies (it's the most critical, isn't it?). What do you think of this idea?

Well, the formal invitation is here, and the informal invitation, both. Apologies for the lateness of the invitations going via mail today.

. . .

Elana

São Paulo, August 31, 1971

Dear Udi-Udi!

Hi, everything OK?

Eh, I don't even know what to say. I just feel like shooting the breeze with you. Hey, why don't you answer? Well, alone, I'm not talking. Well now, Udi, without joking. I've resolved my decision about the "trips." After confusing you for years, talking, deciding, planning, I've decided. I'm . . . NOWHERE! I'm going to get married. December 23. So, I ask you, is there a chance for you to come here? You know how I'd love that. You know if you weren't with . . . I won't annoy you. I know coming here is not like taking a bus, and here you are. And I know you are not on holidays. BUT if you have any opportunity, it's the reason I already am revealing the date.

Udi, it was very hard to decide. Danko had already agreed we'd marry after I came back in February or March, and my documents would be ready this October (the dispatcher told me yesterday). But Udi, I feel like getting married YESTERDAY. And not, of course, in March. Ay, Udi, it is so hard to write you this, because I know it's a dream going down the river, and I start changing my mind. But it will be as it will be. It's better not to overthink it. If it happens that I can go, amen. But in the meantime, I won't badger you with my plans. But I still ask you, if you know what. No. Nothing. Forget it . . .

And Udi, please, don't be mad at me, please. I'm sorry for all the mess, writing you something different in every letter. If you want to curse, I accept, you have reason. Then fill a whole page with curses and mail them, I'll accept it.

Let's change the subject. Yoni's wedding is in 2.5 weeks. I hope you received the invitation. What did you think? I hope there will be a lot of photos to send you. Today I am going to try on a dress. It's turquoise blue. Well, you know I don't draw well [drawing of the dress]. *It's a long dress. I am on a strong diet. Lost 4kg. Since the beginning of the year, I gained 8! I was 72kg. On the 16th I started and today I am 67 kg. I hope to be 60kg by the wedding. It will be hard. You know how I love to eat. I am taking a pill to lose my appetite (but believe me I haven't lost it). Udinha, I will end here, I still have to write to Danko's parents. He is traveling. Write soon, OK?*
A huge kiss from your friend,

Elana

New York, August 1971

Confused by hormones setting her off, perhaps, or the suspense she felt about the near future, she was torn between wanting to take off and go to Europe, or the United States, and being at the doorstep of her own wedding. How she held those two dispositions at the same time, I don't know. She loved to dream and form unavailing plans. If I were to say to her, "But Elana, that can't work out!," I'd just be a spoilsport and naysayer. In writing to her, I always cheered her plans. Who knew, maybe she'd make them work out. I was the reluctant realist, and not stricken by first love.

The following months Elana and I were in different personal universes. Although she continued her studies, the weddings (Yoni's, then hers) were a major factor in her life. What drove me was my academic work as I was embarking on my senior year.

I had a double major, linguistics and French literature, subjects I loved. My goal was to proceed to graduate school the following year. There was no young man to distract me from that goal. My fellow cohorts, literary and linguist friends, were the center of my life. Several of them remained my friends well into midlife, maintaining a long-distance connection.

São Paulo, September 14, 1971

Dear Udi-Udi!

In the first place, I want to wish you a happy birthday. How about it? How does it feel to reach adulthood? I so wish you to take good advantage of adulthood, and that for the rest of your life, which will be long, and I wish it to go on forever, full of happiness, surprises and delights. That you continue to always be the same Udinha who I like so much, and that you find everything you want in this journey of our life. Finally, I wish you happiness, not just for your birthday, but for always. Ah yes, I have another wish: always be a good girl, watch when you cross the street or in the car, and . . . never forget to write to your silly friend.

. . .

Yoni . . . went and sweetly got married! The event was beautiful, and there were many people. After the champagne and cake, we snatched the newlyweds, and drove in different cars, with harmonica, flute and violin, to the restaurant area where we made a huge commotion dancing and singing with the couple.

. . .

We only got home at 3 a.m.! We took a lot of photos, we'll see how they come out, and for sure, I'll send you some. Ah! speaking of photos, I still didn't have the negatives you sent developed!! No problem, right?

Mid-Day:

Udi, the telegram you sent was such a pleasant surprise. You know, my first thought was when I get married will you be there at my side? Or just a telegram? That's just my thought but I felt a knot to my throat. You know, Udi, I'd like to win the lottery! If I won, I'd send passage to everyone far away who I'd like to celebrate with me. And then, to go visit my grandmother. I think if she would be part of this wedding, it would be an infinite happiness. You know I don't "believe" in anything, but sometimes I think: is it possible my grandmother sees me? hears me? where would she be? Oh, Udi, don't mind me, it's just that I continue to love her, and I think about her because to me, she'll never go away.

. . .

Udi, I ask semi-seriously semi-jesting, could you possibly come? You are on vacation at that time, and here it's summer, you could come to rest. I know it's easy to propose this, and that it's not easy for you. But I ask, perhaps you could, and maybe your parents would also want to come around here to shoot the breeze with my parents.

We still don't know what to do. Maybe just go to the marriage bureau, sign the civil then bye-bye. If Danko's parents come, then we'll have a feast and a religious ceremony too. Either the parents will come, or you will come; we'll have a feast. If not, I think . . . ah well, we'll see. But I'd love to hear (or read) that you will appear. In any event, Udi, my wedding is not a parting. On the contrary! Danko is earning a good living and if it continues like this, we'll travel a lot. Our first destination is Czechoslovakia and Hungary and 2nd, New York and Tarrytown. Ah, what a dream!

Udi I must write to my future in-laws and it's already 12:45 a.m. Please write soon, I'm anxious to hear news from you. Kisses and hugs from your friend who again congratulates you.

Elana

[Letters received together.]

São Paulo, September 15, 1971

Dear Udi-Udi!

My letter to you is already sealed, but yours arrived today, so I'll write just a little because my pointer finger is red and inflamed, swollen and delicious! Yesterday was Sandrinha's final. . . . OK so my agony is over [her star student's performance result], *but the reward was worth it. I'm happy and satisfied.*

. . .

Yesterday I called the dispatcher, and he said my naturalization will be effective this month. So, I asked him if someone who lives here 3 years can be naturalized. He said maybe if the person has property, a factory, a Brazilian child . . . or . . . or . . . a spouse. Then I asked what if she's a naturalized wife, and then he figured out I meant Danko and he burst out laughing, saying "You will do." (It's another reason for Danko to marry me! See, I "fish" really well?) This means, right after the wedding, he can be naturalized. And if he continues to earn well, it means we will come visit you. One thing is certain. I will go or we will go. When is the question.

Udi, I already wrote in the other letter, how much it hurts to think you will not be near me when I take this step in my life, and I get a lump in my throat. But . . . let's hope that we can still meet before this! Now I'm not thinking of any particular study-course, just visiting you.

How's college? What is "Graduate school?"

OK, Academia Paulist de Música [APM] *is the name of where I am studying music.*

. . .

Udi, my fingers hurt. Please write real soon, and a lot, whenever you can, even if you don't receive a letter from me. I will do the same.

Udi—tomorrow Sept 16, 1971, I'd like to give you a big hug—there it goes! I'm sorry if I squeezed you too much.

Kisses, your friend

Elana

New York, September 1971

It saddens me to say that as I was reading her letters, I was not contemplating traveling to Brazil for her wedding. My parents and I did not attend Yoni's. But Elana's? She pleads in several letters for me to be at her side. I think I must have been experiencing my callous side by not taking her wishes seriously. In 1971 I had never attended anyone's wedding. It was not meaningful to me, but to not do this favor for a friend . . . ? The trip would have been costly, my parents would certainly not have come, but knowing what I know now, it's not easy to hang around a bride and her family as the big day approaches. I was not going to hang out in S.P. at some hotel waiting and getting ready. Although we were twenty-one, and adults, we were quite immature.

São Paulo, October 19, 1971

Dear Udi-Udinha!

I took a letter, saw the date "October," and came here at the workshop so my mother can go lie down a bit. [Vera was getting fatigued.] *I opened the letter and it's from 1970! I don't have your latest in my hand. But I remember what you wrote.*

Udi-Udi you know I'd like to win the lottery (believe it, I buy sport lotteries) so that I can win the fare to have all my friends from far away come here. Who knows, will it happen? Udi, you know I just can't imagine getting married without you here. Believe me, Udi, I think you know, because you were the first and only one who knew for seven months and 14 days about our engagement.

My father decided we'll also have a religious ceremony. On Thursday we'll go to the civil clerk to mark the day December 23. Udi maybe you will hijack a plane to come here? I'm not kidding, why don't you return here? OK, in reality there's more there than here. But I'd love for you to be here. When I have a child, and he gets sick how is your mother going to bring him "floating islands"? [It's an egg and milk dessert.] *So, I'll have to take extra care of him! Speaking of children, the doctor said I can't get pregnant for 1.5 years because of that nasty tooth problem. I didn't want to take birth control pills, because I am not sure it's a safe medicine. They know that in most cases it doesn't affect the women. But babies of women on the pill are small and it's still not known how it affects them later. It makes me afraid. Kati is on it, and Tzipora is also on the pill, and I know others who are and already have a baby and they're OK. But I still have my doubts. I always menstruate on time, only varying by a day. I can figure that I will start menstruating on December 23rd!! I told Danko but he doesn't want to change the date. Between us: too bad for him! Just joking. Actually, it's OK, this way we'll rest for 3 or 4 days. I think we'll go to Itanhaėm, to the Miami hotel. After that we'll go to Boqueirão, and when we're sick of the beaches, we'll go somewhere else.*

Udi, my mother is a little sick. I am worried. She has a problem with her uterus. But the doctor said it's not serious. Her belly is really big, and she's getting injections and takes medicine. I hope she'll get better! She's very dispirited and tired.

Udinha, believe me I want the Bahia photos! And I will return the negatives to you when I have them developed. So, don't talk ugly to me!! eh? I'm sorry for the delay. But it's only been one year! No joke, soon you'll get them. But first I'll send you a photo of Yoni's wedding.

Miki wrote she's coming here at the end of the year. But it's been a long time since she wrote, so I don't know if she'll get here for the wedding. [She didn't.] *I'll write her now.*

Udi Udi I didn't send you a Rosh Hashanah card. But you know that I wish you a most happy year, not just this year but every year. I didn't send one to anyone, shame on me. You'll see, next year I'll be better: organized and on time. It's good not to promise too much, right?

...

Udinha, I'm going to eat lunch, my father is coming to take me to the dentist and then to school.
Give everyone a thousand embraces and write soon! real soon, OK?

Here goes a smooch for you from your friend of always,

Elana

I found this letter I didn't send you. [Our] *apartment is not the one I wrote about.*

Thousand kisses, your always

Elana

New York, October 1971

Elana's mother, Vera, was weakening with uterine cancer. My mother was not showing any signs of illness yet. She worked as a hairdresser and had a few friends in Tarrytown, and deceivingly, she seemed content. I was distracted by taking a busy course load of senior seminars in linguistics and French literature. There were only three of us pursuing a degree in linguistics in 1971 at Lehman, Tobin, Dalgish, and me. I did not become an academic linguist; they did. Our friendship extended outside campus. Tobin was married with a toddler, and Dalgish loved to hang out. Academic life and social life were intertwined. Elana's friendship was relegated to a subplot of my life just as she was desperate for me to come to her wedding and be at her side.

São Paulo, November 25, 1971

Dear Udi-Udi

I apologize, Udi, I'm really sorry. I'm sending this invitation at the last minute, but believe me, I couldn't earlier, imagine my condition. Already at Yoni's wedding my mother was not well. But she didn't talk about it, only afterwards. She went to the doctor when her abdomen started to get large. The doctor gave her injections. It didn't help. Changed doctors, and after 2 months, this one operated. They did a hysterectomy and took out the ovaries, too. She faltered a little but is getting better. She went to the doctor for an examination.

Udi, she speaks so much nonsense that I'm afraid. My father is pale, and the two don't eat. I don't know what to do. You know, maybe I think we shouldn't do the wedding so soon after. My parents dedicated their life to us. What did they have, what do they have aside from us? Who do they look to if not to us? Now I don't know what they'll do.

But Udi, what can I do? You know Danko and I have been talking about it and will do everything we can for them to be happy. We will stop by here every day, and we'll have a life my parents can be part of. I think we won't have the little common arguments. I think that's normal in a family. But when you only see someone 2 or 3 hours, this will change. We might even miss it.

Finally, I'm very worried about them. I feel they really miss Yoni. He rarely comes, because he's interning, and he's tired, and when he comes, it's with 50 kgs of books under his arm! When he arrives, it looks like my parents get younger by 10 years!

Yoni is living at that apartment on R. Helvetica. We will live on Barão de Limeira at the corner of Alameda Glete. Each of us lives 2 blocks away from the other. I don't have the exact address; I will send it in the next letter.

We don't want to have a baby right away. First, we want to see the financial situation. We want to be secure and confident. Children can sense it if not. But 2 people who grew up in different places with different kind of parents need time to adapt. We've gotten to know each other a lot, but there are things we'll find out after being married. This is the layout of the apartment [a drawing is included] *with good size bath and kitchen. My wedding shower is now complete.*

. . .

The civil ceremony will be on the 23rd at 11 a.m. and the religious will be at 9 p.m. Then cocktails.

We're going to Itanhaém for one week at the Miami then to Mongaguá (also a big beach), where we'll spend New Year's Eve with a gang . . .

Soon after we'll go to Santa Catarina do Sul [southernmost state in Brazil] *since Danko has business to do there.*

So, all that's missing is my parents' health, and you to be here. And Danko's parents who are not allowed to come.

I must end here. Udi, write a lot and fast. I need your letters. "Lembranças" to all. How about a photo of you all? A thousand embraces, your friend always, Elana

Diverging Personal Quests: Friendship with Differences

São Paulo, March 8, 1972

Dear Udi-Udi,

Thank you, thank you for everything.
Thank you for not stopping to write to me while I didn't write to you.
Thank you for your words, thank you for the birthday card.
Finally, thank you for proving your eternal friendship.

Udi, I'm sorry if I didn't write since getting married. Not that I lacked time, it's an old excuse. But it's everything at once. I didn't write to anyone. . . . Let's continue. I have too much to tell you, I don't know where to begin. They're happy things, and I'm content. But since nothing in life is perfect, I don't know why it must be this way.

Udi, my mother is very sick, and I'm so scared. She doesn't deserve this, Udi. Just now, when they [parents] *could take advantage of relaxation, and now that they don't have to kill themselves working for us. Now she gets sick. When they operated, I was happy that the problem would end.*

No. It just started. Medicine, blood tests, then radiotherapy. It has made her weak. She's in pain. She lost 10 kg. And there are still 6 more sessions. But sometimes they must stop because her white blood count is too low. Now she's at 1/4 level and she doesn't want to increase it. They're talking about transfusions. This scares me, Udi, I have nightmares, and worst of all is watching this and not being able to lift a finger to help. Worse still, she continues to work like she did when you were here.

Before the wedding I thought things would be different, that they would move to a better place, a calmer place, and start a new life. I talk about it, but I know nothing like this will happen. My father is downcast, sad, and inanimate all the time. He just looks at my mother. Nothing else interests him. Sometimes I think I made a mistake getting out of there. It was a huge shock for them. They're suffering. Maybe they should be happy, their children have moved on with their lives. When we are there, their mood changes and they get animated, they look like they wake up. We go there every day. Sometimes I bring ice cream or something I made, in other words, anything to make them feel better. Danko is spectacular, he pays attention to all this like me, if not more! He goes by there, he talks to them, he takes my father out, they get along. Udi, I think you understand this disgrace that hit our family, this illness we don't know where it comes from, when and why. And worse we don't know how to save her from it. This always happens to someone who doesn't deserve it. We hope for the best, for a miracle which sometimes happens, or for the drug that maybe tomorrow will be invented. After speaking about this I feel selfish, ungrateful or something like it, writing about this particular part of my life. But I think you've read enough, no?

I got married during the holidays, and I had the entire holiday to get adjusted, to learn to cook, to arrange the house, in other words to be a homemaker. Now school has started, and I'm done for.

. . .

Udi, it's 6 p.m. and I must go to see my mother, we'll eat dinner there and celebrate Yoni's 6th month anniversary. I ask you, please write always and constantly, it brings me happiness.

I didn't read your letter before writing this, maybe I left out some things, but will be for next time.

A big hug from your friend forever,

Elana

New York, March 1972

I now marvel at the naive assumptions about cancer treatments in 1971 and 1972. Vera's very aggressive cancer was hard to treat then, and maybe would be hard to treat even today. It's also possible that health care in the twenty-first century, with the self-awareness, early tests, and preventive procedures, would have made a difference. The biggest difference is the pharmaceutical advancements that have taken place: the miracle that Elana was hoping her mother would receive.

In 1972 many women denied their illness and did not seek help soon enough. Fewer doctors were competent enough in early treatment and care; or when women were seeking a rare specialist, more precious time was wasted as the cancer spread.

It was also common then, not just to keep the illness private, but also not to say the word "cancer." One either denied that one was sick or pretended that one's illness was not serious. Vera did not want us to know, and so Elana had asked that my mother not mention an illness in her letters. I was not acquainted with anyone who had cancer. My family was young and healthy at that time. Cancer was not a new ailment, but it was terrifying even then, perhaps more so. I didn't relate well to her family's predicament, but I was pained by it.

São Paulo, April 14, 1972

Dear Udi-Udi,

Why don't you write me? You know this is so important for me. I wrote to you, didn't I? My head is so mixed up I don't know what I'm doing, or what I did. I'll go see at home if the letter isn't there.

Udi how are you? and everyone? Seems like years I haven't had news from there. Please, write always, Udi.

We are now at my mother's because my father has to go out and we don't want to leave her alone. After the operation she got better a little, and now her abdomen is larger than before. She's not well, very weak. On Friday the doctor will take out water and maybe she'll improve. We are useless, it seems.

Udi, I ask you to be careful if one of you write to her. We are all pretending all is well. It is she who wants to convince us of this. It won't be good for her to receive a letter that's scared, only one that knows she's well. You understand, right? This is disgraceful, I can only write about this, there's nothing else on my mind.

Aside from this, I have nothing in life to complain about. I have an incomparable husband, you can't even imagine how he tends to my parents, as if they were his. And he's so good to me, too, interested in everything I do, and does so much at home. My parents really like him, you would not recognize the atmosphere between them. Danko is making peace with his uncle, as I asked him. Our opinion of him is the same [not sure what the problem was], *but in the end, he's a relative, and if they don't make peace now, then they never will.*

Udi, I stopped taking the pill, it scares me. One person says it's bad, another that it's OK. I don't trust it. What are we to do? Nothing. Maybe be careful during fertile days (tomorrow to Saturday) and this is on Danko.

I send you photos of the wedding, write me right away when you receive them, and what you think. I did not forget the photos of Bahia. But now times are hard, and I ask for more time. They're well-guarded, OK?

I end here, and I ask you to write to me always. With a tender kiss from your friend

Elana

São Paulo, April 26, 1972

Dear Udinha,

As you can see, I wrote but I didn't mail. Doesn't matter, does it? Today I'll wait until half past midnight to take a medicine. I have a urinary tract infection. I tested today but won't know the result till Saturday. Until then, my brother gave me a double dose of antibiotics, because my kidneys hurt. Now it's better.

My mother felt better, since on Thursday (April 20) they removed 10 liters from her abdomen. Saturday and Sunday she went out strolling almost till Maccabi. But today her abdomen is the same size and she's not feeling well. The doctor will do a procedure for direct drainage.

Udi, I must write to my aunt, as my mother has been asking me to do for a while. I think she wants her sister to know she's sick. But I can't. I must do it today, because from today on I have a lot of exams, and I won't have the time or be brave enough to write her. So, forgive me for this Udi, if my letters seem dry and unnatural.

Udi, I did not answer some of your questions in your last letter, but I did not forget. I will write to those as soon as I can sit and write calmly. But if I forget, remind me. I ask you to please write me a lot, even if just postcards, and so I will feel that you are with me, and believe me, I miss that, Udi.

Write about your parents your grandmother and your relatives.

Udi, a huge embrace, full of "saudades," from your forever friend

Elana

PS Any possibility of you coming here in July? Think about it, I beg you! Kisses, Elana

New York, May 1972

I graduated from Lehman College in May. It felt like a momentous occasion. There were no celebrations; instead, I spent summer in close social contact with Lehman friends and went shopping for household items to set up an apartment off campus in Rochester. That's not a "trousseau," but it's a rite of passage, and unlike a move to undergraduate school, this was going to be the permanent move I had been dreaming about. I had been living someone else's life until I was eighteen (my parents'). Then college was a prep period to overcome my family's migratory habit. Now was my chance to do things my way, right or wrong, folly or consequence. This was an emotional state that moved a scrim between

Elana's Brazilian life and mine.

São Paulo, June 21, 1972

Dear Udi,

I already know this is not the letter I would have liked to write, or the kind you'd like to get. But I prefer to write you anyway, if not, you would not write to me.

Udi, my mother is very sick, today they started to infuse her, and I don't think it will stop. She doesn't eat and is now 40 kg maybe 1 or 2 more (her normal weight was 62–62 kg). You understand, I cannot write about what I am fearing. I would have liked to write to you about my ideas regarding what you write, but I will do it when I can, even if your response does not arrive. Funny, Miki wrote about a similar topic. Do you know what I'd like? For the 3 of us to meet and to talk a little. Who knows, one day? [Eventually we did!]

Udi, thank you for your long letter, you can't imagine what emotions it brought me. It arrived on a day that was very difficult. It was last Tuesday, the 12th. OK. That day. First, let me say: you don't want to visit me. But I got a little news, we will have a LITTLE visitor. Do you know what it is? Why not? OK. I also don't know. But it is tiny, and it cries like hell. Did you guess? Yes, it is a baby that's coming. It's a shame to say it, but in the phase we are going through, I can't figure out how this little creature can enter our lives and bring us such joy.

As I said it was the first time when my period didn't come within a 12-hour delay. After 14 hours, I knew, and I told Danko "I think a little visitor will knock on our door." In the afternoon we went to visit

Rachel who laughed at us for suspecting pregnancy after 5 hours, not 5 days' delay. But I'm super regular. On the 5th I called the doctor, and he asked me to take a test. [Elana describes a routine her doctor prescribed, now incomprehensible . . .]

Udi, I must go help my father in the kitchen. Write soon, you can imagine what expectation I have for your letter. Miki will be there/ was there? How was your meeting with her? Write a lot!

A huge embrace and "lembranças" to everyone,

Elana

PS what is your address in Rochester? CONGRATULATIONS!

PS John gave us your regards. I am so happy you won a scholarship. Well-done!

Elana

New York, June 1972

While Elana's life was being upended by the tragedy at home, just six months after she got married and then becoming pregnant soon after, I was realizing my dream to go to graduate school. She had congratulated me when I wrote to her that I won a scholarship to attend a master's program in the foreign language and linguistics department at the University of Rochester. I was also awarded an assistantship (as a TA) tutoring undergraduate students in German. Not only would my master's education not cost me anything, but I would also have some income to cover my basic needs, including rent at a modest apartment building off campus. In addition, I also landed a job teaching Hebrew in a local synagogue's Hebrew school.

I was off on a personal quest that diverged from Elana's, and this took us in different directions for the next decade. She was married but suffering an intense loss; I was ecstatic to start a new life.

São Paulo, July 6, 1972

Dear Udi,

It is so hard to write or to do anything. I am so lost. We are so broken by these past 8 months of constant suffering, tension, hope. All for nothing. Udi, mommy went away. Went away forever, I don't know why. It's so hard to believe that she's down there, that she doesn't move, that she doesn't think. And that she never stopped running, working, and preoccupying herself with us. Udi, I had hope until the last instant. But her body just would not respond to any medication.

This damned illness that swallows so many people, whoever, whenever, no matter how. This is so unjust. She never kept anything for herself. Now that she could have seen the result of her children's success with the education and everything she gave us. Now that she could close everything [work] *and start traveling with dad like another honeymoon without cares, indulge in grandchildren, happiness, everything, now that she could get her rewards, this damned illness took her. Udi, I didn't think that I'd miss her this much, but I do. She stopped breathing day before yesterday (7/4/72) at 12:30 p.m., and I still don't believe I don't have my mother, and not just me, but all of us are lost here.*

Udi, I keep thinking will I be as good a mother as she was; this woman who was such a workhorse, and so dedicated to her family. Worse thing is that a child is ungrateful and only sees the parents' faults, criticizing as if it is easy to be a parent. But when a mother starts slipping through our fingers, and when we are without her, that's when we finally value her. Then we start feeling the whole immensity of what a mother does for us.

Poor mother. She didn't want to go. No, Udi, I know no one wants to go, even at 100! But for her, the good times were just going to start. She was only 47 years old. Where is justice? Where is retribution? If she didn't deserve justice, who does? Oh, Udi, I'm sorry I'm writing like this. But there's nothing else in my mind. I'm disgusted with anger and with rancor.

And how cruel that with the end of her, with her not being here, the cars still drive around, as if nothing is missing in this world. But in my world, she's missing, missing!

Udinha, write to me, write a lot please. Your new address, how you're doing, did you start studies? Is your mother accommodated? and your father? Udi, please write. Embraces from your friend who would like you near.

Elana

New York, July 1972

As I read this letter to translate it, I cried like I never cried the day I received it. I grieved for Vera's loss, and therefore, Elana's loss, in a decades-long delayed response. How I wish that at the age of twenty-one I had the emotional empathy of old age! I was surely saddened by Elana's news, but I didn't act on it, and the memory was not stored long-term, and so I lost this memory of grief.

I know I was capable in providing comfort by writing to her, although I now consider that a gesture that falls short of adequate. I can't place myself in my July 1972 shoes. Instead of feeling guilty, with my memory letting me down, I choose to hope that I had the wherewithal to be sympathetic and comforting. Never having lost a close relative, except for my mother's loss of a full-term baby in 1964, I was unacquainted with death as personal loss, and so I was truly deficient in how to act and what to do to comfort the grieving. It's easy today to think: "just get on an airplane"; it's what I should have done, according to this faraway perspective.

Vera's death at forty-seven was tragic. Elana calls it a wrong against her mother that should be set right. She wanted retribution. I feel a deep guilt, decades later, forgetting the date and the letter until I reread it to translate it. I cannot comprehend in my current frame of mind, why I did not book a flight and go to her. It reinforces what a driven impulse I must have had to make my trip in 1970 succeed. Air travel became easier some years later. During Carter's presidency, in 1978, the airline industry was deregulated, and these changes made air travel commonplace. In addition, in 1972, I was still not a naturalized American citizen or the bearer of a US passport. That was to happen in the latter half of 1973.

São Paulo, September 10, 1972

Dear Udi-Udi,

I don't know how to explain it, I have no sufficient justification for not writing even a card until now. Either there's no time or disposition and so 2 months have passed.

But Udi, in the first place, here goes a huge embrace, a kind that squeezes hard, and congratulations to you. My wish for you to enter your 23rd year on the right foot, and that you take advantage in your new life that starts now, with everything you learned in the past 22. Udi, I want you to be happy and satisfied, and everything that you want I wish for you, too.

Udi, it's been a while since we restarted our correspondence normally. I re-read your last letters, and I found so much that I didn't answer but wanted to except for the lack of patience, willingness and mood. Believe me, Udi, since November, my life changed, I feel drunk.

It was in November, after my mother's surgery that I though my life will start anew, that our relationship would improve, and show my parents how I loved them and respected them, and that everything until then was immaturity. That I wanted to show them that yes, they prepared me to confront life's problems, and as I imagined everything beautifully and everything going well, we found out my mother, that woman who dedicated her life to her children, and who wanted NOTHING *for herself, that instead of starting a good life she deserved, and that woman got cancer.*

That was a tough jolt. I did not imagine that's what she suffered from, and that we didn't rearrange our plans. We couldn't have done it, because she would have asked why. But I am certain that she always knew and kept to herself that she had cancer. She suffered a lot and showed little of her suffering.

I went to buy my trousseau alone, missing her at my side, without her support and help. But she had no strength.

So, we got married. Believe me, Udi until July 4 I only spent one night at home [new home with Danko], *on my birthday. I'd go to her after school, came home for lunch, straightened out, took my books, and when I didn't have a student here, I went there, had dinner and at midnight came here to sleep. I couldn't do any less for them. When I was there, it brought happiness each time. My mother reanimated, and she preoccupied herself with our affairs. We had hope. I really did, Udi, even when I heard her breathing slowing down. But these miracles only happen to some people, not us. This is such a tragedy for our family—my mother going away. I never thought that I'd miss her so much, and I still can't get used to the idea she will not return. It's impossible for me to tell you how I feel about this. I just hope—no, I don't hope. After all, what is there to hope, when a person like her is not requited.*

Forgive me. I want to talk about many things. For example, regarding your wish to be independent of your parents. Remember how much I fought at home and how I invented problems? Our parents are alike. I know yours also sacrificed so much for you. Please Udi, see it this way now. Don't be sorry for this later. Don't think I have any kind of regret today. No, because I think my childhood and adolescent attitudes were normal. And I know these past 2 years I have been able to show my parents that I was grateful, respectful and admiring. They have done well, because I am not alone: I have the piano she got for me, and with her sacrifice I was able to study, and books I know how to read, an ability to choose the right husband, therefore she left me a moral education, a culture for company, and beautiful memories of my childhood. I think she understood and that she noticed she did well for me, the best she could do, and for that I am grateful. Yoni is too.

I don't know your relations with your parents. Unfortunately, when you were here, we did not talk about it. It was after the visit that I also started to think about my relations with my parents.

But your letter left a bad impression on me. I agree with you that now your life will open to spectacular, useful and needed experiences. But you are an only child. I believe your parents live for you. Why break away so fully and so suddenly from them? Why deny your mother if she wants to go with you to an unknown place for her, where you will be living alone, why don't you let her experience that? I know you are 22 years old, we are the same age, but believe me, Udi, independence is something relative. You will always need them, and they will always need you more.

I started noticing all this when I started to date Danko seriously, and maybe you'll see it too, when you're alone in Rochester, and when you go home seeing how your parents are, especially what you mean to them.

Udi I am not reprimanding you. It's just my opinion. Maybe I misunderstood your letter. Whether I'm right or wrong, please write to me what you really feel, what you think. I would so want us to be together now! Speaking about this, you wrote in one of your letters that I didn't want you to come to the wedding. Udi, you know I didn't want to say that, maybe I expressed it incorrectly. [The letters show she did not say that, and I did not either; I think Elana misunderstood some English expression I used in my letter, a misunderstanding.] *I know how hard it is, and to this day I am amazed at your battle to make it possible for you to come here once, something I did not accomplish. It would have been unjust for me to think that you didn't want to come.*

Udi, your grandmother went to visit Israel? Has she returned yet? What does she say? And how are your parents? Write about them. And the university? How is it? And the photo of you and Miki that you promised? I must stop here. Please write soon—today!—about everything and everyone.

I am well, I started to gain weight. I'm 3 months and 26 days pregnant. That's so you'll know the "age" of the baby in the photos. Soon it will start moving. I can't express what I feel. How in this life being pregnant and the disappearance of my mother are in such conflict. It's making me so bewildered.

Udinha, PLEASE NOW—write to me.

Kisses, your always,

Elana

Rochester, September 1972

I moved from home, and I felt emancipated. I arrived in Rochester, New York, feeling lonely, but at least I was in control: expanding my social realm and engaging with people I enjoyed meeting. Academic environments can occasionally provide "home and family" at least provisionally. There's a temporary but enveloping security in academic pursuits, attending classes, doing research, interacting with professors and other doctoral students, and forming social connections with like-minded transients on the university campus. I wasn't fooling myself; I knew this migration was more like tourism, and it was temporary for the next two years, until degrees were earned.

Elana and I were not just living in different hemispheres, we were also living incongruous lives. I had become Americanized, living with American values, and had become very different from a dear friend who married at the age of twenty-one, got pregnant soon after, and had never lived on her own. I was perturbed by how she felt about medicine, whether it was due to Brazilian culture or a less advanced state of medicine (of course they have caught up by now), because I was comparing it to what I felt. I was disquieted by how she was afraid to take the pill yet not about having children right away, because I was comparing it to my lack of fears about the new contraceptive. I couldn't get the pill fast enough, and I was happy that it was easily available and part of the sexual culture of the time, thanks to the current women's movement, which I embraced with conviction. (Or maybe the late twentieth-century women's movement was kick-started by a new and safe oral contraceptive.) Before I walked out of a doctor's office with a prescription, I agonized over and was terrified of an unwanted pregnancy. I did not have a steady boyfriend, so this added to my insecurity about casual experiences. I thought the pill was the best thing that ever happened to women. And in her letters, Elana is equivocating in a mire of misinformation as she was quoting some of the young women in her circle. I don't know where else she got such information.

Her mother hid her cancer, and Elana lived with a delusion that her mother's mysterious illness would somehow be healed. Elana was a dreamer; I was some concrete, calculating realist. Who was the gentler of the two of us? She was. And she tolerated and indulged me. And occasionally lectured me.

She pleaded with me to be sympathetic to my parents. I was. Nevertheless, I felt stifled by them. I wanted a life different from theirs, even as I embraced their past as an important heirloom that later in life became more and more inestimable to me. At the time, I did not think about my parents' turbulent life story; naiveté had made me think of them as ordinary, and they were not.

Vera's death was a life-altering event for Elana. It was an event that changed the perspective of a daughter who in years past constantly argued with her mother and fumed over her mother's stipulations. We battle with our parents, and when they die, we do an about-face. A friend of mine, one who always groused about her elderly mother who then died suddenly, once told me, "Wait till your mother dies; you will miss her to the bottom of your soul." Elana missed her mother to the bottom of her soul.

Every description Elana made about her mother was

something I saw in Vera before we emigrated from Brazil. But I was not her daughter; I saw her with a removed perspective. Did I disrespect my own parents for wanting emancipation and for my lack of perspective regarding their unique history? No, I needed to break away and they were not so obliging, because they needed me; that's a lamentable circumstance, but not an abnormal one. Elana was married, out of the house, establishing her own family with a man she was in love with. It's easy to quickly cleave to your parents when they've "given you away in matrimony"—a very old-fashioned sort of social pact—and find that now that you are independent from them, you actually have more in common with them. Vera and Ernö were so happy that Elana married Danko (after initial concerns and doubts), but Elana got a ticket out of her parents' home, and they, a ticket back into her heart.

I would not marry for another eleven years. I was about to live alone, independently, self-sufficiently for another decade. My parents didn't "give me away" in a socially acceptable filial disengagement. To live my own life, and not one like a recluse or spinster, I had to break my parents' hearts, especially my mother's.

My parents married in June 1949, when my mother was seventeen and my father was not yet twenty. My mother was pregnant within six months. That path was unacceptable to me. I always felt that my parents were children raising a child, particularly my mother. It was my grandmother who always lived near us and followed us from continent to continent who represented the adult figure in my life.

And yet, this determination to break out consigned me to a solitary life. I enjoyed it wholeheartedly, but for ten years, while I had many friends, I had no lasting acceptable intimate companion, and I craved companionship. After a pleasant academic experience, I bailed out of my doctoral work (linguistics) because I saw academia as another stifling environment and moved to New York City for work and a career. I was Mary Richards at last. And

I was the envy of more than a few women whom I ignored, while finding like-minded young women working in the city.

Elana, on the other hand, married, pregnant, and reeling from the loss of her mother, gave me the impression she was cooling off with her studies at university and at the conservatory of music. She abandoned it all to concentrate on raising a large family.

Her old upright piano still sits in a room next to her bedroom, a sentinel to a life gone off on a tangent.

São Paulo, October 10, 1972

Dear Udi-Udi,

Let's see if I can do this straight.

First, thank you for the Rosh Hashana card. I also wish you a year full of satisfaction and success in this new life you started. Now forgive me for this delayed letter. Believe me, lately I don't know where my head is. Since my mother went away in July, I returned home and realized it was totally neglected. So, I've paid a little more attention to my home. I had a maid 3 times a week. When I have the baby I'll need one every day, and I decided to start finding one right away. But ay, Udi, they're all monsters. One felt she was a visitor here. The other came from the interior and looking for adventures, slower than a turtle, decided she liked our things, and lifted towels, cremes, combs and house shoes. Moved everything around and had no idea about hygiene, however used 3 times the soap others have used.

Udi what do I do? I thought my mother was exaggerating when she complained about maids. But now I see she managed well! And then I think about your mother who always managed alone. As did my mother in Israel. Why can't I?

It feels like I want to let everything go, studying, and just take care of house, husband and child. Ha ha ha, right? It's not long ago that I used to say, "I will never be a housewife, I prefer to work at a profession and pay a maid with what I earn."

Hey Udi, what nonsense talk, right? But do you have any idea of what I should do? Or do I remain enslaved by these people like others. Ah, forget it! It's just that I just arrived home, and everything was rearranged to my dislike. But I got over it. Thank you for listening to this.

Udi, of course I'd like to have a photo of your graduation, naturally, if possible. And thank you for the other photos, it was exquisite to see you and Miki, you looked so good together, I would have recognized you anywhere anytime. [I went to London, where I had the opportunity to meet Miki.]

I'll take a picture of me and my belly and will send you. The baby is already playing football, or boxing. Never rests. Starting at 4 months and not the usual 4 and 1/2. But they say it's possible, and it means it is really a strong baby. I told the doctor to beware when the baby comes not to be punched in the face.

Udi, you said that you didn't pay attention to my mother's condition and that it makes you feel disappointed in yourself. But Udi, I never wrote to you what was wrong with her, or that she wasn't well. Maybe it's because I didn't believe it either.

Udi, forgive me for misunderstanding your words in your last letter regarding your parents. I'm glad I was wrong, and I should have remembered how you were so close together when you lived here.

Ay Udi, how I'd love to talk to you, I think we have so much to talk about, and I miss it. Yes, the letters help, but it isn't the same. Ay, Udi, what is life going to bring us?

...

I must dine, and then go to college this evening, I have classes. Dad is well, but I think inside he's broken. When we have free time, we're together. Danko is well, he's working hard. Yoni and Tzipora are well, too.

Udi, write me soon, and a lot, like last time. About your studies, your apartment, your new life. Everything. "Lembranças" to your parents, with all my affection,

Elana

Rochester, October 1972

The last letter of our twenty-second year ushered us into a divergence in the state of our lives. She went one way and I another.

I moved to Rochester and set myself up at a rented studio apartment off campus. I drove to Rochester with the old Buick Special my father had given me, and so I could drive to campus nearby and park there. The University of Rochester was such an easy school to attend. Living as a graduate student was a world apart from the high-spirited mischief of undergraduate life. We were the adults, the serious academics who had access to professors on a friendly level, who bantered with postgrads and foreign students attracted to so many departments at Rochester: physics, chemistry, medicine, neurolinguistics, and modern languages. I was nervous living alone; it made me feel like a greenhorn. But I found my footing, I found friends, and I was independent. My father had gifted me $2,000 for unforeseen expenses and emergency needs. I never touched this money. I earned enough to live on in this frigid upstate New York town that burst into an effervescence of lavender lilac blossoms in early May after seven months of cloud cover. I loved having a car. I could go exploring around Rochester and take friends when we planned outings. I could drive home whenever I felt like it. I was the lucky only child of generous parents. But my mother started to suffer. Because I was away from her, she perceived she was losing me, which precipitated the descent to mental illness within two years.

What Elana suffered when her mother was ill and dying, I was to experience soon. But I was not seasoned yet: I sympathized with Elana, but I did not have the capacity to empathize. My trial was a couple of years away. When my mother succumbed to mental illness, I had to experience what the psychologist Pauline Boss called "ambiguous loss," the grieving for the loss of someone still alive. The pain I learned to carry was as deep as one caused by a loss from death, and it may have caused a delayed impact on how I regarded Elana and her mother's death.

Although the next couple of years saw a decline in our correspondence, the ties that bound us did not falter. We just got too busy, especially Elana, with her marriage and motherhood. I was distracted in a different way, but not in one that affected the friendship. My distraction was due to my emancipation, our differing cultural environments, the move to Rochester where I was living alone, adjusting to graduate school, and mostly, experiencing the difficult process of accepting my mother's intensifying illness. The terms of our friendship were set, the feelings were declared, the physical distance remained the same but became less important with the advent of easier travel and less expensive phone service, and so we were able to "let go" and write less often.

From 1973, Lacking Spare Time: Parallel Lives

In 1973 Elana gave birth to her first daughter, Rivkah, named after Vera's Hebrew name. She wrote to me in January about the imminent birth, and then in February announcing the occasion.

In early 1973 I became an American citizen and fulfilled a dream that had eluded me through two previous migrations. I was no longer a migrant; I was now the bearer of an American passport. And with it I could go on many travels. In June I went to Israel, Paris, and London with my mother, before the awful Yom Kippur War that took place in October.

We found Israel bursting with hubris, but the war soon wiped out that atmosphere. My mother started to falter and came home deeply depressed. And then she started hallucinating. I don't know if the trip to Israel triggered her psychosis, but she was never the same after that.

In 1974 there was only one letter from Elana, in March. She gave birth to a second daughter, Rina. I got my master's degree in linguistics at the University of Rochester and moved to New York City to live and work.

In 1975, I received two letters from Elana in March and in October. I was working as a data coordinator at Rockefeller University, where I met Leonard, whom I was to marry nine years later. I traveled alone to Israel to visit a friend from college, Charles Tobin, who became a renowned linguist. My friend Judy died of liver cancer in Toronto, Canada; she was a newlywed. I was shaken.

In 1976 there were only three letters from Elana, in June, September, and November.

My mother was admitted to a psychiatric hospital. Her breakdown was complete, twelve years after her last trauma. While working at Rockefeller University as a data manager, I started to study computer programming, to expand my career prospects. I pivoted to working at Metropolitan Life Insurance Co. as a computer programmer/analyst.

I traveled west to Idaho and California with an Israeli colleague of Charles Tobin's.

In 1977 there were six letters from Elana, in February through May, then July, and a card in August. She had more time during a reprieve in raising the two girls and before having two more children, boys.

I continued working as a programmer at Met Life. My parents divorced, and my mother's illness intensified. I spent a summer month in Europe with a friend I met at Rockefeller University, Nancy, traveling through Switzerland, Italy, and Greece, each of us carrying nothing but one small bag. It was her first trip abroad, and I felt like an expert. I dated Leonard occasionally, after he moved to Philadelphia.

In 1978, again, there was only one letter in April.

I was still working at Met Life as a computer programmer. I went rafting on the Colorado River with a friend from work, Steve. Sadly, he died of AIDS in 1983. I also traveled to Bermuda with another friend from Met Life, Scharolyn. My relationship with Len was still intermittent. I dated others, none that I care to remember.

From 1979 to 1982 there were no letters. Yossi was born in 1980, and Beni was born 1981.

I was working at American Express teaching computer programming and technology. I also taught computer programming at the New York University School of Continuing Education. I started working at IBM as a Systems Engineer, a consultant to IBM clients.

I traveled to California with Len to visit national parks. I traveled to France with Len on his first trip outside the United States. Len's father died in 1982, and Len concluded that it was time to get married.

From 1983 to the Age of Email

Mature Women: One Is Brazilian and the Other American

The letters came sporadically. Her last letter to me was sent in September 1988. And then our form of communication changed completely. When the internet and computer messaging arrived, we could email and text each other. The first such message system we used was ICQ. It was the precursor to SMS messaging or voice over internet (VoIP). Now we can text and call each other using WhatsApp, in addition to FaceTime on our cell phones. We've communicated frequently, at least once a month, and sometimes more often when planning a reunion.

Thanks to the age of easy jet travel, we have seen each other and our families at least a dozen times over the years somewhere around the world.

Our friendship seemed to have expanded as our family life expanded. We each married and had children, and all understood that Elana's and my relationship was a lifelong bond, one that started with our parents. What we have accomplished with this friendship is to show our children how it's possible to be connected to someone very far away who is not a blood relative, but as if she were.

It was not until I tackled translating the letters and writing this memoir that I became fully conscious of what those letters meant to me as an uprooted and lonely immigrant. And then I also understood why the correspondence lasted so long: because we were dedicated to each other and dedicated to the friendship. There was Elana, there was me, and there was the friendship.

Emotional Maturity: Holding On to What Matters

I thought that while translating the letters and writing my retrospective contemplations and meditations, in hindsight, I would find keen insights about friendship. All I found was that the letters themselves explain the meaning of this friendship.

Does this particular friendship exist because, and only because, we wrote to each other? We wrote because we were friends, and we were friends because we wrote? Why be tautological when twenty-four years of letters are demonstrative. Any other explanation is redundant. And yet, there was a predisposition in both of us: to write, to document, and to express our devotion. We didn't keep diaries, we didn't journal, but we just had to write to each other. That need was fulfilled and reinforced, and each exchange spurred a continued cycle that did not end for as long as postal mail was the vehicle of delivery. Had we not corresponded for so long, the friendship would have withered.

This correspondence is a synecdoche, it is pars pro toto of this friendship. The words the letters impart are declarations of eternal friendship. Their intensity and frequency prove the friendship. Instead of ruminating over something that touches me deeply, I just let my feelings convey a reality that is meaningful to me: that this correspondence is very significant for me and for Elana.

Collected letters are a goldmine, but the letters must have a physical form. That does not include printed emails. Preferably they ought to be private and mundane. The entirety of a computer inbox folder or archived email folder does not have the power to be a treasure; at most, it's a commercial commodity. Witness the millions of emails that are sifted through in a legal case. My husband told me one time he was not allowed to delete any emails: there was a legal case against the pharmaceutical company and a new pill that ground through the courts and made some people rich (the lawyers), but no one healthier (the patients who could no longer get that medicine). Or the stolen emails of Hillary Clinton, which became a political commodity, meant to embarrass, then were forgotten, yet they changed the course of an election. Emails are documents totally different in nature from a personal correspondence on paper with ink. They're too casual, too glib and easily sent, whether in business or the personal sphere.

While writing to each other, Elana and I had crossed the historical watershed with the onset of the telecommunications revolution. The letters peter out not only because we were busier, even after we retired and had more time, but because there was no need to write when we could just pick up the phone. Or we could book a flight and go visit. Ironically, those letters came by plane. They were written on rice paper to make them light; the thin envelopes in the green and yellow Brazilian national colors were stamped *Par Avion*; otherwise they would have been consigned to a lengthy maritime transport. But it is the twenty years of corresponding that brought us to the telecommunication age without a gap.

We are old enough to have lived and become friends prior to this revolutionary change in communications. Fortuitously, I was fastidious enough to save all the letters as I moved through two countries. I can now see why: they alleviated the trauma of my dislocations, they were the lifeline that stabilized my cultural instability, they were a connection to the past, and that connection proceeded to evolve and create its own history between us. We became the subjects of this evolution; we created our own history. And even when we later became too busy to write, visit, or call, as friends we shared a cherished history, and so the friendship lived on for our lifetime.

Part Three

The Revelation

Remembrance has a Rear and Front —
'Tis something like a House —
It has a Garret also
For Refuse and the Mouse,

Besides the deepest Cellar
That ever Mason laid —
Look to it by its Fathoms
Ourselves be not pursued —

—Emily Dickinson, *The Poems of Emily Dickinson*

Bridging the Continents and Time

Emails are a poke, but letters are a caress.

—Simon Garfield, *To the Letter: A Celebration to the Lost Art of Letter Writing*

In January 2016, I planned a trip to Brazil to visit Elana, her husband, Danko, and their family. When moving from New Jersey to a new apartment in New York City, I set aside my collection of Elana's letters dating back to 1964. It was time to bring them into the light.

I placed the package of letters in my carry-on bag for the flight to São Paulo. I was to arrive in Brazil for the sixth time in my life, not as a migrant or a tourist, but this time, as a devoted friend.

Over the years, Elana and I had visited each other several times. She came to the United States with her children and I went to Brazil with mine. And just for the sake of visiting each other, Elana, Miki, and I reunited without families on trips to various places in the world.

Our friendship had matured during the later years after we were done raising our children and our careers were waning. We had many opportunities to talk about the past, to convey how we felt about our parents and about being immigrants. We revealed ourselves in ways we couldn't while we were children and adolescents. Miki told us about leaving Brazil and her relationship with her stepfather. Elana told us about her father's life and tribulations as a widower. We finally were able to talk about memories in the past tense, interpreted by our mature selves. Elana admired my parents, the way I admired hers. Despite this, I revealed in one of these reunions something she did not know when I lived in Brazil: that my mother was abused. My father had a serious temper. I had watched the yelling, the cursing, and the hitting while sitting cowered and timid in the corner of the room. Sometimes my grandmother stepped between them trying to restrain it. Timidity came naturally to me; I think it's a natural trait in children who grow up in a volatile household. Perhaps timidity is also an inherited trait, and my mother had her own problem with it, until years later, schizophrenia ripped open her inhibitions.

As adults, whenever Elana, Miki, and I reunited, we'd pose in the same manner for an updated photograph. This cherished photo collection sits on top of a cabinet near my desk. We planned to continue our reunions every few years.

Reuniting the Letters with Their Writer

During my visit to her in 2016, Elana and I were not planning on traveling; we were to have a stay-at-home visit with her family in their city apartment, and in a change of scenery, at their farm. I hoped that we would have time to sit and talk. I intended to make this the "reveal" of the cache of letters. I told Elana I was bringing them and asked her to find mine. By the time I arrived she was still not able to find them. She eventually revealed that she had to clear her apartment at some point, especially a room where old boxes were piled high, and everything must have been tossed out. So, my letters were lost, and she was remorseful.

It did not stop us, however. We were to reunite with our former selves. One letter at a time in chronological order, reluctantly at first, but then relentlessly, Elana read out loud words she wrote more than fifty years earlier in letters she had not seen since they were mailed.

This was an emotionally solemn experience—a rare and unique one. A black swan event comes to mind, but this was different. Black swan events are not predicted. This was expected; after all, I had saved the letters and retrieved them. Perhaps what was unpredictable was what we were going to find in the letters. Neither she nor I had remembered the contents of the letters.

What we experienced was an antecedent voice spoken in the concrete voice of the present. It was like the unearthing of a long-lost diary. It was personal archaeology. As we grow older, we change over time. Events, personal and external, change our attitudes, our actions, our understanding of ourselves and of others. Our brain and our emotions evolve. And the accumulated experience of many decades re-creates us into what we become at any given time, only to change some more with more time and more experience. Elana and I had not experienced trauma during the intervening years, no earthquake to alter our archaeological layers; we had safe and successful lives, with bearable losses and normal joys. We did not suffer psychiatric illness, and not much physical illness up to that point. As adults, we were ordinary and fortunate. And so, the layers of sediment that daubed us into what we are today kept us within the same outlines. The retreat into a past voice could have been distressing; it wasn't. It could have been dramatic; I think it was. It was revealing, as in an uncovering, because the decades had buried our adolescence in layers of life and experiences.

While we were reading the letters, the rest of the household left us alone. As much as our friendship had strengthened over the years, this emotionally touching encounter affected each of us even more deeply. To me, it bordered on a spiritual experience, as a revelation meant by the Greek *apokalypsis* (appropriately, also meaning unveiling).

After many years, the memories from adolescence are either lost, buried, or altered. What we remember may be correct or may not be. Memory isn't static, it's constantly edited; some experiences may be etched, but many others are evanescent. There is nothing ordinary about being sixty-six years old and hearing our fourteen-year-old voice. We did not expect to hear our own words as written, so this surprised us. Who knew, who remembered, that as teens we were capable of expressing ourselves in historical terms and leaving our words to our future selves.

In a process of unveiling, reading one letter after another, Elana was fourteen years old again. And I, too, was fourteen years old again, hearing news from her life far away. Fifty-two years were bridged in January 2016. Each letter sent was meant to bridge the continent and the weeks that had passed with us being apart. Each letter was a means to bridge our separation. But eventually, each became a bridge across a lifetime, and a reunion with our former selves.

While reading her own letters, Elana made comments as she interrupted her reading, usually with a mild expletive: the Brazilian *puxa!* ("Darn!"), or "Why did I write it this way?," or "Look what a fancy word I used!" like an editor displeased with the wording. Sometimes she was even surprised at the mature vocabulary. She alone heard her words with self-criticism; I did not. My reaction was surprising amazement at the maturity of the letters. They were interesting.

These did not represent some silly blathering to me; what struck me was their earnestness. Separated from each other, we were informing the other of our life. Like a shared journal or diary, we meant to keep each other abreast of our experiences and feelings. And in each letter, the declaration of friendship and protestation of absence was expressed with ardor.

Every letter read prompted moving conversations about the circumstances around the time the letter was written, so this took a long time, with long reminiscences and heartfelt dialogue.

When it was time to leave, I packed up my precious collection and brought it home to New York. This time, the letters traveled north bearing more emotional weight and treasured value.

Prompting to Translate: How to Hold On to the Past

It was the revelation, both emotional and conceptual, that I experienced during the letter reading that gave me the impetus to think about our correspondence in wider, more universal terms that would transcend our individuality, and be meaningful to others who have not experienced migration and separation. And yet it was the recognition that it was the unique nature of our friendship's predigital platform, in addition to the depth of our friendship, that awoke in me the need to share my revelation. In this age of instant communication, letters can be quaintly historical and concretely revelatory.

Four years had passed since our visit, and the year 2020 brought a worldwide pandemic and self-isolation. Life became curtailed enough, that during the long Northern Hemisphere winter, secluded from exposure to the virus, I decided to start writing an introduction and to translate the letters from Portuguese to English. With Elana's permission, I wished to publish the translated letters. I wished to share the emotional lessons expressed in a world not connected electronically, where waiting and yearning was a commonplace experience, and when patience was truly a virtue that was doubly rewarded by a deep friendship.

Among my other reasons to do so, first was that writing personal, long-form letters to be mailed via post is now quite rare. The telephone, the internet with email, text, Facebook and WhatsApp, video calls, and now Zoom have made letter writing and airmail posting obsolete—or I'd prefer to say, historical.

Another reason is that this long and intact correspondence is uncommon nowadays. This kind of communication, frequent and detailed, written in longhand, with a one-week to ten-day delay in delivery, is a far cry in breadth and intensity from our modern methods of communicating using the internet. The letters are physical objects; email is not. Both can be stored, but only one can become a cherished treasure. The instant delivery of the modern internet can elicit more compact and pithy communication. In addition, our story traversed from the predigital to the digital age in the 1990s onward. The letters are a collection of their time; in other words, they're archival. Thus, I am also motivated to scan the letters and store them digitally and photographically, to save them for a longer period of time, allowing them to be shared more easily. My motivation is also driven by the universal nature of the contents of these insightful letters, particularly the passing of time spanning the maturation period of the correspondents. They were letters about growing up. And finally, the cultural and historical milieu of our lives, across cultures and countries, and mostly across a lifetime, renders our experience somewhat exotic, and our story worthy of being autobiographical.

Epistolary literature and published letter collections have appeared on the literary scene for several hundred years. Madame de Sévigné was an avid letter writer in the seventeenth century, and the collection of her daily letters to her daughter and others makes up dozens of volumes. Of course, hers, and the letters of other famous people, get published. Perhaps there is room for published letters of two keen and good friends who were quite ordinary during unusual times, except for their extraordinary friendship. Perhaps there's a captivating story in their innocent intimacy.

Another factor integral to the correspondence is that the correspondence took place in two languages, with a third interjected occasionally. The bilingual aspect of our communication also stands out in contrast to any of our compatriots because it was so fluid. We started out as migrants, but even with our permanently adopted citizenship—hers arrived at before mine, which was delayed by more migration—we remained multilingually fluid for the rest of our lives. We each speak our adopted language natively, but we can transition to another language with natural ease. Multilingualism gives us a wide-angle view of the world even as it focuses on the uniqueness of our past. Elana and I can flow from English to Portuguese to Hungarian to Hebrew.

Finally, Elana remained in Brazil. Time and distance recast her environment as foreign to me, the same way that my environment in North America was foreign to her. I moved to Canada and then the United States, countries that were exotic and alien to her, even as American life was romanticized because of film, literature, and the overall American self-proclaimed exceptionalism. Her letters reveal her wonder at, and yearning for, life in the North. As for me, with each year that passed and I adjusted to an entirely new environment, the one I left behind receded in my mind. Elana's descriptions of her daily life, in an environment in which I could no longer picture myself as having a part, produced a looking-through-the-store-window longing in my heart.

How Do You Translate "Saudades"?

The national language of Brazil is Portuguese, not Spanish. Thanks to the 1494 Treaty of Tordesillas, the world was divided among Spain and Portugal (by Spain and Portugal). Speaking of hubris, world powers such as the United States, China, or Russia are not different in the twentieth and twenty-first centuries. In 1494, a longitudinal line was drawn down the globe, with the East belonging to Portugal, the West to Spain. Brazil is mostly situated East of this imaginary line, so Brazil was colonized by the kingdom of Portugal, under King João II. Everyone else knows Ferdinand and Isabella, but João was no laggard.

Portuguese is a Romance language. Meaning that Portuguese, Brazilian and continental Portuguese (also spoken in Mozambique and Angola), split from Middle Spanish, which developed from Latin after the fall of the Roman Empire. It is therefore a Romance language like its sibling Spanish (with its many, many dialects), French (and its various dialects), Italian, and Romanian.

The nature of the language and the nature of its speakers is very romantic, that is, emotional. In Brazil, the emotional aspect of life, especially love, can be carried by Portuguese practically "on its sleeve." Speech oozes with sentimentality, because the Brazilian population is an ardent population. Unlike Nordic, Germanic, or even English speech, there's no "cool" reserve or detachment. Brazil is a country of volatile emotional warmth. Being by nature reserved, in the long run, I did not fit this modality of communication.

When I arrived in Brazil and could not understand the language, I would listen to local radio stations and be astounded by the emotional tone of announcers. The music played on local stations was a gush of broken hearts spilling their cloying verses on vocal cords to the accompaniment of string guitars and native instruments. The music I heard and the lyrics I was trying to decipher were melodramatic odes to romantic suffering. Of course, there is danger in crossing the line from the emotional to the melodramatic. In Brazilian popular music this crossing was a point of national pride.

Just as we arrived in Brazil in January 1959, a new wave of a Brazilian musical form swept into the airwaves and the streets. Just like the cowboy epitomizes an American icon, the *Sertanejo,* the loner from the *Sertão,* the interior of Brazil, epitomized the Brazilian icon. It is Brazil's "country" music. From the combination of the weepy and lamenting *Sertanejo* music, and the Afro-Latin music particular to Brazil—the samba—played, sung, and danced to during Carnaval over decades, there came a melding with some influence from jazz, breaking out into a new genre: bossa nova.

It then rocketed to North America and Europe, as more musicians and singers wrote and interpreted this music derived from samba starting in late 1959. For example, "The Girl from Ipanema," Antônio Carlos Jobim's ode to the young, bikini-clad beauty on the beaches of Rio de Janeiro, became the anthem of love in the early 1960s and won a Grammy in the United States in 1965. It was written by Jobim in 1962, with lyrics by Vinícius de Moraes.

The first love anthem of this genre, in about 1959, "Chega de Saudades" (translates as "Saudades Have Arrived" or "Abundant Saudades") was a classic bossa nova written and sung by its creator and foremost vocal interpreter, João Gilberto. (His wife, Astrud Gilberto, sang the English lyrics in Stan Getz's American version of "The Girl from Ipanema" hit.)

There is no English word for *saudades*. The feeling is expressed in English by a variety of words, none of which entirely capture the Portuguese word: nostalgia, longing, yearning, hunger for, ache for, lust after, pine over, dream of, suffer the lack of, miss the presence of, and suffer the distance between. *Saudades* is all of the above and none of the above. It is a feeling that represents an emotional, and hurtful, empty space—a loss. It is not a noun phrase or a verbal phrase, but a solitary noun. *Saudades* is a concrete word for a nonconcrete concept, a feeling.

Expressions of *saudades* appear every time in Elana's letters. I've translated them as an American would have written the letter, like "I miss you," but in English it does not even come close. I tried . . . but sometimes the context of the word does not allow for a translation. So, at times I don't translate it and simply say, "The *saudades* are . . ." because *saudades* are so concrete. The grammatical congruence of the quantifying adjectives that precede it throws English on its end. *Muitas saudades* translates as "many," not "much," a peculiarity that breaks English rules for indefinite pluralization.

Translating it to "I miss you a lot" just doesn't express in English the depth of meaning in Portuguese. In her letter valedictions, when Elana closes her letters with the nominal adjective *saudosa,* she is also using a Portuguese word that has no one-word counterpart in English. It means the one (female) who feels *saudades.*

Epilogue

To tell the past is to take ownership of a memory.

—Walter Benjamin

Emily Dickinson's poem "Remembrance Has a Rear and Front . . ." started me thinking about memories, how they form and how we retrieve them. Two people experiencing the same event will not have the same memories. Take note of how Elana and I reacted to our trip to Bahia. Each interpreted an event and stored memories of it differently. Instead of focusing on memory as a psychological process, I take a more concrete and literate approach to Dickinson's poem, as follows:

> Letters stored in a box. Transported from city to city, packed up along with boxes of shoes, photo albums, diplomas, and birth certificates, to move from apartment to house to apartment, across national borders and across towns. Never opened, never examined, but always held in the topmost rank of items to be packed and moved. Without a thought, that is, with certainty. The box unpacked and placed in a similar and fresh location for security after each move.
>
> And one day the box is opened, and a letter is unfolded. And out comes a key: the key to the house of remembrance; the house which has different levels.

- The pretty memories displayed like the artsy books stacked on a living room coffee table.

Photo albums stored on the library shelf showing my wonderful trips, my wedding, my babies.

- The old keepsake memories stored in boxes in the attic.
  Keepsakes from my grandmother, my wedding dress, my babies' first shoes, my first shoes.
- The counterfeit memories invented to mask embarrassments, insecurities, and lies that are stored next to the collection of useless records and tapes that morph into CDs and DVDs and digital playlists over the years as technology advances.
  My unwelcome thoughts about a reason for a job loss, the rationale for a love gone astray, the wrong dealt to a friend, or the insult dished out by a friend, and the anguish of an offended parent.
- The quotidian memories needed to function week to week and month to month, like reminders on the kitchen corkboard, the month-at-a-glance desk calendar, or the kitchen catchall drawer.
  My family members' birthdays, anniversaries, itineraries, social security numbers.
- The painful and haunting ones relegated to the dark and dank cellar to collect cobwebs of neglect, hopefully to be forgotten.
  The unwanted memories that provoke my fear of being found out. The ones not even a memoir dares to unearth.

The childhood memories unlocked by the letters from Brazil were stored in closets through multiple migrations. Letters I reread after decades and then translated into a new native tongue provided the key to remembrances abandoned long ago. I had to choose which remembrances to air out. I chose the ones that were written to Elana, the stories of my circumstances as an immigrant dislocated for the first, second, and third time, until finally I found a home.

Bibliography

Aciman, André. *Out of Egypt: A Memoir* (Farrar Straus & Giroux, 2007).

Aciman, André. *Roman Year* (Faber & Faber, 2024).

Behar, Ruth. *Letters from Cuba* (Nancy Paulsen Books, 2020).

Brooks, Geraldine. *Foreign Correspondence: A Pen Pal's Journey from Down Under to All Over* (Knopf Doubleday, 1999).

Coetzee, J. M., and Mariana Dimópulos. *Speaking in Tongues* (Liveright, 2025).

Cohen, Roger. *The Girl from Human Street* (Vintage, 2015).

Dickinson, Emily. *The Complete Poems of Emily Dickinson* (First Rate Publishers, 2013).

Dreyer, Benjamin. *Dreyer's English: An Utterly Correct Guide to Clarity and Style* (Random House, 2019).

Ernaux, Annie. *Écrire La Vie* (Quatro Gallimard, 2013).

Ferrante, Elena. *My Brilliant Friend* (Europa Editions, 2012).

Garfield, Simon. *To the Letter: A Celebration to the Lost Art of Letter Writing* (Gotham, 2014).

Hakakian, Roya. *A Beginner's Guide to America: For the Immigrant and the Curious* (Albert A. Knopf, 2021).

Hanff, Helene. *84, Charing Cross Road* (Penguin Publishing Group, 1996).

Hesse, Karen. *Letters from Rifka* (Square Fish, Henry Holt, 1992).

Hoffman, Eva. *Lost in Translation: A Life in a New Language* (Penguin Books, 1990).

Klebanoff, Susan. "The Romani Woman and the (non)Wandering Jew: Immigration, Dissociation, and the Search for Belonging," *Psychoanalytic Perspectives* 20, no. 2 (2023): 170–88, DOI: 10.1080/1551806X.2002.2133305.

Lahiri, Jhumpa. *In Other Words* (Penguin Random House, 2017).

Lomnitz, Claudio. *Nuestra América: My Family in the Vertigo of Translation* (Other Press, 2021).

Morgenthaler, Goldie, ed. *Letters from the Afterlife, The Post-Holocaust Correspondence of Chava Rosenfarb and Zenia Larsson* (McGill-Queen's University Press, 2025).

Pinker, Steven. *The Sense of Style* (Penguin Books, 2015).

Rosner, Elizabeth. *Survivor Café: The Legacy of Trauma and the Labyrinth of Memory* (Counterpoint, 2018).

Sanders, Ella Frances. *Lost in Translation: An Illustrated Compendium of Untranslatable Words from Around the World* (Ten Speed Press, Crown Publishing, 2014).

Stavans, Ilan. *On Borrowed Words: A Memoir of Language* (Penguin Putnam, 2001).

Stavans, Ilan, ed. *The People's Tongue: Americans and the English Language* (Restless Books, 2023).

Stein, Sarah Abrevaya. *Family Papers: A Sephardic Journey Through the Twentieth Century* (Picador, 2019).

White, E. B. *Here Is New York* (The Little Book Room, 1999).

Acknowledgments "Reconhecimentos"

It started with an introduction, a few letters, and then it grew into a manuscript that needed a lot of work. Along the way, there were commenters, critics, and beta readers. I want to thank everyone who heard me talk endlessly about Brazilian letters and then read parts or the whole of my growing work. Aside from dedicating this book to her, I want to acknowledge that Elana is also an author of this book. She's my correspondence partner, and she wrote her letters to me as a young woman not realizing that she was becoming an author. I want to thank Ruth Edelman, Sarah Birnbach, Nancy Gorrell, Estare Weiser, Lucinda Zoe, Candace Styron, Phyllis Cohen, Ava Weinberger, Ronit Fisher, and Leonard Oppenheimer, who read it in its entirety, at various stages of development, and the many people who helped me work out parts of it, namely, Anya Yurchyshyn's group: Jae Sun Park, Lucinda Zoe, Lily Klebanoff Blake, Patrick Morrissey, Jane Bowers, Maryann Kenney, Jessica Prusa, Ana Busto, and Sarah Vogwill; Wendy Salinger's group: Jennifer Reid, Joseph Bernardo, Meg Giles, Lily Klebanoff Blake, Samuel Freeman, J Hinds, Dennis Sherman, and Charlotte Morrissey; Betsy Bonner's group: Georgette Blau, Nancy Novick, Marilynn Talal, Susan Sherman, Rimma Kranet, Allison Somers, Pam Groff,

Shari Adler, and Barbara Janoff; Karol Neilsen's group: Linda Movish, Sarah Frank, Amy Edelman, Lucy Raubertas, Myra Friedman, Anne Schulman, Estare Weiser, Lily Klebanoff Blake, and Virginia Schorr. I am indebted to Brooke Warner for her leadership as a publisher, securing such a talented team and creating an environment that welcomes so much talent. It is humbling to be included among her publications.

About the Author

Author photo © nyheadshots

RUTH ZELIG migrated three times and lived in four countries before the age of twenty, changing languages (at least five), cultures, and school systems. She got a master's degree in linguistics at the University of Rochester, New York, after a bachelor's in linguistics and French at Lehman College, CUNY. To expand her opportunities for a career, she added computer languages to her studies. She was a programmer and Systems Engineer at IBM. After changing her focus to raise her children, she spent years volunteering in a New Jersey community at various levels of leadership and became the president of a Conservative synagogue. As an only child, Ruth has taken care of her senescent parents for many years. English remains her primary language for writing. Ruth is also a photographer and gardener. She was a Master Gardener in Somerset County, New Jersey. Her social media name is Zeligova, a nickname she got from a fellow linguist in graduate school even though neither of them is Slavic—it was just a patronymic twist out of fondness for language. Ruth lives in Manhattan, New York, with her husband of forty-three years. They also spend much time at their Rhinebeck home in the Hudson Valley. When in neither residence, they travel to Marin County, California, to visit family that includes a granddaughter. Ruth sings to her in Hebrew and Hungarian and translates Spanish books, hoping to encourage the child to become bilingual.